HARRAP'S

PARDON MY GERMAN!

POCKET GERMAN SLANG DICTIONARY

English-German / German-English

by
Joaquín Blasco

D1057588

HARRAP

First published in Great Britain 2006
by Chambers Harrap Publishers Ltd
7 Hopetoun Crescent
Edinburgh EH7 4AY

© Chambers Harrap Publishers Ltd 2006
Reprinted 2007

ISBN 978 0245 60766 0

Designed and typeset by Chambers Harrap Publishers Ltd, Edinburgh
Printed and bound by WS Bookwell, Finland 2007

Author/Autor
Joaquín Blasco

German editor/Redaktion Deutsch
Veronika Schnorr

With/Mit
Alexander Brock, Kristin Davie

Thanks to/Dank
Helen Galloway, Max Brock, Nina Middel, Felix Schnorr,
Oliver Schnorr, Philipp Tommasi

Publishing Manager/Gesamtleitung
Patrick White

Prepress/Druckaufbereitung
Sharon McTeir

Based on an original idea by Joaquín Blasco and Tony Gálvez

Trademarks

We have made every effort to mark as such all words which we believe to be trademarks. We should also like to make it clear that the presence of a word in the dictionary, whether marked or unmarked, in no way affects its legal status as a trademark.

Warenzeichen

Als Warenzeichen geschützte Wörter sind in diesem Wörterbuch durch das Zeichen © gekennzeichnet. Die Markierung mit diesem Symbol, oder sein Fehlen, hat keinen Einfluss auf die Rechtskräftigkeit eines Warenzeichens.

Preface

Slang, or informal language, is now covered to a greater or lesser extent by the various general English-German dictionaries available on the market. However, since slang terms are treated just like any other term in these dictionaries, their coverage tends to be somewhat arbitrary and the translations provided often fail to reflect the nuances of the item being translated. Slang is a very rich and productive area of language, and there is often a whole range of slang terms referring to the same concept (e.g. sex, parts of the body, madness). The beauty of slang is that all these apparently synonymous terms are in fact used in slightly different ways in slightly different contexts and by different people. These subtleties, which are precisely what makes slang such a fascinating and creative type of language, are generally not reflected in the equivalents provided by bilingual dictionaries, where more often than not ten different slang terms meaning "excellent", for example, all have the same translation, despite the fact that they actually have different shades of meaning. The author of this dictionary, Joaquín Blasco, and his colleague Tony Gálvez have devised a sophisticated methodology designed to ensure that the translations given come as close as possible to conveying all the nuances of the term being translated. It is our hope that this will allow users to gain a much better understanding of how the items in this dictionary are actually used in real-life situations. This in turn will put them in a position to use the items productively in as natural a way as possible, should they wish to do so. In short, we hope you will have just as much fun recognizing common informal expressions on the English-German side of the dictionary as you will delighting in the carefully-considered and natural-sounding translations on the German-English side.

What is slang?

"Slang" is a term that might at first sight appear easy enough to define. However, closer inspection reveals that the word in fact has a number of different interpretations. For example, "slang" is often used to refer to the jargon of particular social or professional groups such as soldiers, criminals or even dentists. This type of slang is usually not familiar to the population at large, and has not been included in this dictionary. We have opted for a broader definition of slang as language that is generally considered to be informal in nature. This book aims to provide in-depth coverage of the most common informal terms used in spoken and written English and German, with abundant example sentences highlighting the most important contexts. The words included may range from colloquial to vulgar in register, but will always be among the informal words most frequently heard by anyone staying in the UK or in German-speaking countries.

Register

The register of a word refers to how informal it is. The majority of bilingual dictionaries label slang terms as either informal, very informal or vulgar. You will notice, however, that these labels are not used in this dictionary. This is because, in practice, the register of many slang terms varies depending on the specific context in which they are used. It is by no means uncommon for the same word to be informal in some contexts and very informal or even vulgar in others. Rather than arbitrarily tying a word to one register or another, the authors have sought to provide translations that work in exactly the same way, i.e. that change in register according to context just like the source language item. Where this was not possible, a range of examples have been provided, showing different usages and with translations that match the register of each specific usage. A few extremely vulgar words and expressions are followed by the symbol !! which draws the user's attention to the fact that these are among the most taboo terms in the language and they should not use them if they wish to avoid causing offence. Furthermore, in the few cases where no slang translation exists, translations that are neutral in register have been provided, followed by either the label [*not slang*] or [*nicht Slang*].

Racist, sexist, homophobic and other offensive terms

While the authors deplore the use of such terms, it is inevitable that a slang dictionary will contain a considerable amount of racist, sexist and homophobic language, as well as terms that are offensive to other groups in society, such as people with disabilities. All such items are clearly labelled, alerting readers to the fact that their use is likely to cause offence to the groups in question. Furthermore, in those cases where the translations do not necessarily reflect all the nuances of usage in every context, usage boxes have been provided giving additional information about some of these terms. Our aim is in no way to promote the use of terms which cause offence, but a slang dictionary is by definition obliged to record them.

Extra help

A very rigorous methodology was used in the compilation and translation of this dictionary in an attempt to ensure that the translations reflect the precise register and usage of the source language item as accurately as possible. In those cases where we felt that no translation adequately covers the full range of usage, we have provided the missing information in the form of usage boxes.

In view of the fact that slang is a very fluid form of language and the same terms can be understood differently in different regions or by different individuals, all headwords, senses and phrases have been given explanations in brackets to make it absolutely clear to the user which meaning is being translated. This contrasts with most bilingual dictionaries, where explanations are only retained for some headwords and phrases.

All insults have been clearly identified as such so that non-native speakers will be aware of the dangers of using such items. Humorous and ironic items are also labelled.

All euphemisms are not only labelled as such, they also carry an explanation of the term that the euphemism is replacing, e.g.:

effing *adj Euphemism [fucking]* ...

We have made every effort to avoid using arcane abbreviations and symbols in this dictionary. While it has been necessary to use some abbreviations for reasons of practicality, these are mainly confined to parts of speech. Wherever possible, we have sought to make the dictionary easier to use by writing things out in full.

A comprehensive cross-reference system has been employed, making it as easy as possible for users to find the item they are looking for.

Our friends across the pond

The emphasis of this dictionary is on British English and standard German. However, the influence of American English in the media means that American terms are increasingly understood and even used by speakers of British English. For this reason, and also to aid German users who come across American slang terms in books, films, etc, a representative sample of the most common American English slang terms has also been included on the English-German side of the dictionary, as have a few widely recognized terms from other parts of the world where English is spoken.

Vorwort

Slang, oder Umgangssprache, wird heutzutage zum Großteil in diversen frei auf dem Markt erhältlichen allgemeinen Englisch-Deutsch Wörterbüchern abgehandelt. Da die Slangausdrücke jedoch in den Wörterbüchern wie jedes andere Wort behandelt werden, ist ihre Handhabung meistens eher willkürlich, und die angebotene Übersetzung wird oft dem Nuancenreichtum des übersetzten Begriffes nicht gerecht. Slang ist ein reichhaltiger und produktiver Aspekt der Sprache, und oft wird ein bestimmtes Konzept von einer ganzen Reihe verschiedener Slangausdrücke abgedeckt (z. B. Sexualität, Körperteile, Geisteskrankheit). Was den Reiz der Slangausdrücke ausmacht, ist dass diese anscheinend synonymen Begriffe jeweils in leicht veränderter Form in leicht unterschiedlichen Zusammenhängen und von verschiedenen Leuten benutzt werden. Diese Feinheiten machen aus Slang eine so faszinierende und kreative Sprachgruppe, aber sie spiegeln sich häufig nicht in den von den zweisprachigen Wörterbüchern angebotenen Definitionen und Entsprechungen wider. Dort wird z. B. anstelle der zehn verschiedenen Slangausdrücke für "excellent" jeweils immer die gleiche Übersetzung angeboten, trotz der Tatsache, dass sie eigentlich leicht unterschiedliche Bedeutungen haben. Der Autor dieses Wörterbuches, Joaquín Blasco, hat mit seinem Mitarbeiter Tony Gálvez eine ausgefeilte Methodik entwickelt, die garantieren soll, dass die angebotene Übersetzung so gut wie möglich alle Nuancen des übersetzten Begriffes angibt. Wir hoffen, dass unsere Benutzer dadurch einen besseren Einblick bekommen, wie die Begriffe in diesem Wörterbuch eigentlich im wahren Leben benutzt werden. Im Gegenzug werden sie dadurch in die Lage versetzt, bei Bedarf die Begriffe produktiv und so natürlich wie möglich anzuwenden. Kurzum, wir hoffen, dass Sie bei der Entdeckung umgangssprachlicher Begriffe auf der englisch-deutschen Seite des Wörterbuches viel Spaß haben, als auch Freude an den gewissenhaft ausgewählten und natürlich lautenden Übersetzungen der deutsch-englischen Seite empfinden.

Was ist „Slang"?

„Slang" ist ein Begriff, der auf den ersten Blick leicht zu verstehen scheint. Bei näherem Hinsehen jedoch wird klar, dass es eine Reihe unterschiedlicher Interpretationen von „Slang" gibt. Er bezieht sich z. B. häufig auf den Jargon bestimmter sozialer oder beruflicher Gruppen, so z. B. Soldaten, Kriminelle oder gar Zahnärzte. Diese Art von Slang ist meistens der weiteren Bevölkerung nicht bekannt und ist in diesem Wörterbuch nicht enthalten. Wir haben eine weitreichendere Definition von Slang gewählt, dessen Wesensart im Allgemeinen umgangssprachlich ist. Dieses Buch zielt darauf ab, die bekanntesten umgangssprachlichen Begriffe im schriftlichen und mündlichen Englisch und Deutsch detailliert zu behandeln. Dies beinhaltet eine Fülle von Beispielsätzen, die die wichtigsten Zusammenhänge illustrieren. Die enthaltenen Wörter können im Stil von bloßen umgangssprachlichen Begriffen bis hin zu extrem vulgären Ausdrücken variieren, sind aber immer unter den meist gebräuchlichen Slangwörtern zu finden, die jeder, der sich in englisch- oder in deutschsprachigen Ländern aufhält, tagtäglich hören kann.

Stilebene

Die Stilebene eines Wortes bezieht sich auf den Grad seiner Umgangs- sprachlichkeit. Die meisten zweisprachigen Wörterbücher bezeichnen Slang entweder als salopp, derb oder vulgär. Sie werden jedoch sehen, dass diese Definitionen in diesem Wörterbuch nicht gebraucht werden. Der Grund dafür ist, dass die Stilebene der meisten Slangwörter in der Praxis vom Zusammenhang abhängt, in dem sie gebraucht werden und daher variiert. Es ist häufig durchaus der Fall, dass ein Wort in einem Zusammenhang salopp, in anderen Umständen jedoch derb oder gar vulgär ist. Hier aber werden Begriffe nicht willkürlich in feste Stilebenen eingeteilt. Die Autoren streben stattdessen nach Übersetzungen in die Zielsprache, die auf genau die gleiche Art und Weise funktionieren wie die Begriffe in der Quellsprache, d. h. sie haben eine andere Stilebene, je nach dem in welchem Zusammenhang sie benutzt werden. Ist dies jedoch nicht möglich, illustriert eine Reihe von Beispielsätzen den unterschiedlichen Gebrauch des Begriffes, und die Übersetzung passt sich jeweils der Stilebene des speziellen Gebrauchs an. Ein paar extrem vulgäre Wörter und Begriffe sind mit dem Symbol ‖!!‖ bezeichnet, welches den Benutzern anzeigen soll, dass diese Begriffe zu den am stärksten tabuisierten Worte in der Sprache gehören und möglichst nicht gebraucht werden sollen, wenn man vermeiden will, Anstoß zu erregen. Ferner, in den wenigen Fällen, wo es keine Slangübersetzung gibt, wurden Übersetzungen im neutralen Stil gewählt, die mit der Bezeichnung [*not slang*] oder [*nicht Slang*] versehen sind.

Rassistische, sexistische, schwulenfeindliche und andere beleidigende Begriffe

Obwohl die Autoren den Gebrauch solcher Begriffe nicht gutheißen, muss ein Slangwörterbuch wohl zwangsläufig eine beträchtliche Anzahl an rassistischer, sexistischer und schwulenfeindlicher Sprache beinhalten, als auch Begriffe, die andere Bevölkerungsgruppen als beleidigend empfinden, wie z. B. Behinderte. Jeder dieser Begriffe ist eindeutig als solcher bezeichnet und soll Benutzer darauf hinweisen, dass der Gebrauch dieses Wortes eine Beleidigung der fraglichen Gruppen darstellt. Ferner, in den Fällen wo eine Übersetzung nicht notwendigerweise alle Nuancen des Gebrauchs in jedem Zusammenhang aufzeichnet, wurden weitere Informationen über den Gebrauch der Begriffe in Form von Textkästchen gegeben. Es ist absolut nicht unser Ziel, den beleidigenden Gebrauch dieser Begriffe zu unterstützen, aber ein Slangwörterbuch ist nun mal per definitionem dazu angehalten, diese festzuhalten.

Zusätzliche Hilfestellung

Eine hoch entwickelte Methodik wurde in der Zusammenstellung und Übersetzung dieses Wörterbuches angewandt, um sicherzugehen, dass die Übersetzungen die richtige Sprachebene und den präzisen Gebrauch des quellsprachlichen Begriffs so akkurat wie möglich wiedergeben. In den Fällen wo es uns nicht möglich erscheint, mit der Übersetzung die volle Spannweite des Gebrauchs zu umfassen, stellen wir die fehlende Information in Form von Textkästchen zur Verfügung.

Im Hinblick auf die Tatsache, dass Slang keine sehr stabile Sprachform ist, und dass ein Begriff in verschiedenen Regionen oder von verschiedenen Individuen unterschiedlich aufgefasst werden kann, wurden alle Stichwörter, Bedeutungsbeschreibungen und Redewendungen mit Erklärungen in Klammern versehen, um die Bedeutung, welche übersetzt wird, dem Nutzer eindeutig klar zu machen. Das unterscheidet dieses Wörterbuch von den meisten zweisprachigen Wörterbüchern, wo solche Erklärungen nur für einige Stichwörter oder Redewendungen gegeben werden.

Alle beleidigenden Ausdrücke wurden eindeutig als solche gekennzeichnet, sodass Nichtmuttersprachler auf die Gefahr hingewiesen werden, die der Gebrauch solcher Worte nach sich zieht. Humorvolle oder ironische Begriffe sind auch als solche gekennzeichnet.

Alle Euphemismen sind nicht nur als solche bezeichnet, sie werden zusätzlich noch von einer Erklärung begleitet die klarstellt, welchen Begriff der Euphemismus ersetzt, z. B.

effing Euphemism [fucking] ...

Wir haben uns alle Mühe gegeben, den Gebrauch undurchdringlicher Kürzel und Symbole in diesem Wörterbuch zu vermeiden. Obwohl es notwendig ist, einige Abkürzungen aus praktischen Gründen beizubehalten, sind diese hauptsächlich auf die Wortarten reduziert. Wenn möglich haben wir versucht, den Gebrauch des Wörterbuches durch das Ausschreiben von Wörtern zu erleichtern.

Die Verwendung umfassender Querverweise soll es den Benutzern erleichtern, gesuchte Begriffe schnell zu finden.

Unsere Freunde überm großen Teich

Die Betonung dieses Wörterbuches liegt auf britischem Englisch und Hochdeutsch. Der Einfluss von amerikanischem Englisch durch die Medien ist jedoch so, dass amerikanische Begriffe mehr und mehr von britischen Sprechern verstanden und sogar benutzt werden. Aus diesem Grund, und auch um den Deutschen zur Hilfe zu kommen, denen amerikanische Slangbegriffe in Büchern, Filmen etc. begegnen, haben wir eine repräsentative Auswahl der gebräuchlichsten amerikanischen Slangbegriffe auf der englisch-deutschen Seite dieses Wörterbuches aufgenommen, wie auch eine Anzahl weithin bekannter Begriffe aus anderen englischsprachigen Teilen der Welt.

Structure of Entries

Artikelaufbau

> **boozer** n (a) (pub) Kneipe f [not slang]
> (b) (person) Säufer,-in m,f

> **Eurone** f (Euro) euro [nicht Slang]

• clear labelling of the cases where a slang translation does not exist

• klare Kennzeichnung der Fälle, in denen es keine Slangübersetzung gibt

> **coon** !! n Racist (black person) Bimbo m

• symbol to identify the most taboo terms in the language

• dieses Zeichen kennzeichnet die am stärksten tabuisierten Wörter der Sprache

> **fahrbar** → Untersatz

• comprehensive system of cross-references to help you find the phrases you are looking for

• umfassendes Verweissystem, das beim Auffinden von Wendungen hilft

> **effing** Euphemism [fucking] 1 adj (for emphasis) **the effing car won't start** das bescheuerte Auto springt nicht an

• euphemisms clearly labelled and followed by an explanation of the term they are replacing, in square brackets

• Euphemismen sind klar bezeichnet, und in eckigen Klammern steht das Wort, das sie eigentlich ersetzen

> **Geist** m den Geist aufgeben
> *(sterben, kaputtgehen)* to give
> up the ghost; **jemandem auf den
> Geist gehen** *(nerven)* to get on
> somebody's wick

- comprehensive explanations of the meaning of all senses and phrases, to avoid ambiguity
- umfassende Erklärungen der Bedeutung eines Wortes oder einer Wendung, um absolute Klarheit zu schaffen

> **Gelber** !! m, **Gelbe** f
> *rassistisch (Chinese)* chink

> **bent** *adj* (a) *Homophobic
> (homosexual)* andersrum; **he's as
> bent as a three pound note** der
> ist 'ne richtige Schwester; **stop
> hugging me, you bent bastard!**
> hör auf, mich zu umarmen, du
> warmer Bruder!
> (b) *(criminal)* **a bent copper** ein
> geschmierter Bulle

> **Mieze** f *sexistisch (Frau)* bird

> **cretin** n *Insult (stupid person)*
> Schwachkopf m; **you (stupid)
> cretin!** du Schwachkopf!

- clear labelling of racist, homophobic and sexist items, as well as insults
- klare Kennzeichnung von Ausdrücken, die rassistisch, schwulenfeindlich, sexistisch oder beleidigend sind

> **frühstücken** *vi* rückwärts
> frühstücken *scherzhaft
> (erbrechen)* to do a technicolour
> yawn

fat *adj Ironic* **do you expect to get a pay rise? – huh, fat chance (of that)** *(no chance)* meinst du, du kriegst eine Gehaltserhöhung? – ha, einen Dreck werd' ich kriegen; **did she help you? – yes, and a fat lot of good it did us too** *(it did no good)* hat sie euch geholfen? – ja, und viel hat's uns gebracht!; **I don't know how it works – a fat lot of use you are** *(you're no use)* ich weiß nicht, wie das funktioniert – du bist aber auch gar keine Hilfe

- humorous and ironic expressions identified
- scherzhafte und ironische Ausdrücke werden bezeichnet

actress *n* **it won't go in... as the actress said to the bishop** *(expresses double-entendre)* das geht nicht rein... wie sie so schön zu ihm sagte

ⓘ **As the actress said to the bishop** ist eine witzelnde Wendung, die benutzt wird, wenn man sich darüber klar wird, dass das, was man gesagt hat, als sexuell zweideutig interpretiert werden kann, obwohl man es so nicht unbedingt gemeint hat. Ein weiteres Beispiel zum Gebrauch in diesem Zusammenhang wäre: **that's a big one... as the actress said to the bishop** *(das ist aber ein großes Teil... wie sie so schön zu ihm sagte)*.

> **Pimmel** *m (Penis)* cock
>
> ⓘ The term **Pimmel** was originally a mild term used by and of children, and would have been translated by the English term *willy*. However, it has recently become widely used in pornography and is thus now almost never used in its original context.

- usage notes to explain subtleties than cannot be fully conveyed by a translation
- Erklärungen in Kästen verdeutlichen Feinheiten, die durch eine Übersetzung nicht vermittelt werden können

> **zip, zippo** *n US (nothing)* **we won six to zip(po)** wir haben sechs zu null gewonnen [*not slang*]; **how much food is left? – zip(po)** wie viel Essen ist noch da? – null; **you don't know zip(po) about that subject** du hast davon ja null Ahnung

> **sheila** *n Australian (woman)* Tussi *f*

- coverage of key American English slang terms and widely recognized terms from other parts of the world where English is spoken
- Behandlung der wichtigsten amerikanischen Slangausdrücke und solcher anderer anglophoner Länder, soweit sie allgemein bekannt sind

Abbreviations

Abkürzungen

adj	adjective/Adjektiv
adv	adverb/Adverb
art	article/Artikel
esp	especially/besonders
f	feminine/Femininum
interj	interjection/Interjektion
inv	invariable/unveränderlich
m	masculine/Maskulinum
m,f	masculine or feminine/Maskulinum und Femininum
n	noun/Substantiv
npl	plural noun/Substantiv im Plural
nt	neuter noun/Neutrum
pl	plural noun/Substantiv im Plural
präp	preposition/Präposition
pref	prefix/Vorsilbe
prep	preposition/Präposition
pron	pronoun/Pronomen
reflexiv	reflexive verb/reflexives Verb
sing	singular/Singular
US	American English/amerikanisches Englisch
vi	intransitive verb/intransitives Verb
vt	transitive verb/transitives Verb
vt insep	inseparable transitive verb/nicht trennbares transitives Verb
vt sep	separable transitive verb/trennbares transitives Verb
[!!]	extremely offensive term/sehr beleidigendes Wort
→	cross-reference/Querverweis

A

ace 1 *adj (excellent)* spitze
2 *interj (expresses pleasure)*
Spitze!

actress *n* **it won't go in... as
the actress said to the bishop**
(expresses double-entendre) das
geht nicht rein... wie sie so schön
zu ihm sagte

> ⓘ **As the actress said to the
> bishop** ist eine witzelnde
> Wendung, die benutzt wird,
> wenn man sich darüber klar
> wird, dass das, was man gesagt
> hat, als sexuell zweideutig
> interpretiert werden kann,
> obwohl man es so nicht
> unbedingt gemeint hat. Ein
> weiteres Beispiel zum Gebrauch
> in diesem Zusammenhang wäre:
> **that's a big one... as the actress
> said to the bishop** *(das ist aber
> ein großes Teil... wie sie so schön
> zu ihm sagte).*

airhead *n (stupid person)*
Strohkopf *m;* **he's a bit of an
airhead** der hat nicht viel in der
Birne

all right → **bit**

anorak *n (boring person)*
uncooler Typ; **her brother's
a real anorak** ihr Bruder ist

ja so was von uncool; **he's a
computer anorak** er ist so ein
Computerfuzzi

ape, apeshit *adj* **to go ape** *or*
apeshit *(get angry)* die Krise
kriegen

argy-bargy *n (quarrelling)*
Krach *m;* **there was a bit of
argy-bargy next door last night**
gestern Abend gab's nebenan
Krach

arse 1 *n* **(a)** *(backside)* Arsch *m;*
**get off your arse and do some
work!** lass jucken und tu mal
was!; **get your arse over here!**
(come here quickly) beweg mal
deinen Arsch hierher!; **she kicked
him** *or* **gave him a kick up the
arse** sie hat ihm einen Tritt in
den Arsch gegeben; **she needs a
good kick up the arse** *(needs a
talking-to)* die muss man mal zur
Sau machen; **it's my arse that's
on the line here!** *(I stand to lose)*
hier geht's um meinen Arsch!; **to
fall** *or* **go arse over tit** *(fall head
over heels)* auf die Schnauze
fallen; **get your arse into gear
and give me a hand!** *(get a move
on)* lass jucken und hilf mir mal!;
**I've been getting it up the arse
from the boss** *(being victimized)*
mein Chef hat mich echt gefickt;

they'll have my arse for this *(punish me)* die kriegen mich deswegen am Arsch; **he doesn't know his arse from his elbow** *(he's clueless)* der hat doch keinen blassen Schimmer; **move your arse!** *(hurry up)* beweg deinen Arsch!; *(get out of the way)* verzieh dich da!; **my arse!** *(expresses disbelief)* verarsch mich nicht!; **aromatherapy my arse!** *(expresses contempt)* Aromatherapie, meine Fresse!; **you couldn't see her arse for dust** *Humorous (she left quickly)* die hat ganz schnell den Abflug gemacht; **shift your arse!** *(hurry up)* beweg deinen Arsch!; *(get out of the way)* verzieh dich da!; **(stick or shove it) up your arse!** *(get stuffed)* leck mich am Arsch!; **you can stick your job up your arse!** *(forget it)* den Job kannst du dir in den Arsch schieben!; **we had a bloke in a Ford Fiesta right up our arse the whole way** so ein Typ in einem Ford Fiesta hat uns die ganze Strecke am Arsch geklebt; **I'm up to my arse in work** *(overwhelmed)* ich hab' arschviel zu tun → **bit, face, fuck, head, kiss, out, pain, piece, rat, screw, sun, talk**

(b) *Insult (person)* Arsch *m*; **he's a stupid arse** er ist ein blöder Arsch; **you stupid arse!** du Arsch!; **he made an arse of himself at the wedding** *(behaved stupidly)* er hat sich bei der Hochzeit voll zum Arsch gemacht

  2 *vt (break) (machine, object)* in Arsch kriegen

arse about, arse around *vi (mess about)* rumarschen

arsed *adj* (a) *(bothered)* **do you fancy going to the cinema? – no, I can't be arsed** hast du Lust, ins Kino zu gehen? – nö, null Bock; **I can't be arsed to do it** *or* **doing it now** ich hab' null Bock, das jetzt zu machen

  (b) *(broken)* im Arsch

arsehole *n* (a) *(anus)* Arschloch *nt*; **this town is the arsehole of the universe** *(unpleasant)* diese Stadt ist das letzte Scheißloch

  (b) *Insult (contemptible man)* Arschloch *nt*; **he's an arsehole** das ist ein Arschloch; **what an arsehole!** so ein Arschloch!; **you (stupid) arsehole!** du (blödes) Arschloch!; **you fucking arsehole!** !! du Arschficker!

arse-licker *n (sycophant)* Arschkriecher,-in *m,f*

arse up *vt sep (make a mess of)* versauen

ass *n (backside)* Arsch *m*; **get off your ass and do some work!** lass jucken und tu mal was!; **get your ass over here!** *(come here quickly)* beweg mal deinen Arsch hierher!; **she kicked him** *or* **gave him a kick in the ass** sie hat ihm einen Tritt in den Arsch gegeben; **it's my ass that's on the line here!** *(I stand to lose)* hier geht's um meinen Arsch!; **get your ass in gear and give me a hand!** *(get a move on)* lass jucken und hilf mir mal!; **they'll have my ass for this** *(punish me)* die kriegen mich deswegen am

Arsch; **he doesn't know his ass from his elbow** *(he's clueless)* der hat doch keinen blassen Schimmer; **move your ass!** *(hurry up)* beweg deinen Arsch!; *(get out of the way)* verzieh dich da!; **my ass!** *(expresses disbelief)* verarsch mich nicht!; **shift your ass!** *(hurry up)* beweg deinen Arsch!; *(get out of the way)* verzieh dich da!; **(stick** or **shove it) up your ass!** *(get stuffed)* leck mich am Arsch!; **you can stick your job up your ass!** *(forget it)* den Job kannst du dir in den Arsch schieben!; **I'm up to my ass in work** *(overwhelmed)* ich hab' arschviel zu tun → **bit, fuck, haul, head, kick, kiss, out, pain, piece, rat, screw, talk**

awesome *adj (excellent)* geil

AWOL *adj Humorous* **my dad goes AWOL whenever it's time to do the washing-up** *(disappears)* mein Vater macht die Flatter, sobald der Abwasch gemacht werden muss; **my calculator seems to have gone AWOL again** *(disappeared)* mein Taschenrechner hat sich mal wieder in Luft aufgelöst

B

babe *n* (a) *(attractive woman or man)* Schnitte *f*; **check out those babes over there** guck dir mal die Schnitten da drüben an; **babe magnet** *(attractive man)* Traumboy *m*

(b) *Sexist (form of address)* Baby *nt*

backside → **pain**

bad 1 *adj* (a) *(good)* Wahnsinns-; **it's one bad video game** das ist ein Wahnsinnsvideospiel; **hey, that's bad, man!** Wahnsinn, Mann!

(b) *(not good)* **her boyfriend's bad news** ihr Freund ist eine üble Marke; **that company's bad news** das ist eine ganz üble Firma

2 *adv* **he's got it bad for her** er ist total verknallt in die

badass *adj esp US* (a) *(good)* saustark

(b) *(tough)* knallhart; **her husband's some badass Mob guy** ihr Mann ist so ein knallharter Mafiatyp

bad hair day *n (difficult day)* **I'm having a bad hair day** heut' geht auch alles in die Hose

bag 1 *n* (a) *Insult (woman)* **she's a bag** *or* **an old bag** sie ist eine blöde Ziege; **you (old) bag!** du (dumme) Kuh!

(b) *(scrotum)* Sack *m*

2 *npl* **he's got bags of money/talent** *(a lot)* er hat jede Menge Geld/Talent

ball *vt (have sex with)* pimpern

ballistic *adj* **to go ballistic** *(get angry)* am Rad drehen

balls 1 *npl* (a) *(testicles)* Eier *pl*; **we've been breaking** *or* **busting our balls to finish on time** *(working hard)* wir haben uns den Arsch aufgerissen, um das rechtzeitig fertig zu kriegen; **she's been breaking** *or* **busting my balls about me always arriving late** *esp US (nagging me)* sie hat mich zur Sau gemacht, weil ich immer zu spät komme; **they've got us by the balls** *(in a difficult position)* die haben uns am Arsch

(b) *(nonsense)* **what he said is complete and utter balls** er hat die totale Scheiße erzählt; **stop talking balls!** hör auf, Scheiße zu erzählen!; **that's a load of (old) balls!** das ist doch totale Scheiße!

(c) *(courage)* Traute *f*; **it takes balls to do a thing like that** um so was zu machen, darf man keinen Schiss haben; **to have the balls to do something** die Traute haben, etwas zu tun; **his balls are bigger than his brains** der denkt mit den Muckis statt mit dem Hirn

2 *n (mess)* **to make a balls of something** etwas verhunzen

3 *interj (expresses annoyance)* verflucht!; *(expresses disbelief)* du willst mich wohl verscheißern!; **he wants us to work all weekend – balls to that!** *(no way)* er will, dass wir das ganze Wochenende arbeiten – der ist ja nicht ganz sauber!; **balls to you!** *(get stuffed)* leck mich!

balls up 1 *vt sep (make a mess of)* versauen

2 *vi (mess up)* Scheiße bauen

balls-up *n (mess)* Murks *m*; **to make a balls-up of something** etwas versauen; **I made a real balls-up of trying to tell her I loved her** ich hab's versaut, als ich ihr eine Liebeserklärung machen wollte

bang 1 *n* (a) *(sex)* Bumsnummer *f*; **to have a bang** orgeln

(b) *esp US (enjoyment)* **he gets a bang out of seeing other people suffer** er kann sich daran aufgeilen, wenn andere leiden

2 *vt* (a) *(have sex with)* orgeln; **to bang somebody's brains out** jemanden bis zur Bewusstlosigkeit durchorgeln

(b) **to bang the bishop** *(masturbate)* die Schlange würgen

3 *vi (have sex)* orgeln

4 *adv* **bang go my chances of getting the job!** *(I've no chance)*

und das war's dann mit meinen Chancen, den Job zu kriegen

barf *esp US* **1** *n (vomit)* Kotze *f*

2 *vi (vomit)* kotzen

3 *interj (expresses disgust)* kotzwürg!

barking *adj (crazy)* **to be barking (mad)** völlig bekloppt sein

bastard 1 *n* (a) *Insult (nasty man)* Scheißkerl *m*; **he's a right bastard to his wife** seiner Frau gegenüber ist er ein richtiger Scheißkerl; **you bastard!** du Scheißkerl!; **you bloody bastard!** du Sauhund!; **you fucking bastard!** ‖!!‖ du blödes Arschloch!

(b) *(any man)* **he's a clever bastard** er ist ein schlauer Sack; **he's a big bastard** er ist ein Mordsbrocken; **some bastard nicked my pen** irgend so'n Sack hat meinen Stift geklaut; **you jammy bastard!** du verdammter Glückspilz!; **what a stupid bastard!** was für 'n blöder Sack!; **all right, you old bastard?** *(greeting)* alles klar, du alter Sack?

(c) *(difficult thing)* **this sum's a real bastard** die Rechnung ist saumäßig schwierig; **this door's a bastard to open** die Tür geht saumäßig schwer auf

(d) *(unpleasant situation)* **his wife left him – what a bastard!** seine Frau hat ihn verlassen – was 'ne Kacke!; **it's a real bastard having to get up so early** es ist total Kacke, immer so früh aufstehen zu müssen

2 *adj (annoying)* **I can't get**

the bastard lid off ich krieg den Kackdeckel nicht auf

beat vt tell him to **beat it** (go away) sag ihm, er soll abhauen; **beat it!** (go away) hau ab! → **crap, shit, shite**

beefcake n (a) (attractive man) heißer Typ
(b) (attractive men) heiße Typen pl; **check out the beefcake by the pool!** guck dir mal die heißen Typen am Pool an!

bend → **round**

bender n (a) Homophobic (homosexual) warmer Bruder; **he's a bender** er ist vom anderen Ufer; **stop hugging me, you great bender!** hör auf, mich zu umarmen, du warmer Bruder!
(b) **to go on a bender** (go drinking) eine Kneiptour machen

bent adj (a) Homophobic (homosexual) andersrum; **he's as bent as a three pound note** der ist 'ne richtige Schwester; **stop hugging me, you bent bastard!** hör auf, mich zu umarmen, du warmer Bruder!
(b) (corrupt) **a bent copper** ein geschmierter Bulle

berk n Insult (stupid man) Blödmann m; **I felt a right berk** ich bin mir wie ein Blödmann vorgekommen; **shut up, you (stupid) berk!** halt die Klappe, du Blödmann!

bevvied adj (drunk) **to be bevvied** fett sein; **I got bevvied** ich hab' mich abgefüllt

bevvy n (drink) **I went down the pub for a few bevvies with my mates** ich war in der Kneipe und hab' mit meinen Kumpeln ein paar gezischt

bible basher n (evangelist) **he's a bible basher** er ist so ein Betbruder

big adj (a) Ironic (generous) **that's big of you!** wie nobel von dir!
(b) (phrases) **I passed my exam – big deal! I passed mine ages ago** (so what?) ich hab' meine Prüfung bestanden – ja toll! Ich hab' meine schon lang bestanden; **she gave him the big E** (left him) sie hat ihn in die Wüste geschickt; **she's a big girl** (has large breasts) sie hat viel Holz vor der Hütte; **don't be such a big girl's blouse!** (pathetic) sei nicht so 'n Weichei!; **he's a big shot in the party** (important) er ist ein großes Tier in der Partei; **they've messed up big time** (badly) sie haben's total versaut; **she fancies him big time** (a lot) sie ist total in ihn verknallt; **he's into chess in a big way** (seriously) Schach ist total sein Ding; **he's the big white chief** (person in charge) er ist der große Häuptling → **one**

big up vt sep **to big it up for somebody** (applaud) jemandem 'ne Runde Applaus spenden; **big it up for my main man Darren who saved our lives** (expresses acclaim) alle Achtung für unseren Freund Darren, der uns das Leben gerettet hat; **big it up for companies that promote equal opportunities**

(they deserve credit) alle Achtung vor Unternehmen, die Chancengleichheit praktizieren; **to big something up** *(hype it)* einen Riesenhype um etwas machen; **ministers are bigging up London as the venue for the next Olympics** *(hyping it)* die Minister machen einen Riesenhype um London als Austragungsort für die nächsten Olympischen Spiele

Bill *n* **the (old) Bill** *(police)* der Wachtmeister

bimbo *n (woman)* **his girlfriend's a right bimbo** seine Freundin ist ein kleines Dummchen

bird *n* (a) *Sexist (woman)* Mieze *f*
(b) *Sexist (girlfriend)* Kleine *f*

bishop → **bang**

bit *n* **she's/he's a bit of all right** *(attractive)* sie/er ist nicht übel; **he was with a gorgeous bit of fluff** *or* **stuff** *or* **skirt** *Sexist (woman)* er hatte 'ne tolle Schnecke dabei; **a bit of arse** *or* US **ass** *Sexist (attractive woman)* 'ne geile Sau; **he's got a bit on the side** *(a lover)* er hat was nebenher laufen; **he's not her husband, he's her bit on the side** das ist nicht ihr Mann, mit dem hat sie nur was → **crumpet**

bitch *n* (a) *Insult (nasty woman)* Miststück *nt*; **she was a real bitch to me** die Schlampe hat mich echt gemein behandelt; **you bitch!** du Miststück!; **you stupid** *or* **old bitch!** *(as general insult)* du blödes Miststück!; **you fucking bitch!** !! du blöde Fotze!

(b) *(woman)* Tuss *f*; **she's a clever bitch** sie ist eine ganz gescheite Tuss; **you jammy bitch!** du hast ein Schwein!; **the poor bitch broke her leg** die arme Tuss hat sich das Bein gebrochen; **what a stupid bitch!** so eine doofe Tuss!
(c) *Sexist (girlfriend)* Braut *f*
(d) *(difficult thing)* **this sum's a real bitch** die Rechnung ist brutal schwierig; **this door's a bitch to open** die Tür geht brutal schwer auf

bitchin *adj esp US (excellent)* bockstark

bite *vt US* **bite me!** *(get stuffed)* verpiss dich!

blast **1** *n esp US (great time)* **how was the party? – it was a blast** wie war die Party? – spitzenmäßig; **we had a blast** wir haben uns saugut amüsiert; **he gets a blast out of seeing other people suffer** *(enjoys it)* er kann sich daran hochziehen, wenn andere leiden
2 *interj (expresses annoyance)* Mist!

bleeding **1** *adj (for emphasis)* **he's a bleeding idiot** er ist ein Vollidiot; **it's a bleeding pain in the neck** das ist zum Abgewöhnen; **bleeding hell** *or* **heck!** *(expresses annoyance)* Herrgottnochmal!; *(expresses surprise)* ach du grüne Neune!
2 *adv (for emphasis)* **the film was bleeding awful** der Film war total schrecklich; **don't be so bleeding stupid!** sei nicht

so verdammt doof!; **there was a bleeding great hole in the bottom** da war ein verdammt großes Loch im Boden; **no bleeding way am I doing that!** einen Dreck werd' ich tun!; **too bleeding right!** das kannst du laut sagen!; **you'd bleeding well better do what I say!** du solltest verdammt noch mal tun, was ich dir sage!

bling, bling bling 1 *n* *(jewellery)* Klunker *pl*
2 *adj (cool)* angesagt
3 *vt* **to bling bling it** *(wear ostentatious jewellery)* beklunkert sein

blink *n* **the telly's on the blink again** *(playing up)* der Fernseher tut schon wieder nicht

blinking 1 *adj (for emphasis)* **he's a blinking idiot** er ist ein Volltrottel; **it's a blinking pain in the neck** das ist echt zum Abgewöhnen; **blinking hell** *or* **heck!** *(expresses annoyance)* Herr im Himmel!; *(expresses surprise)* ach du grüne Neune!
2 *adv (for emphasis)* **the film was blinking awful** der Film war voll schrecklich!; **no blinking way am I doing that!** ich kann mich bremsen, das zu tun!; **you'd blinking well better do what I say!** ich will dir schwer geraten haben zu tun, was ich dir sage!

block *n* **she's off her block** *(crazy)* sie hat einen Vogel

bloke *n (man)* Typ *m*; **he's a good bloke** er ist ein netter Typ

bloody 1 *adj (for emphasis)* **the bloody car won't start** das Scheißauto springt nicht an; **he's a bloody bastard** er ist ein Scheißtyp; **you bloody idiot!** du saublöder Idiot!; **I can't hear a bloody thing** ich kann verdammt nichts hören; **it's a bloody pain in the neck** das ist echt ätzend; **bloody hell** *or* **heck!** *(expresses annoyance)* verdammt und zugenäht!; *(expresses surprise)* ach du dickes Ei!; **who the bloody hell does she think she is?** für wen zum Teufel hält die sich eigentlich?; **bloody Nora!** *(expresses surprise)* heiliger Strohsack!
2 *adv (for emphasis)* **the film was bloody good/awful** der Film war saugut/sauschlecht; **we had a bloody marvellous time** wir haben uns saugut amüsiert; **it's bloody freezing** es ist scheißkalt; **we were bloody lucky** wir hatten ein Schweineglück; **don't be so bloody stupid** sei nicht so saublöd; *Ironic* **that's bloody brilliant, now what do we do?** na klasse, und was zum Teufel machen wir jetzt?; **a bloody great lorry** ein scheißgroßer Lastwagen; **you did bloody well** das hast du saugut gemacht; **you'd bloody well better do what I say!** verdammt noch mal, mach, was ich sage!; **no bloody way am I doing that!** den Teufel werd' ich tun!; **are you going? – not bloody likely!** gehst du hin? – den Teufel werd' ich tun!; **too bloody right!** das kannst du, verdammt noch mal, laut sagen; **it's bloody difficult**

das ist scheißschwierig; **he's bloody clever** der ist sauklug; **I can't be bloody bothered** ich habe verdammt keine Lust; **I'm not bloody going, you can go on your own** verdammt noch mal, ich geh' da nicht hin, du kannst alleine gehen; **just bloody (well) shut up!** ach verdammt, halt doch die Klappe!; **you can bloody well put up with it!** du wirst dich, verdammt noch mal, dran gewöhnen müssen!

blooming 1 *adj (for emphasis)* **he's a blooming idiot** er ist ein Vollidiot; **it's a blooming pain in the neck** das ist echt zum Abgewöhnen; **blooming hell or heck!** *(expresses annoyance)* Himmel, Arsch und Zwirn!; *(expresses surprise)* Himmel!

2 *adv (for emphasis)* **the film was blooming awful** der Film war total schrecklich; **no blooming way am I doing that!** einen Dreck werd' ich tun!; **you'd blooming well better do what I say!** tu verdammt noch mal, was ich dir sage!

blotto *adj (drunk)* **to be blotto** stramm sein; **I got blotto** ich hab' mich voll laufen lassen

blow 1 *vt* (a) *(ruin)* **that's blown it!** jetzt ist alles vermasselt!
(b) *(spend)* auf den Kopf hauen; **he blew all his savings on a holiday** er hat seine ganzen Ersparnisse für einen Urlaub auf den Kopf gehauen
(c) *(fellate)* **she was blowing him** sie hat ihm einen geblasen
2 *vi (be terrible)* für 'n Kübel

sein; **it blows chunks** *(it's really terrible)* das ist totaler Kack
3 *n* (a) *(cannabis)* Shit *m*
(b) *US (cocaine)* Schnee *m*

blow job *n (fellatio)* Blowjob *m*; **she gave him a blow job** sie hat ihm einen geblasen

bog *n (toilet)* Klo *nt*; **I need (to go to) the bog** ich muss aufs Klo

bogey *n (piece of mucus)* Popel *m*

bog-standard *adj (ordinary)* stinknormal

bollocking *n (telling-off)* **the teacher gave me a bollocking** der Lehrer hat mich zur Schnecke gemacht; **we got a bollocking** wir sind zur Schnecke gemacht worden

bollocks 1 *npl* (a) *(testicles)* Eier *pl* → **dog**
(b) *(nonsense)* Scheiß *m*; **what he said is complete and utter bollocks** er hat den totalen Scheiß erzählt; **stop talking bollocks!** hör auf, Scheiß zu erzählen!; **that's a load of (old) bollocks!** das ist doch der totale Scheiß!; **their new record is (utter or a load of) bollocks** *(bad)* ihre neue Platte ist (totale) Scheiße
2 *n (mess)* **to make a bollocks of something** etwas versaubüxeln
3 *interj (expresses annoyance)* verdammte Scheiße!; *(expresses disbelief)* du willst mich wohl verscheißern!; **she's getting married – bollocks she is!** *or* **is she bollocks!** sie heiratet – erzähl kein' Scheiß!; **he wants us to**

work all weekend – bollocks to that! *(no way)* er will, dass wir das ganze Wochenende arbeiten – der ist ja nicht ganz sauber!; **bollocks to you!** leck mich am Arsch!

bone *vt esp US (have sex with)* poppen

boner *n (erection)* Latte *f*; **he got a boner** er hat eine Latte gekriegt; **he had a boner** er hatte eine Latte

bonk 1 *n (sex)* **d'you fancy a bonk?** hast du Lust zu bumsen?; **to have a bonk** bumsen

2 *vt (have sex with)* bumsen; **did you bonk him?** hast du ihn gebumst?; **she bonked my brains out** sie hat mich durchgebumst, dass mir Hören und Sehen verging

3 *vi (have sex)* bumsen

bonkers *adj (crazy)* bescheuert; **that music is driving me bonkers** *(annoying me)* die Musik macht mich ganz kirre; **to go bonkers** *(get angry)* durchdrehen

boob *n (breast)* Titti *f*; **boobs** Busen *m*; **she's got big boobs** sie hat einen großen Busen

boogie 1 *n (dance)* Schwof *m*; **to have a boogie** schwofen

2 *vi (dance)* schwofen; **let's boogie on down!** lass uns das Tanzbein schwingen!

boost *vt US (steal)* klauen

booty *n (woman's bottom)* Knackpo *m*; **she was shaking her booty** *(dancing)* sie tanzte 'ne heiße Nummer

booze 1 *n (alcohol)* Stoff *m*; **have you been on the booze?** hast du gesoffen?

2 *vi (drink)* saufen; **to go boozing** einen saufen gehen

boozer *n* **(a)** *(pub)* Kneipe *f* [*not slang*]

(b) *(person)* Säufer,-in *m,f*

booze-up *n (party)* **to have a booze-up** 'ne Party schmeißen

bop 1 *n* **(a)** *(dance)* Schwof *m*; **to have a bop** schwofen

(b) *(discotheque)* Disko *f*

2 *vi (dance)* schwofen

bore → shit, shite, shitless

bored → shitless

bottle 1 *n* **(a)** **she's been on the bottle again** *(drinking excessively)* sie hat wieder gesoffen

(b) *(nerve)* **she showed a lot of bottle** sie war ganz schön cool; **will he have the bottle to tell her?** ob er den Schneid hat, es ihr zu sagen?; **he lost his bottle** er hat Nerven gezeigt; **I was going to tell my Mum I'm gay but I lost my bottle at the last minute** ich wollte meiner Mutter sagen, dass ich schwul bin, dann hat mich in der letzten Minute aber doch der Schneid verlassen

2 *vt (mess up)* **she needed one game to win the title, and she bottled it** sie brauchte nur ein Spiel, um den Titel zu gewinnen und hat's verbockt

bottle out *vi (pull out)* kneifen; **he bottled out of asking her** er hat gekniffen und sie nicht gefragt

box n (a) (woman's genitals)
Dose f
   (b) he was out of his box
(drunk) er hatte die totale
Gesichtslähmung

brains → bang

brass 1 n (money) Knete f;
he's earning loads of brass der
verdient jede Menge Knete
   2 adj it's brass monkeys out
there (cold) draußen ist es
saukalt

brassed off adj (annoyed) sauer;
I'm really brassed off about what
she said ich bin echt sauer über
das, was sie gesagt hat; she's
brassed off with her boyfriend
sie ist sauer auf ihren Freund;
I get really brassed off seeing
him sit around doing nothing all
day long es kotzt mich an, wenn
ich ihn den ganzen Tag so faul
rumsitzen sehe

bread n (money) Moos nt

break → balls

brick 1 n → shit, short
   2 adj he's built like a brick
shithouse (strong) der ist ein
richtiger Kleiderschrank
   3 vt I was bricking it all the
way home (terrified) ich hatte
die Hosen gestrichen voll, bis ich
endlich daheim war

broad n esp US (a) Sexist
(woman) Schickse f
   (b) (prostitute) Hure f

browned off adj (annoyed)
sauer; I'm really browned off
about what she said ich bin echt
sauer über das, was sie gesagt

hat; she's browned off with her
boyfriend sie ist sauer auf ihren
Freund; I get really browned
off seeing him sit around doing
nothing all day long es kotzt
mich an, wenn ich ihn den
ganzen Tag so faul rumsitzen
sehe

buff n to be in the buff (naked)
nackig sein

bugger 1 n (a) (any man or
woman) he's a clever bugger das
ist ein schlauer Typ; he's a big
bugger das ist ein Mordsbrocken;
some bugger nicked my pen
irgendein Depp hat meinen Stift
geklaut; she's a cheeky bugger
sie ist ein Frechdachs; don't be
such a daft bugger! sei nicht
so ein Blödmann!; you jammy
bugger! du Glückspilz!; the little
buggers have eaten all the cake
die Blagen haben den ganzen
Kuchen gegessen → silly
   (b) Insult (nasty person)
Armleuchter m; you bugger! du
Armleuchter!
   (c) (difficult thing) this sum's
a real bugger die Rechnung ist
sauschwer; this door's a bugger
to open die Tür geht sauschwer
auf; it's a real bugger having
to get up so early das ist echt
Scheiße, wenn man so früh
aufstehen muss
   (d) (phrases) you've done
bugger all today (nothing)
einen Scheißdreck hast du heut'
gemacht; I went to the record
shop, but they had bugger all ich
war im Plattenladen, aber einen
Scheißdreck hatten die da; we

got bugger all help from them *(none)* einen Scheißdreck haben sie uns geholfen; **I got bugger all for my efforts** *(nothing)* einen Scheißdreck hab' ich für meine Mühe bekommen; **you know bugger all about it, so shut your face!** *(you know nothing)* einen Scheißdreck weißt du darüber, also halt die Klappe!; **there's bugger all else to do, so we might as well watch the film** *(nothing else)* sonst gibt's verdammt null anderes zu tun, also können wir uns auch den Film ansehen; **I don't** or **couldn't give a bugger what they think!** *(don't care)* es interessiert mich einen feuchten Mist, was sie meinen!

2 *vt* **(a)** *(break) (machine, object)* kaputtmachen

(b) *(injure)* versauen; **I buggered my back playing tennis** ich hab' mir beim Tennisspielen den Rücken versaut

(c) *(ruin) (plan, hopes)* vermurksen

(d) *(exhaust)* schaffen

(e) *(forget)* **bugger the consequences, let's just do it** scheiß drauf, machen wir's doch einfach; **bugger the cost** scheiß auf die Kosten; **bugger the lot of them** ich scheiß doch auf die alle

(f) *(phrases)* **bugger it!** *(expresses annoyance)* Mist!; **bugger it, I've had enough of waiting around, I'm off** scheiß drauf, ich hab' genug von der Rumwarterei, ich hau ab; **bugger me!** *(expresses surprise)* meine Nerven!; **bugger me, did you**

hear what he just said? meine Nerven, hast du gehört, was er gerade gesagt hat?; **they want us to work at the weekend – bugger that!** *(no way)* die wollen, dass wir am Wochenende arbeiten – die sind ja nicht ganz sauber!; **I think you're being stupid – well bugger you, then!** *(get stuffed)* du bist blöd! – leck mich doch!

3 *interj (expresses annoyance)* Mist!

bugger about, bugger around 1 *vt sep (waste time of)* verschaukeln; **I'm fed up of being buggered about by this airline** ich hab' die Nase voll, von der Fluggesellschaft dauernd verschaukelt zu werden

2 *vi (mess about)* blöd rummachen; **stop buggering about with the computer** hör auf, mit dem Computer rumzumachen

buggered *adj* **(a)** *(broken)* kaputt

(b) *(injured)* versaut; **my knee's buggered** ich hab' ein versautes Knie

(c) *(exhausted)* geschafft

(d) *(in trouble)* **we're really buggered now** jetzt sitzen wir in der Scheiße

(e) *(phrases)* **well I'll be buggered!** *(expresses surprise)* nicht zu fassen!; **well I'll be buggered, he's the last person I'd have expected to get married!** nicht zu fassen! Von ihm hätte ich am wenigsten erwartet, dass er heiratet; **I'm buggered**

if I know! *(I don't know)* bin ich Moses?; **I'm buggered if I'm going to help them!** *(I'm not going to)* 'nen Teufel werd' ich tun und denen helfen!

bugger off 1 *vi (go away)* **I buggered off halfway through the afternoon** ich hab' mich mitten am Nachmittag verkrümelt; **I told him to bugger off** ich hab' ihm gesagt, er soll abschieben

2 *interj (go away)* zieh Leine!; *(expresses refusal)* verpiss dich!; *(expresses disbelief)* mach kein' Scheiß!

bugger up 1 *vt sep (make a mess of)* versauen

2 *vi (mess up)* Scheiße bauen

bull → **dyke**

bullshit 1 *n (nonsense)* Scheiße *f*; **what he said is complete and utter bullshit** er hat die totale Scheiße erzählt; **stop talking bullshit!** erzähl keinen Scheiß!; **that's a load of (old) bullshit!** das ist doch der totale Scheiß!

2 *vt (lie to)* **don't bullshit me!** erzähl keinen Scheiß!

3 *vi (talk nonsense)* Scheiße erzählen

4 *interj (expresses disbelief)* kein Scheiß?

bum 1 *n (bottom)* Hintern *m*; **she kicked him** *or* **gave him a kick up the bum** sie hat ihm einen Tritt in den Hintern gegeben

2 *adj (bad)* kaputt; **I got a bum deal** ich bin hundsgemein behandelt worden

3 *vt* **(a)** *(scrounge)* **she's always bumming fags off me** sie schnorrt dauernd Kippen von mir; **I bummed a ride off him** ich hab' mich von ihm mitnehmen lassen

(b) *Homophobic (have anal sex with)* **he was bumming his boyfriend** er war gerade dabei, seinen Freund von hinten zu stechen

4 *interj (expresses annoyance)* Scheibenkleister!

bummer *n (unpleasant situation)* **my girlfriend left me – (what a) bummer!** meine Freundin hat mit mir Schluss gemacht – das is' ja blöd!; **it's a real bummer having to get up so early** es ist total blöd, immer so früh aufstehen zu müssen

bunk off 1 *vt insep (not attend)* **to bunk off school** die Schule schwänzen

2 *vi (from school)* schwänzen

buns *npl esp US (buttocks)* Po *m*; **he's got a gorgeous pair of buns on him** der hat einen knackigen Po

bush *n (woman's pubic hair)* Pelz *m*

business *n* **right, we're in business** *(ready to start)* jetzt kann's losgehen; **my new camera is the business** *(really good)* meine neue Kamera ist voll der Renner; **has the dog done its business?** *Euphemism (defecated)* hat der Hund sein Geschäft gemacht?; **did you do the business (with her)?** *(have sex)* ist was (mit ihr) gelaufen?

bust → balls

butcher's n *(look)* let's have
a butcher's (at it) lass mal
beaugapfeln

butt n *(bottom)* Hintern m; **get
your butt over here!** *(come here*
quickly) beweg dein Hinterteil
hierher! → kick, pain

buy vt **do you think they'll buy
it?** *(believe it)* meinst du, die
kaufen uns das ab?; **he bought it
a while ago** *(died)* den hat's vor
einiger Zeit erwischt

C

can n US (a) (toilet) Örtchen nt
(b) (prison) **in the can** hinter
schwedischen Gardinen

cathouse n US (brothel) Puff m

chat up vt sep (flirt with)
anbaggern

chav n Proll m

> (i) Unter **chavs** versteht
> man junge Briten aus nicht
> sehr feinen Stadtteilen.
> Man erkennt sie an ihrer
> Einheitskleidung. Dazu gehört
> eine Baseballmütze, ein T-Shirt
> mit einem Werbeaufdruck,
> weiße Turnschuhe, auffälliger
> Goldschmuck und irgendein
> Kleidungsstück aus
> Burberrystoff. Sie mögen Rap,
> R&B und Tanzmusik, sind stolze
> Besitzer von Kampfhunden
> und hängen meist an ihrem
> Handy. Wenn sie nicht gerade
> telefonieren, sind sie meist in
> eine Prügelei verwickelt. In
> Schottland nennt man sie **neds**.

check out vt sep (look at) **check
out those babes over there** achte
auf die Schnitten da drüben;
hey, check out these trainers!
guck dir bloß mal die geilen
Turnschuhe an!; **check this out,**

**there were 18 robberies in our
street** nicht zu fassen, da hat es
18 Einbrüche in unserer Straße
gegeben

cheers interj (a) (thank you)
dankeschön! [not slang]; **let me
give you a hand – cheers, mate!**
komm, ich helf' dir – danke,
Kumpel!
(b) (goodbye) tschüss!

cheesed off adj (annoyed)
genervt; **I'm really cheesed
off about what she said** was
sie gesagt hat, hat mich echt
genervt; **she's cheesed off with
her boyfriend** sie ist genervt
von ihrem Freund; **I get really
cheesed off seeing him sit
around doing nothing all day
long** es nervt mich, wenn ich
ihn den ganzen Tag so faul
rumsitzen sehe

chick n Sexist (woman,
girlfriend) Puppe f

chicken 1 n (coward)
Waschlappen m
2 adj (cowardly) **are you chicken
or what?** hast du Schiss oder
was?; **don't be chicken** sei nicht
so ein Waschlappen!; **he's too
chicken to do it** der hat zu viel
Schiss, um das zu tun

chicken out vi (back out)
kneifen; **he chickened out of
going on the rollercoaster** er
hatte Schiss, mit der Achterbahn
zu fahren

chief → **big**

chill vi (a) (relax) relaxen; **I was
chilling to some music** ich hab'
bei ein bisschen Musik relaxt
(b) (hang out) **what are you
doing here? – just chilling** was
machst du hier? – einfach nur
abhängen

chill out vi (a) (relax) chillen; **I
was chilling out to some music**
ich hab' bei ein bisschen Musik
gechillt; **hey, chill out, man!**
(calm down) he Mann, chill mal
ein bisschen!
(b) (hang out) **what are you
doing here? – just chilling out**
was machst du hier? – nur
chillen

chopper n (a) (penis) Gerät nt
(b) Insult (contemptible man)
Saftsack m; **you chopper!** du
Saftsack!; **I felt a right chopper
in my kilt** ich bin mir in dem
Kilt wie ein Arsch mit Ohren
vorgekommen; **stop being such
a chopper!** hör auf, dich wie ein
Saftsack aufzuführen!

chronic adj (very bad)
sauschlecht

chuck vt (a) (throw) schmeißen;
can you chuck us the keys?
kannst du mal die Schlüssel
rüberschmeißen?
(b) (end relationship with)
abservieren

chuck down vt sep **it was
chucking it down** (raining hard)
es hat geschüttet

chuck in vt sep (job, studies)
schmeißen

chuffed adj (pleased) **I was really
chuffed with my present** ich
fand mein Geschenk total gut;
**I was really chuffed about her
getting the job** ich fand das total
gut, dass sie den Job gekriegt hat

city n **that area's yuppie city**
in der Gegend gibt's voll die
Yuppies; **her apartment was
barf city** esp US (revolting) ihre
Wohnung sah aus wie Sau

clapped-out adj (car, machine)
klapprig; **she drives a clapped-
out old car** sie fährt so 'ne alte
Klapperkiste

cleverclogs, cleverdick n
(person who thinks they are
clever) Neunmalkluger m,
Neunmalkluge f

cock n (penis) Schwanz m

cock up 1 vt sep (mess up)
versauen
2 vi (mess up)
he's gone and cocked up again
er hat schon wieder Scheiße
gebaut

cock-up n (mess) Murks m; **what
a cock-up!** so ein Scheißsalat!; **to
make a cock-up of something** bei
etwas Scheiße bauen

coke n (cocaine) Koks m; **to do
coke** koksen

come 1 n (semen) Soße f
2 vt **don't come it with me, son!**
(stop being rude) komm mir bloß

nicht so, mein Freundchen!

3 vi **(a)** *(have orgasm)* kommen

(b) come again? *(pardon?)* was hast du gesagt?; *(you must be joking!)* wie bitte?

commando n **to go commando** *(not wear any knickers or underpants)* nichts drunter haben

con 1 n **(a)** *(swindle)* Beschiss m; **it's a con, they told me the job would be well paid!** das ist Beschiss, sie haben mir gesagt, der Job würde gut bezahlt!

(b) *(prisoner)* Knastbruder m

2 vt *(deceive)* bescheißen; **you can't con me!** mich kannst du nicht bescheißen!; **they conned him into leaving them all his money** sie haben ihm sein ganzes Geld abgeluchst; **they conned me out of £20** sie haben mir 20 Pfund abgeluchst

conk n *(nose)* Zinken m

conk out vi **(a)** *(stop working)* den Geist aufgeben

(b) *(fall asleep)* einpennen

(c) US *(die)* **he conked out** er hat ins Gras gebissen

cool 1 adj **(a)** *(fashionable)* cool; **he's a cool dude** das ist ein cooler Typ

(b) *(good)* cool; **that's really cool!** echt cool!; **it's cool runnings** *(everything's fine)* alles fit

(c) *(not concerned)* **I'm cool about that** ich hab' damit kein Problem; **I told my mother I'm gay and she was cool about it** ich hab' meiner Mutter gesagt,

dass ich schwul bin, und sie hat's ganz relaxed genommen; **are we cool?** *(still friends)* kein Stress zwischen uns?

(d) *(acceptable)* **don't worry, it's cool** ist in Ordnung, null Problemo; **is it cool to smoke a joint?** alles klar, wenn ich einen Joint rauche?

(e) *(not carrying drugs)* sauber

2 vt **cool it!** *(calm down)* reg dich ab!

3 interj *(great)* cool!

coon !! n Racist *(black person)* Bimbo m

cop 1 n **(a)** *(police officer)* Polyp m; **the cops** die Polente; **a cops and robbers film** ein Krimi

(b) *(phrases)* **it wasn't much cop** *(wasn't very good)* das war nicht gerade der Schlager; **it's a fair cop** *(I can't complain about being caught)* geschieht mir recht

2 vt *(get)* **I copped a beating from my dad** ich hab' von meinem Vater Prügel bezogen; **cop hold of this end of the rope** halt mal das Ende des Seils [*not slang*]; **he copped it** *(died)* er hat ins Gras gebissen; **we'll cop it from the teacher if she finds out** *(get in trouble)* wenn die Lehrerin das rausfindet, dann gibt's Zoff; **cop a load of this!** *(look at this)* guck mal!; *(listen to this)* hör dir das mal an!; **to cop some Zs** esp US *(have a nap)* 'ne Runde abliegen

cop out vi *(back out)* kneifen; **he copped out of asking her to dance** er hat Fracksausen bekommen und sie nicht zum Tanzen eingeladen

cop-out n (cowardly decision) Drückebergerei f; **that's a total cop-out** das doch reine Drückebergerei; **that sounds like a cop-out to me** das klingt nach Kneifen

copper n (police officer) Polyp m

couch potato n (person who watches too much TV) Couchpotato f

cough up 1 vt sep (a) (pay) rausrücken
(b) (vomit) **I coughed my guts up** ich hab' mir die Seele aus dem Leib gespuckt
2 vi (pay up) die Kohle rausrücken

count → out

cow n (a) Insult (nasty woman) Kuh f; **she's a cow to her sister** sie ist saugemein zu ihrer Schwester; **you (old or stupid) cow!** du dumme Kuh!; **she's a miserable old cow** sie ist eine alte Zimtzicke
(b) (woman) Tante f; **she's a clever cow** die Tante ist ganz schön clever; **some cow nicked my pen** irgend so 'ne Tante hat meinen Stift geklaut; **look at that fat cow over there!** guck dir mal die fette Tante dort drüben an!; **you jammy cow!** du hast ein Schwein!; **the poor cow broke her leg** die arme Tante hat sich das Bein gebrochen; **don't be such a silly cow!** sei nicht so 'ne doofe Ziege!

crack n (a) (of bottom) Kimme f

(b) (situation) **what's the crack, guys?** was geht, Leute?
(c) esp Irish (fun) **the crack's great there** da ist schwer was los; **what's the crack like in Spain?** was ist in Spanien so los?

crack up 1 vi (a) (start laughing) sich einen ablachen; **I cracked up when I heard what had happened** ich habe mir einen abgelacht, als ich gehört habe, was passiert ist
(b) (have mental breakdown) mit den Nerven fix und fertig sein; **she is gradually cracking up** die dreht langsam völlig durch
2 vt sep (cause to laugh) **she/ that programme cracks me up** die/das Programm ist zum Schreien
3 vt insep **it's not all it's cracked up to be** so toll ist das dann auch wieder nicht

crap 1 n (a) (excrement) Kacke f
(b) (act of defecation) **I need a crap** ich muss kacken; **to do a crap** kacken; **to go for a crap** kacken gehen; **to have a crap** kacken
(c) (bad thing) Kacke f; **that album's a load of (old) crap** das Album ist Kacke; **you can't expect me to eat that crap** du meinst doch wohl nicht, dass ich so 'ne Kacke esse
(d) (nonsense) Scheiße f; **what she said is complete and utter crap** sie hat die totale Scheiße erzählt; **that's a load of (old) crap!** das ist doch alles

Scheiße!; **cut the crap!** erzähl keine Scheiße!; **you're full of crap!** *(you're a liar)* erzähl doch keinen Scheiß!; **don't give me that crap!** erzähl mir doch nicht so'n Scheiß!; **to talk crap** Scheiße erzählen; **don't start on about that New Age crap!** fang bloß nicht mit der New-Age-Scheiße an!

(e) *(hassle)* Scheiße *f*; **I don't have to take that crap from him, he can get stuffed!** so 'ne Scheiße muss ich mir von ihm nicht gefallen lassen, der kann mich mal!; **I don't need this (kind of) crap** so 'ne Scheiße muss ich mir nicht geben

(f) *(stuff)* Scheißzeugs *nt*

(g) *(anything)* **you don't know crap** 'nen Scheiß weißt du; **we didn't get crap** einen Scheiß haben wir bekommen

(h) *(bad heroin)* Scheißstoff *m*

(i) *(phrases)* **he beat** *or* **kicked** *or* **knocked the crap out of me** *(beat me up)* er hat mich zu Matsch geschlagen; *(defeated me heavily)* er hat mich in den Sack gesteckt; **he bores the crap out of me** *(I find him very boring)* der ödet mich total an; **you lied! – did I crap!** *(I didn't)* du hast gelogen! – Scheiße, hab' ich nicht!; **he's got a new car – has he crap!** *(he doesn't)* er hat ein neues Auto – 'nen Scheiß hat er!; **it's good to meet some other people who actually give a crap about animal rights** *(care)* toll, noch andere Leute zu treffen, die sich beim Tierschutz reinhängen; **I don't** *or* **couldn't give a crap about it/them** *(don't care)* das ist/die sind mir scheißegal; **he couldn't give a crap** *(doesn't care about anything)* das ist ihm alles scheißegal; **who gives a crap what she thinks?** *(no-one cares)* das interessiert doch keine Sau, was sie meint; **like crap!** *(expresses disbelief, disagreement)* das ist doch gequirlte Scheiße!; **I already phoned her – like crap you did!** *(no you didn't)* ich hab' sie schon angerufen – 'nen Scheiß hast du!; **I feel like crap** *(ill)* mir geht's beschissen; **it hurts like crap** *(a lot)* das tut brutal weh; **he treats me like crap** *(badly)* er behandelt mich wie die letzte Scheiße; **you scared the crap out of me** *(frightened me to death)* du hast mir eine Scheißangst eingejagt

2 *adj* (a) *(bad)* beschissen; **their music is crap** die machen beschissene Musik; **he's a crap singer** er ist ein beschissener Sänger; **I'm crap at physics** in Physik bin ich beschissen schlecht; **I feel crap** *(ill)* mir geht's beschissen; **we had a crap holiday** der Urlaub war beschissen; **this hi-fi sounds crap** die Stereoanlage klingt beschissen

(b) *(remorseful)* **I feel crap about what I said/did to her** ich fühl' mich beschissen, dass ich das zu ihr gesagt habe/ihr das angetan habe

3 *vt* **I was crapping myself** *(scared)* ich habe mir vor Angst

in die Hose geschissen
 4 vi (defecate) kacken
 5 interj (expresses disbelief, disagreement) erzähl' keinen Scheiß!; **I couldn't find it – crap!** (expresses disbelief) ich hab's nicht gefunden – erzähl' keinen Scheiß!

crappy adj (a) (bad) beschissen; **a crappy computer** ein beschissener Computer; **we had a crappy time** es war beschissen
 (b) (ill) **I feel crappy** mir geht's beschissen
 (c) (nasty) **that was a really crappy thing to do** das war hundsgemein, so was zu tun

crash vi (sleep) pennen; **can I crash at your place?** kann ich bei dir pennen?

crash out vi (sleep) einpennen; **he crashed out on the sofa** er ist auf dem Sofa eingepennt

creek n **we're really up the creek (without a paddle) now** (we've had it) jetzt sitzen wir in der Tinte → **shit**

creep **1** n (a) Insult (nasty man) Kotzbrocken m; **get lost, you creep!** hau ab, du Kotzbrocken!
 (b) (sycophant) Schleimer,-in m,f
 2 vi (be sycophantic) **you're always creeping (up) to the teacher** du schleimst dich immer beim Lehrer ein

cretin n Insult (stupid person) Schwachkopf m; **you (stupid) cretin!** du Schwachkopf!

ⓘ Obwohl das Wort **cretin** (*Kretin*, *Schwachsinniger*) kaum noch verwendet wird, um einen geistig Behinderten zu bezeichnen, ist es, wenn es als Schimpfwort für einen dummen Menschen benutzt wird, dennoch eine Beleidigung für Menschen mit einer geistigen Behinderung.

crucial **1** adj (well) crucial (excellent) spitzenmäßig
 2 interj (excellent) spitzenmäßig!

crummy adj (a) (bad) mies
 (b) (ill) **I feel crummy** mir geht's bescheiden
 (c) (nasty) **that was a really crummy thing to do** das war fies, das zu tun

crumpet n (a) Sexist (women) geile Bräute pl; **look at that bit of crumpet over there** guck dir mal die Braut da drüben an
 (b) (men) Schnuckelchen pl; **look at that bit of crumpet over there** guck dir mal den schnuckeligen Typ da drüben an
 (c) (sex) **he hasn't had any crumpet for ages** er hat schon ewig keine Schnitte mehr gehabt; **I fancy a (nice) bit of crumpet** ich könnte jetzt gut 'ne (hübsche) Schnitte vernaschen

cunt !! n (a) (vagina) Fotze f
 (b) Insult (contemptible man) blöder Sack; **you cunt!** du blöder Sack!; **you fucking cunt!** du Arschficker!
 (c) (any man or woman) **she's a clever cunt** das ist ein ganz

schlaues Arsch; **some cunt nicked my pen** irgend so ein Arsch hat meinen Stift geklaut; **you lucky cunt!** du hast ein Arschglück!; **the poor cunt buggered her leg** die arme Fotze hat sich das Bein kaputtgemacht; **what a stupid cunt!** so eine blöde Fotze!

(d) *Sexist (woman)* **look at that bit of cunt over there!** guck dir mal die Fotze an!

(e) *Sexist (sex)* **I fancy a bit of cunt** ich brauch' jetzt 'ne Fotze zum Ficken

(f) *(difficult thing)* **this sum's a real cunt** die Rechnung ist arschschwierig; **this door's a cunt to open** die Tür geht echt arschschwer auf

> ⓘ Fast jeder kann bestätigen, dass **cunt** das beleidigendste Wort der englischen Sprache ist, und in der Tat benutzen es viele Leute nie und deuten es nur mit der Beschönigung **the C-word** an. In der Wendung **you fucking cunt** benutzt, stellt es die schlimmste Beleidigung im Englischen dar. Kein deutsches Wort gibt den Grad der Beleidigung wieder. Wenn es in Bezug auf eine Frau oder auf den Sex mit einer Frau benutzt wird, hat es eine ungeheuer sexistische Bedeutung. Obwohl es eigentlich auch sexistisch ist, die weibliche Vagina so zu bezeichnen, wird es doch seit kurzem von einigen Frauen selbst dafür benutzt.

D

dago *Racist* **1** *n* **(a)** *(Spaniard)* Südländer *m*

(b) *(Spanish language)* **I can't speak a word of dago** ich kann kein Wort Spanisch [*not slang*]

2 *adj (Spanish)* spanisch [*not slang*]; **you dago bastard!** du schleimiger Südländer!

ⓘ Der Ausdruck **dago** ist rassistisch, wenn damit ein Spanier bezeichnet wird. Im Zusammenhang mit der Sprache ist es nicht so abwertend und wird manchmal sogar als leicht humorvoll empfunden.

damn 1 *n* **I don't** *or* **couldn't give a damn about them** *(don't care)* die sind mir doch verdammt noch mal egal; **I don't** *or* **couldn't give a damn about what you think** *(don't care)* was du meinst ist mir doch verdammt noch mal egal; **he couldn't give a damn** *(doesn't care about anything)* das ist ihm alles verdammt egal; **you've done damn all today** *(nothing)* du hast den ganzen Tag keinen Strich getan; **I asked her nicely, but damn all good it did me** *(it did me no good, it was no use)* ich hab' sie nett gefragt, aber das hat mir null genutzt; **you know damn all about it, so shut your face!** du weißt doch null darüber, also halt die Klappe!

2 *adj (for emphasis)* **the damn car won't start!** das verdammte Auto springt nicht an!; **I can't hear a damn thing** *(anything)* ich kann verdammt noch mal nichts hören; **she's a damn sight cleverer than he is** *(a lot)* sie ist ein verdammtes Stück klüger als er

3 *adv (for emphasis)* **the film was damn good/awful** der Film war verdammt gut/schlecht; **don't be so damn stupid** sei nicht so verdammt doof; **you did damn well** das hast du verdammt gut gemacht; **you'd damn well better do what I say!** du solltest verdammt noch mal tun, was ich dir sage!; **you know damn well who I mean** du weißt verdammt genau, wen ich meine; **no damn way am I doing that!** das werde ich verdammt noch mal nicht tun!; **too damn right!** verdammt richtig!

4 *vt* **damn you!** *(get stuffed)* zum Teufel mit dir!; **damn the lot of them!** *(they can get stuffed)* sie können sich alle zum Teufel scheren!; **I'm damned if I'm going to take that sort of**

treatment from them! ich werd' mich verdammt noch mal nicht so von denen behandeln lassen!; **well I'll be damned!** *(expresses surprise)* ich fass' es nicht!; **damn it!** *(expresses annoyance)* verdammt!; **as near as damn it** *(very nearly)* so gut wie

5 *interj (expresses annoyance)* verdammt!

dead 1 *adj* **over my dead body!** *(no way)* nur über meine Leiche!; **she was dead to the world** *(fast asleep)* sie hat tief und fest geschlafen → **drop**

2 *adv (very)* total; **he's dead nice** er ist total nett; **it was dead difficult/easy** das war total schwierig/leicht; **he was dead beat** *(exhausted)* er war todmüde

def *adj (excellent)* fetzig; **he's got this well def motor** er hat diese fetzige Karre

dick *n* **(a)** *(penis)* Schwanz *m* **(b)** *Insult (stupid man)* Arschloch *nt*; **you (stupid) dick!** du (blödes) Arschloch!; **I felt a right dick in my kilt** ich bin mir in dem Kilt wie das letzte Arschloch vorgekommen; **stop being such a dick!** sei nicht so ein Arschloch! **(c)** *esp US (anything)* **he didn't do dick at the office today** einen Kack hat er heut' im Büro getan; **you don't know dick** einen Kack weißt du

dickhead *n Insult (stupid man)* Arschloch *nt*; **you dickhead!** du Arschloch!; **I felt a right dickhead in my kilt** ich bin mir in dem Kilt wie das letzte Arschloch vorgekommen; **stop being such a dickhead!** sei nicht so ein Arschloch!

dike → **dyke**

dildo *n Insult (stupid person)* Blödhammel *m*; **you dildo!** du Blödhammel!

dipshit *n US Insult (contemptible person)* Trottel *m*; **you dipshit!** du Trottel!

dire *adj (terrible)* **the film/ weather was dire** der Film/das Wetter war zum Abgewöhnen

dirty 1 *adj Humorous* **we went away for a dirty weekend** wir sind auf ein Sexwochenende weggefahren

2 *adv (for emphasis)* **there was a dirty great hole in the bottom** da war ein brutal großes Loch im Boden

dis, **diss** *vt (criticize)* dissen

div *n Insult (stupid person)* Doofie *m*; **you div!** du Doofie!

dive *n (unpleasant place)* **that bar is a real dive** die Kneipe ist ein übler Schuppen

do *vt* **(a)** *(cheat)* **we've been done** wir sind reingelegt worden; **they did us for fifty quid** sie haben uns fünfzig Mäuse abgeknöpft **(b)** *(punish)* **dad'll do you when he finds out** wenn Papa das rausfindet, dann setzt es was; **I got done for talking in class** es hat was gesetzt, weil ich im Unterricht gequatscht habe **(c)** *(prosecute)* **she got done for speeding** sie ist wegen zu schnellem Fahren verknackt worden

(d) *(have sex with)* Sexist knallen; **did you do her?** hast du sie geknallt?

(e) *(drug)* nehmen [*not slang*]; **I don't do hard drugs** ich nehme keine harten Drogen

(f) *(imitate)* **he did a Gareth Southgate and missed the penalty** er hat's Gareth Southgate nachgemacht und den Elfmeter verschossen

(g) *(phrases)* **that woman really does something for me** *(I find her attractive)* die Frau ist meine Kragenweite; **to do it (with somebody)** *(have sex)* es (mit jemandem) machen

doddle *n* **it was a doddle** das war kinderleicht

dodgy *adj* (a) *(unreliable, bad)* **the weather's been a bit dodgy recently** das Wetter ist in letzter Zeit auch nicht ganz echt; **the brakes on the car are really dodgy** die Bremsen an dem Auto sind nicht ganz astrein; **we stayed at a well dodgy hotel** wir haben in einem ziemlich üblen Schuppen gewohnt; **the food there's pretty dodgy** das Essen dort ist ziemlich übel; **I've got a dodgy knee** ich hab' was am Knie

(b) *(untrustworthy)* **he's a well dodgy geezer** das ist ein ganz krummer Hund; **that sounds like a pretty dodgy story to me** das kann doch kein Schwein glauben

(c) *(ill)* **I'm feeling pretty dodgy** ich fühl' mich richtig mies

(d) *(tricky)* **it's a dodgy situation** das ist eine beknackte Situation

(e) *(stolen)* geklaut; **he tried to sell me some dodgy tickets** er hat versucht, mir geklaute Karten zu verkaufen

dog *n* (a) Sexist *(ugly woman)* Krähe *f*

(b) *(phrases)* **the food there's the dog's bollocks** *(excellent)* das Essen da ist voll der Knaller

ⓘ Zu dem Ausdruck **it's the dog's bollocks** gibt es mehrere witzige Abwandlungen wie **it's the donkey's knob**, **it's the mutt's nuts** und **it's the canine's testicles**, die alle auf die Hoden von Tieren abzielen.

doh *interj (expresses frustration at stupidity)* bo nnein!

do in *vt sep* (a) *(kill)* **they did him in** den haben sie um die Ecke gebracht; **he did himself in** *(committed suicide)* er hat sich umgebracht

(b) *(beat up)* **I'm gonna do your head in** *(beat you up)* ich mach dich fix und alle; **this crossword is doing my head in** *(confusing me)* das Kreuzworträtsel macht mich wahnsinnig

(c) *(exhaust)* fertig machen

doo-doo *n* Humorous (a) *(excrement)* Aa *nt*; **the floor was covered in doo-doo** der Fußboden war voller Aa

(b) *(piece of excrement)* Häufchen *nt*; **I think the baby's done a doo-doo in its nappy** ich glaube, das Baby hat Stinkerchen in die Windel gemacht

(c) *(trouble)* **we're in deep doo-doo now** jetzt sind wir verraten und verkauft

dope *n* (a) *(marijuana)* Dope *nt*; **to smoke dope** kiffen; **he's a dope fiend** der kifft
(b) *(any illegal drug)* Stoff *m*
(c) *Insult (stupid person)* Doofmann *m*; **you dope!** du Doofmann!

dork *n esp US Insult (idiot)* Kotzbrocken *m*

dosh *n (money)* Kohle *f*; **he's earning loads of dosh** der verdient jede Menge Kohle

doss 1 *n* (a) *(easy thing)* **this degree's a doss** dieser Abschluss ist doch easy
(b) *(sleep)* **to have a doss** ratzen
2 *vi* (a) *(be idle)* **to doss (about** *or* **around)** faul rumhängen
(b) *(sleep)* ratzen; **I spent a month dossing on park benches** ich hab' einen Monat lang auf Parkbänken geratzt

dosser *n (lazy person)* **he's a dosser** er ist ein fauler Hund

douchebag *n US Insult (contemptible person)* Wichser *m*

dough *n (money)* Kies *m*; **he's earning loads of dough** der verdient jede Menge Kies

drama queen *n (over-dramatic person)* **don't be such a drama queen** nun mach mal kein Drama draus; **he's a drama queen** er macht aus allem ein Drama

drip *n (boring, bland person)* Dumpfbacke *f*

drop 1 *vt* **to drop a sprog** *Humorous (give birth)* werfen
2 *vi* **drop dead!** *(get stuffed)* geh zum Teufel!

druggie *n (drug addict)* **he's a druggie** der ist auf Drogen

dude *n* (a) *(man)* Typ *m*
(b) *(term of address)* **yo, dude!** he, Alter! → **cool**

duff 1 *n* **to be up the duff** *(pregnant)* einen Braten in der Röhre haben
2 *adj (bad, faulty)* für 'n Eimer; **it was a duff cartridge** die Patrone war für 'n Eimer; **he took a duff penalty** der Elfmeter ging in die Hose

dump 1 *n* (a) *(unpleasant place)* **the youth hostel was a dump** die Jugendherberge war eine Bruchbude; **that town's a dump** die Stadt ist ein Kaff
(b) *(phrases)* **to have a dump** *(defecate)* ein Ei *or* ein Dampf-Ei legen
2 *vt (split up with)* Schluss machen mit

dweeb *n US Insult (idiot)* Trottel *m*; **you dweeb!** du Trottel!

dyke *n Homophobic (lesbian)* Lesbe *f*; **bull dyke** kesser Vater

ⓘ Obwohl **dyke** ein lesbenfeindliches Wort ist, wenn von Heterosexuellen in Bezug auf Lesbierinnen benutzt, verliert es jedoch jeden beleidigenden Zug, wenn Lesbierinnen sich selbst so bezeichnen.

E

E *n* (a) *(ecstasy)* E *nt*
(b) *(ecstasy tablet)* Bonbon
m or nt; **he had taken at least
five Es** er hatte mindestens fünf
Bonbons eingeworfen

eat *vt* **eat shit (and die)!** *(get
stuffed)* du kannst mich am Arsch
lecken!; **to eat pussy** *(perform
cunnilingus)* lecken

eejit *n esp Irish (idiot)* Dämlack
m; **you eejit!** du Dämlack!

effing *Euphemism* [*fucking*] **1**
adj (for emphasis) **the effing
car won't start** das bescheuerte
Auto springt nicht an; **he's an
effing idiot** er ist ein saublöder
Idiot; **I can't hear an effing thing**
verdammt noch mal, ich kann
kein Stück hören

2 *adv (for emphasis)* **the film
was effing awful** der Film war
total beschissen; **no effing way
am I doing that!** einen Scheiß
werd' ich tun!; **you'd effing well
better do what I say!** verdammt,
tu, was ich dir sage!

eff off *Euphemism* [*fuck off*]
1 *vi (go away)* **I told him to eff
off** ich hab' ihm gesagt, er soll
abschieben

2 *interj (go away)* verfatz dich!;
(expresses refusal) du kannst
mich mal!; *(expresses disbelief)*
mach kein' Scheiß!

end *n* **to get one's end away**
(have sex) einen Stich machen

F

F.A. *n Euphemism* [*fuck all*] *(nothing)* **I got (sweet) F.A. for my trouble** einen Dreck hab' ich für meine Mühe bekommen

face *n* **he was out of his face** *(drunk)* er hatte die totale Gesichtslähmung; *(on drugs)* er war total zu; **I got out of my face** *(drunk)* ich bin total abgestürzt; *(on drugs)* ich hab' mich zugedröhnt; **get out of my face!** *(leave me alone)* zieh Leine!; **she has a face like the back end of a bus** *Humorous (she's ugly)* die hat ein Gesicht wie 'ne Bratpfanne; **he has a face like a slapped arse** *(looks miserable and angry)* dem hängen die Mundwinkel bis zum großen Zeh; **hang on while I put my face on** *(do my make-up)* Sekunde, ich muss mir nur noch etwas Farbe ins Gesicht klatschen → **shut, suck**

faff about, **faff around** *vi (mess about)* rumgammeln; **he does nothing but faff about on the computer** er spielt dauernd nur am Computer rum

fag *n* **(a)** *(cigarette)* Kippe *f* **(b)** *US Homophobic (homosexual)* Schwuli *m*; **stop hugging me, you fag!** hör auf, mich zu umarmen, du warmer Bruder!
(c) *(boring task)* **to be a fag** nerven; **doing the dusting's a real fag** Staubwischen nervt echt

 Obwohl **fag** im Sinne von **(b)** ein schwulenfeindliches Wort ist, wenn von Heterosexuellen in Bezug auf Homosexuelle benutzt, verliert es jedoch jeden beleidigenden Zug, wenn Homosexuelle sich selbst so bezeichnen.

faggot *n US Homophobic (homosexual)* Schwuli *m*; **stop hugging me, you faggot!** hör auf, mich zu umarmen, du warmer Bruder!

 Obwohl **faggot** ein schwulenfeindliches Wort ist, wenn von Heterosexuellen in Bezug auf Homosexuelle benutzt, verliert es jedoch jeden beleidigenden Zug, wenn Homosexuelle sich selbst so bezeichnen.

fair → **cop**

fairy *n Homophobic (homosexual)* Schwuchtel *f*

fanny *n* **(a)** *(vagina)* Muschi *f*; **get your fanny over here!** *(come* *here quickly)* beweg deinen Hintern hierher!

   (b) *US (bottom)* Hinterteil *nt*

   (c) *Sexist (women)* Schnallen *pl*

   (d) I got sweet Fanny Adams for my trouble *Euphemism* [*fuck all*] *Humorous (nothing)* einen feuchten Dreck habe ich für meine Mühe bekommen

far-out 1 *adj* **(a)** *(bizarre)* abgefahren

   (b) *(great)* irre

   2 *interj (great)* ist ja irre!

fart 1 *n* **(a)** *(wind)* Furz *m*; **to do a fart** furzen

   (b) *Insult (stupid person)* **he's an old fart** er ist ein altes Ekel; **stop being such a boring old fart** sei doch nicht so 'n Spießer

   2 *vi (pass wind)* furzen

fart about, fart around *vi (mess about)* rumgammeln; **he does nothing but fart about on the computer** er spielt dauernd nur am Computer rum

fast → **pull**

fat *adj Ironic* **do you expect to get a pay rise? – huh, fat chance (of that)** *(no chance)* meinst du, du kriegst eine Gehaltserhöhung? – ha, einen Dreck werd' ich kriegen; **did she help you? – yes, and a fat lot of good it did us too** *(it did no good)* hat sie euch geholfen? – ja, und viel hat's uns gebracht!; **I don't know how it works – a fat lot of use you are** *(you're no use)* ich weiß nicht, wie das funktioniert – du bist aber auch gar keine Hilfe

favour *n* **do me a favour!** *(don't be ridiculous)* ich glaub', ich hör nicht richtig!

feck *interj Irish (expresses annoyance)* verfluchte Scheiße!

fess up *vi esp US (confess)* singen

fierce 1 *adj (excellent)* krass; **their latest single is fierce, man** ihre neueste Single ist voll krass, Mann

   2 *interj (excellent)* krass!

finger → **pull**

fit 1 *n* **my dad will have or throw a fit when he finds out** *(be angry)* mein Vater kriegt oder bekommt 'nen Anfall, wenn er das rausfindet

   2 *adj (attractive)* schnuckelig

flaming 1 *adj (for emphasis)* **he's a flaming idiot** er ist ein Vollidiot; **it's a flaming pain in the neck** das ist für die Füchse; **flaming hell or heck!** *(expresses annoyance)* Herrgottnochmal!; *(expresses surprise)* Himmel!

   2 *adv (for emphasis)* **it was flaming awful** es war total schrecklich; **don't be so flaming stupid** sei nicht so verdammt doof; **there was a flaming great hole in the bottom** da war ein verdammt großes Loch im Boden; **no flaming way am I doing that!** einen Dreck werd' ich tun!; **too flaming right!** verdamm mich, das kannst du laut sagen!; **you'd flaming well better do what I say!** du solltest verdammt noch mal tun, was ich dir sage!

flasher n *(exhibitionist)* Exhi m

flip 1 vt **my dad flipped his lid when he found out** *(got angry)* mein Vater ist echt ausgeklinkt, als er das rausgefunden hat; **flip it!** *(expresses annoyance)* Kacke!

2 vi **(a)** *(get angry)* ausflippen; **my dad totally flipped when he found out** mein Vater ist total ausgeflippt, als er das rausgefunden hat

(b) *(go mad)* ausflippen

3 interj *(expresses annoyance)* Kacke!

flipping 1 adj *(for emphasis)* **the flipping car won't start** das doofe Auto springt nicht an; **he's a flipping idiot** so ein Doofmann; **I can't hear a flipping thing** ich kann nicht die Bohne hören; **it's a flipping pain in the neck** das ist echt ein Mist; **flipping hell** or **heck!** *(expresses annoyance)* ach du Kacke!; *(expresses surprise)* Mensch Meier!

2 adv *(for emphasis)* **it was flipping awful** das war echt schrecklich; **we had a flipping marvellous time** wir haben uns echt toll amüsiert; **it's flipping freezing** es ist schweinekalt; **we were flipping lucky** wir hatten ein Schweineglück; **don't be so flipping stupid** sei doch nicht so doof; *Ironic* **that's flipping brilliant, now what do we do?** na prima, und was machen wir jetzt?; **there was a flipping great hole in the bottom** da war ein mordsmäßig großes Loch im Boden; **you did flipping well** das hast du echt super gemacht;

you'd flipping well better do what I say! ich würd' dir stark raten zu tun, was ich sage!; **no flipping way am I doing that!** ich denk' nicht im Traum daran!; **are you going? – not flipping likely!** gehst du hin? – ich denk' nicht im Traum daran!; **too flipping right!** das kann man laut sagen!

flog vt **(a)** *(sell)* verkitschen; **he tried to flog me a dodgy computer** er hat versucht, mir einen maroden Computer anzudrehen

(b) he was flogging his log *Humorous (masturbating)* er war gerade dabei, seine Rohre zu reinigen

fluff → **bit**

flunk vt *US (fail)* durchrasseln in; **I flunked physics/my exam** ich bin in Physik/in der Prüfung durchgerasselt

fly adj *(excellent)* hammergeil

fogey, fogy n *(old)* fogey Spießer,-in m,f; **he's a young fogey** er ist schrecklich spießig

footie n *(football)* Fußball m [*not slang*]; **to play footie** kicken

fork out 1 vt sep *(pay)* hinblättern

2 vi *(pay)* blechen; **I had to fork out for a new fridge** ich musste in einen neuen Kühlschrank investieren

freaking *esp US Euphemism* [*fucking*] **1** adj *(for emphasis)* **the freaking car won't start** das beschissene Auto springt nicht an; **he's a freaking bastard** er ist ein Scheißtyp; **you freaking idiot!** du bescheuerter Idiot!; **I can't hear a freaking thing** ich hör' keinen Scheiß; **what the freaking hell is wrong with you people?** was ist eigentlich mit euch Scheißtypen los?

2 adv (for emphasis) **the film was freaking brilliant** der Film war voll krass; **the film was freaking awful** der Film war voll beschissen; **we had a freaking marvellous time** wir haben uns voll fett amüsiert; **don't be so freaking stupid** sei doch nicht so bescheuert; **you must be freaking joking** (no way) du hast sie wohl nicht alle?; Ironic **that's freaking brilliant, now what do we do?** schöne Scheiße, und was machen wir jetzt?; **a freaking great lorry** ein brutal großer Lastwagen; **you'd freaking well better do what I say!** verdammt, du tust, was ich sage!; **no freaking way am I doing that!** 'nen Dreck werd' ich tun!; **are you going? – not freaking likely!** gehst du hin? – 'nen Dreck werd' ich tun!; **too freaking right!** das kannst du verdammt noch mal laut sagen!

freak out 1 vt sep **(a)** (scare) **spiders freak me out** bei Spinnen flippe ich aus

(b) (disconcert) **that guy just freaks me out** der Typ ist mir nicht geheuer [not slang]; **it freaked me out** ich bin total ausgeflippt

2 vi **(a)** (get scared) ausflippen; **he freaked out when he saw the spider** er ist ausgeflippt, als er die Spinne sah

(b) (get disconcerted) ausflippen; **I freaked out when I found out his room was covered in photos of me** ich bin ausgeflippt, als ich rausfand, das sein Zimmer mit Fotos von mir gepflastert war

(c) (get angry) austicken **(d)** (go berserk) ausrasten

frigging Euphemism [fucking] **1** adj (for emphasis) **the frigging car won't start** das bescheuerte Auto springt nicht an; **he's a frigging bastard** er ist ein Scheißtyp; **you frigging idiot!** du bescheuerter Idiot!; **I can't hear a frigging thing** ich hör keinen Scheiß; **it's a frigging pain in the neck** so 'ne Scheiße, das ist voll ätzend; **frigging hell** or **heck!** (expresses annoyance) verfluchte Kacke!; (expresses surprise) Herr im Himmel!

2 adv (for emphasis) **the film was frigging good/awful** der Film war saugut/sauschlecht; **we had a frigging marvellous time** wir haben uns wie die Idioten amüsiert; **it's frigging freezing** es ist scheißkalt; **we were frigging lucky** wir hatten ein Scheißglück; **don't be so frigging stupid** sei doch nicht so bescheuert; Ironic **that's frigging brilliant, now what do we do?** schöne Scheiße, und was machen wir jetzt?; **a frigging great lorry** ein brutal großer Lastwagen; **you did frigging well** das hast du brutal gut gemacht; **you'd frigging wel**

better do what I say! verdammt, du tust, was ich sage!; **no frigging way am I doing that!** 'nen Dreck werd' ich tun!; **are you going? – not frigging likely!** gehst du hin? – 'nen Dreck werd' ich tun!; **too frigging right!** das kannst du verdammt noch mal laut sagen!

fritz n US **the TV's on the fritz again** (playing up) der Fernseher tut schon wieder nicht

Frog 1 n Racist (a) (French person) Froschfresser m
  (b) (French language) Französisch nt [not slang]
  2 adj (French) französisch [not slang]

fruit n esp US Homophobic (homosexual) Schwuli m

> ⓘ Obwohl **fruit** ein schwulenfeindliches Wort ist, wenn von Heterosexuellen in Bezug auf Homosexuelle benutzt, verliert es jedoch jeden beleidigenden Zug, wenn Homosexuelle sich selbst so bezeichnen.

fruitcake n (eccentric person) Spinner m

fuck 1 n (a) (sex) ‼ Fick m; **to have a fuck** ficken
  (b) (sexual partner) ‼ **he's/she's a good fuck** er/sie ist ein guter Fick
  (c) Insult (person) ‼ **he's a useless fuck** er ist ja so ein Arsch; **you stupid fuck!** du saublöder Wichser!
  (d) (anything) **he didn't do fuck at the office today** einen Kack hat er heut' im Büro getan; **you don't know fuck** einen Kack weißt du!; **my opinion isn't worth fuck round here** keine Sau interessiert sich hier für meine Meinung
  (e) (phrases) **they earn a fuck of a lot** (a huge amount) sie verdienen arschviel; **we had a fuck of a job doing it** (it was very difficult) das war arschschwer; **the waterfall was as big as fuck** (very big) der Wasserfall war saugroß; **it's as cold as fuck in here!** (very cold) hier drin ist eine Arschkälte!; **her brother's as stupid as fuck** (very stupid) ihr Bruder ist ja so ein Arschkeks; **for fuck's sake!** (expresses annoyance) Scheiße noch mal!; **for fuck's sake get a move on!** (expresses impatience) verdammte Scheiße, mach voran!; **you've done fuck all today** (nothing) einen Kack hast du heut' gemacht; **we got fuck all help from them** (none) einen Kack haben sie uns geholfen; **I got fuck all for my efforts** (nothing) einen Kack hab' ich für meine Mühe bekommen; **you know fuck all about it, so shut your face!** (you know nothing) 'nen Kack weißt du darüber, also halt die Klappe!; **there's fuck all else to do, so we might as well watch the film** (nothing else) sonst gibt's doch vedammt nichts zu tun, also können wir uns auch den Film ansehen; **fuck knows how we're ever going to finish this on time** (I don't

know) weiß der Geier, wie wir das rechtzeitig fertig kriegen sollen; **how did she do that? – fuck knows** *(I don't know)* wie hat sie das gemacht? – weiß der Geier; **get the fuck out of here!** *(get out)* beweg deinen Arsch hier weg!; **get to fuck!** *(go away)* !! ach, verfick dich!; **it's good to meet some other people who actually give a fuck about animal rights** *(care)* toll, noch andere Leute zu treffen, die sich für den Tierschutz den Arsch aufreißen; **I don't** *or* **couldn't give a fuck about it/them** *(don't care)* das geht/die gehen mir ja so am Arsch vorbei; **I couldn't give two fucks** *(don't care)* das geht mir ja doppelt am Arsch vorbei; **I couldn't give a fiddler's** *or* **flying** *or* **rusty fuck** *(don't care)* das geht mir ja so was von am Arsch vorbei; **he couldn't give a fuck** *(doesn't care about anything)* das geht ihm alles am Arsch vorbei; **who gives a fuck what she thinks?** *(no-one cares)* das interessiert doch keine verdammte Sau, was sie meint; **you fancy her, don't you? – do I fuck!** *(I don't)* du bist scharf auf sie, nicht? – das ist doch verquirlte Scheiße!; **Bury's in Yorkshire, isn't it? – is it fuck!** *(it isn't)* Bury ist in Yorkshire, nicht? – 'nen Scheiß ist es!; **they beat** *or* **kicked the fuck out of us** *(beat us up)* die haben uns die Eier poliert; *(defeated us heavily)* die haben uns die Hosen ausgezogen; **I gave it to my brother – like fuck you**

did! *(no you didn't)* ich hab's meinem Bruder gegeben – 'nen verdammten Scheißdreck hast du!; **he's going out with her – like fuck (he is)!** *(expresses disagreement)* er geht mit ihr – 'nen verdammten Scheiß tut er!; **I'm going to leave now – like fuck you are!** *(no you're not)* ich geh' jetzt – verdammte Scheiße, das wirst du nicht!; **it hurts like fuck** *(a lot)* das tut scheißweh; **shut the fuck up!** *(shut up)* !! halt die Fresse!; **what/when/where/who/why the fuck...?** *(for emphasis)* meine Fresse, was/wann/wo/wer/warum ...?; **that's Claudia Black – who the fuck is she?** *(for emphasis)* das ist Claudia Black – meine Fresse, wer?; **why the fuck didn't you tell me earlier?** Scheiße, warum hast du mir das nicht früher gesagt?; **we can't really afford to take the day off, but what the fuck!** *(we might as well)* wir können es uns eigentlich nicht leisten, einen Tag freizunehmen, aber scheiß der Hund drauf!

2 *vt* **(a)** *(have sex with)* !! ficken; **she'll fuck anything in trousers** *or* **on two legs** *(she's promiscuous)* die fickt doch alles, was bei drei nicht auf dem Baum ist; **he fucked him up the arse** *or* *US* **ass** *(sodomized him)* er hat ihn in den Arsch gefickt; **I fucked his brains out** *(had energetic sex with him)* ich hab' ihn fast bewusstlos gefickt

(b) *(damage)* in Arsch kriegen; **I fucked my leg playing footie** ich hab' gekickt, und jetzt ist mein

Bein im Arsch; **these drugs really fuck your mind** *(cause mental problems)* von den Drogen kriegt man echt 'nen Schaden

(c) *(ruin)* *(plan, chances)* versauen; **my chances of getting the job are fucked** meine Chancen, den Job zu kriegen, sind im Arsch

(d) *(exploit)* ficken

(e) *(phrases)* **fuck a duck!** *Humorous (expresses surprise)* ach du dickes Ei!; **fuck it!** *(expresses annoyance)* verdammte Scheiße!; *(expresses resignation)* scheiß der Hund drauf!; **fuck me!** *(expresses surprise)* heilige Scheiße!; **fuck me gently** or **rigid!** *(expresses surprise)* meine Fresse!; **fuck that!** scheiß drauf!; **they want us to work at the weekend – fuck that!** *(no way)* die wollen, dass wir am Wochenende arbeiten – die haben ja den Arsch offen!; **fuck the lot of them!** *(they can get stuffed)* !! die können mich alle kreuzweise am Arsch lecken!; **fuck this for a laugh** or **a lark** *(this is a waste of time)* das ist doch total für 'n Arsch; **fuck this for a game of soldiers, let's go for a beer!** *(this is a waste of time)* so 'ne Gülle, lass uns ein Bier zischen gehen!; **fuck what they say, let's go anyway!** *(ignore it)* scheiß der Hund drauf, was sie sagen, lass uns trotzdem gehen!; **fuck you!** *(get stuffed)* !! verfick dich!; **go fuck a duck!** *(go away)* fick dich doch ins Knie!; **go fuck yourself** or **your mother** *(go away)* !! verfick

dich, du Arschgesicht!

3 *vi (have sex)* !! ficken; **she fucks like a bunny** or **a mink** *(is very good in bed)* sie ist eine Fickmaschine

4 *interj (expresses annoyance)* verdammte Scheiße!; *(expresses surprise)* heilige Scheiße!; *(expresses fear)* ach du Scheiße!

(i) Fast jeder empfindet **fuck** als das zweitschlimmste Schimpfwort in der englischen Sprache, direkt nach **cunt**. Im Umgangssprachlichen wird es häufig auf kumpelhafte Weise benutzt, ist jedoch in allen anderen Situationen allgemein unakzeptabel. Manche Leute nehmen es tatsächlich nie in den Mund und deuten es höchstens mit der Umschreibung **the F-word** an. Obwohl es im Deutschen ähnliche Wörter gibt, kann keins von ihnen die volle Wortgewalt des englischen Wortes **fuck** wiedergeben.

fuck about, fuck around
1 *vt sep (mess about)* verarschen; **the gas company have been fucking me about** die Gasgesellschaft hat mich voll verscheißert

2 *vi* (a) *(mess about)* Scheiß machen

(b) *(be promiscuous)* herumhuren

fucked *adj* (a) *(broken)* im Arsch

(b) *(injured)* im Arsch; **my knee's fucked** mein Knie ist im Arsch

(c) *(exhausted)* gefickt

(d) *(phrases)* **we're fucked**

(we've had it) jetzt ist die Kacke am Dampfen; **I'm fucked if I know where it is** *(I don't know)* ich hab' keine Scheißahnung, wo das ist; **I'm fucked if I care** das geht mir doch so am Arsch vorbei!; **I'm fucked if I'm going to help them!** ich und denen helfen, die können mich mal am Arsch lecken!; **I can't be fucked going out tonight** *(I can't be bothered)* ich hab' keine Scheißlust, heut' Abend wegzugehen

fucked off *adj (annoyed)* scheißwütend; **I'm really fucked off about what she said** ich bin echt scheißwütend über das, was sie gesagt hat; **I'm totally fucked off with her** ich bin wirklich scheißwütend auf sie; **I get really fucked off seeing him sit around doing nothing all day long** es scheißt mich an, wenn ich ihn den ganzen Tag so faul rumsitzen sehe; **I'm well fucked off with this whole situation** die ganze Situation scheißt mich an

fucked up *adj* (a) *(psychologically damaged)* verkorkst (b) *(terrible)* beknackt; **hey, that's really fucked up** he, das ist ja echt Kacke

fucker *n* (a) *Insult (contemptible man)* !! Ficker *m*; **what a fucker!** so ein Ficker! (b) *(any man or woman)* **she's/he's a clever fucker** die/der ist ein schlaues Stück; **some fucker nicked my pen** irgend so ein Dreckstück hat meinen Stift geklaut; **you jammy fucker!** du hast ein Schweineglück!; **the poor fucker buggered his leg** das arme Schwein hat sich das Bein kaputtgemacht; **what a stupid fucker!** so ein blödes Stück! (c) *(thing)* **it's a big fucker** das ist ja ein saugroßes Scheißteil (d) *(difficult thing)* **this sum's a real fucker** die Rechnung ist scheißschwierig; **this door's a fucker to open** die Tür geht scheißschwer auf (e) *(unpleasant situation)* **his wife left him – what a fucker!** seine Frau hat ihn verlassen – was 'ne Scheiße!

fucking 1 *adj (for emphasis)* **the fucking car won't start** das beschissene Auto springt nicht an; **he's a fucking bastard** !! er ist ein Arschloch; **you fucking idiot!** du beschissener Idiot!; **I can't hear a fucking thing** ich hör' keinen Scheiß; **fucking hell or heck!** *(expresses annoyance)* verdammte Scheiße!; *(expresses surprise)* heilige Scheiße!; **who the fucking hell does she think she is?** und was meint die Scheißtante, wer sie ist?; **fucking Nora!** *(expresses surprise)* heiliger Strohsack!

2 *adv (for emphasis)* **the film was fucking brilliant** der Film war saugut; **the film was fucking crap** der Film war die totale Scheiße; **we had a fucking marvellous time** wir haben uns scheißgut amüsiert; **don't be so fucking stupid** sei doch nicht so scheißblöd; **you must be fucking joking** *(no way)* du

hast wohl den Arsch offen?;
how should I fucking know?
und woher soll ich so'n Scheiß
wissen?; *Ironic* **that's fucking
brilliant, now what do we do?** so
ein Kack! Und was machen wir
jetzt?; **a fucking great elephant**
ein scheißgroßer Elefant; **you
did fucking well** das hast du
scheißgut gemacht; **you'd
fucking well better do what
I say!** verdammt du Arsch, du
tust, was ich sage!; **no fucking
way am I doing that!** einen
Scheiß werd' ich tun!; **are you
going? – not fucking likely!**
gehst du hin? – einen Scheiß
werd' ich tun!; **too fucking right!**
verdammte Scheiße, das kann
man wohl sagen!

fuck off 1 *vi (go away)* sich
verpissen; **I fucked off half way
through the afternoon** ich hab'
mich mitten am Nachmittag
verpisst; **I told him to fuck off**
ich hab' ihm gesagt, er soll sich
verpissen
  2 *vt sep (annoy)* anscheißen;
**her behaviour really fucked me
off** ihr Verhalten hat mich echt
angeschissen
  3 *interj (go away, expresses
refusal)* !! verfick dich!;
(expresses disbelief) erzähl nicht
so 'ne Scheiße!; **fuck off and
die!** *(go away)* !! verfick dich,
du Arsch!; **fuck off out of it!** *(go
away)* !! verfick dich bloß!

fuck up 1 *vt sep* **(a)** *(mess up)*
verkacken
  (b) *(damage psychologically)*
versauen
  2 *vi (mess up)* Kacke bauen

fuck-up *n (mistake)* **there
was a fuck-up over the
travel arrangements** bei den
Reisevorbereitungen hat's Kacke
gegeben; **what a fuck-up!** so
eine Kacke!

full → monty

G

gammy adj (bad) **I've got a gammy knee** ich hab' 'nen Knieschaden

garbage n (a) (nonsense) Quatsch m; **what he said is complete and utter garbage** er hat völligen Quatsch erzählt; **stop talking garbage!** red keinen Quatsch!; **that's a load of (old) garbage!** das ist doch Quatsch mit Soße!

(b) (phrases) **that album's a load of (old) garbage** (bad) das Album ist doch der totale Mist; **you can't expect me to eat that garbage** du erwartest doch wohl nicht, dass ich so 'n Mist esse

geek n (socially inept person) Stiesel m; **he's a computer geek** er ist so ein Computerfuzzi

geezer n (man) Heini m

get vt (a) (understand) kapieren; **I just don't get it, why can't we do it this way?** ich kapier' nicht, warum wir das nicht so machen können

(b) (look at) **get that bloke over there, is he for real?** ich glaub', ich spinne, guck dir bloß mal den Typ da drüben an; **get a load of that!** bo, das ist ja der Hammer!; **get this, the boss says he's going to give us a pay rise!** ich krieg' sie nicht mehr alle, der Chef sagt, er gibt uns 'ne Gehaltserhöhung!

(c) (annoy) auf die Palme bringen

(d) (phrases) **that subject really gets me going** (gets me excited) darauf fahre ich voll ab; **leather boots really get me going** (cause me sexual excitement) auf Lederstiefel fahre ich voll ab

get down vi (a) (dance) 'ne kesse Sohle aufs Parkett legen

(b) US (have sex) **they were getting down in the back of the car** sie machten es hinten im Auto

get off vi (a) (achieve orgasm) fertig werden

(b) (masturbate) **he gets off on pictures of naked women** er guckt sich Fotos von nackten Frauen an und holt sich dabei einen runter

(c) (get high on drugs) **to get off on something** mit etwas abheben

(d) (phrases) **to get off at Edge Hill** or **Gateshead** or **Haymarket** or **Paisley** Humorous (experience coitus interruptus) einen Rückzieher machen; **she gets off on ordering people around** (likes it) sie findet das voll geil, wenn sie andere herumkommandieren kann; **did you get off with him?** *(seduce)* und, hast du ihn rumgekriegt?

get out *vi esp US* **get out of here!** *(expresses disbelief)* ich glaub', ich hör nicht richtig!

ginormous *adj (huge)* elefantös

git *n* (a) Insult *(contemptible man)* blöder Heini; **don't be such a stupid git!** du bist vielleicht ein blöder Heini!
  (b) *(any man or woman)* **he's a lazy git** das ist ein fauler Typ; **she's a fat git** sie ist 'ne fette Tante; **you jammy git!** du Glückspilz!

give *vt* **don't give me that shit!** *(that's a bad excuse)* erzähl doch keinen Scheiß!; **I forgot to type up that report – I'll give you 'forgot', I want it on my desk in five minutes!** *(expresses threat)* ich habe vergessen, den Bericht zu tippen – was heißt hier vergessen, ich will den in fünf Minuten auf meinem Schreibtisch sehen!; **I wouldn't mind giving it to her** *(having sex with her)* der würde ich es gerne besorgen; **did you give her one?** *(have sex with her)* hast du's ihr richtig besorgt?

Glasgow kiss *n* Humorous *(headbutt)* **he gave me a Glasgow kiss** er hat mir 'ne Kopfnuss verpasst

gnarly *adj US* (a) *(excellent)* krass (b) *(terrible)* sauschlecht

go **1** *n* **to have a go at somebody** *(criticize)* jemanden herunterputzen

2 *vt* (a) *(say)* sagen *[not slang]*; **and she goes "no way"** und sie sagt „bestimmt nicht"
  (b) *(phrases)* **I could really go a beer** *(I fancy a beer)* ein Bier würd' jetzt gut reinlaufen; **he was really going it** *or* **some** *(going fast)* er ist echt gedüst

3 *vi* (a) *(go to the toilet)* **I really need to go** ich muss aber ganz nötig
  (b) *(phrases)* **did you go all the way?** *(have sex)* bist du bis zum Äußersten gegangen?; **they were going at it hammer and tongs** *(having vigorous sex)* die gingen dran wie Nachbars Lumpi; **she goes like the clappers** *(she's promiscuous)* die geht ganz schön ab

gob **1** *n* (a) *(mouth)* Maul *nt*; **I smacked him in the gob** ich hab' ihm aufs Maul gehauen; **she gave him a gob job** *(performed fellatio on him)* sie hat es ihm französisch gemacht
  (b) *(spit)* Rotz *m*; **there was a lump of gob on the floor** da war ein Rotzflecken auf dem Boden → **shut**

2 *vi (spit)* rotzen; **he gobbed at me** er hat mich angerotzt

gobshite *n* Insult *(stupid person)* Affe *m*; **you gobshite!** du blöder Affe!

gobsmacked *adj (amazed)* geplättet; **I was totally gobsmacked** ich war total geplättet

go down on *vt insep* **she went down on him** *(performed* *fellatio on him)* sie hat ihm einen abgelutscht; **he went down on her** *(performed cunnilingus on her)* er hat sie geleckt

goof US 1 n (a) *(blunder)* Schnitzer m; **I made a goof** mir ist ein Schnitzer passiert
  (b) Insult *(idiot)* Dösel m; **you goof!** du Dösel!
  2 vi *(make mistake)* **I goofed** mir ist ein Schnitzer passiert

goof about, goof around vi US *(mess about)* rumgammeln; **he does nothing but goof about on the computer** er spielt dauernd nur am Computer rum

goolies npl Humorous *(testicles)* Weichteile pl; **they've got us by the goolies** *(in a difficult position)* die haben uns in der Zange

Gordon Bennett interj Euphemism [God] *(expresses surprise)* ach du liebe Güte!

gormless adj *(stupid)* blöd; **he's gormless** der ist echt blöd; **she just gave me a gormless grin** sie hat mich nur blöd angegrinst

grand n *(thousand pounds or dollars)* Riese m; **ten grand** zehn Riesen

grass 1 n (a) *(marijuana)* Gras nt; **to smoke grass** kiffen
  (b) *(informer) (criminal)* Singvogel m; *(at school)* Petze f
  2 vi *(inform) (criminal)* singen; *(pupil)* petzen; **he grassed on his mates** *(criminal)* er hat seine

Kumpel verpfiffen; *(pupil)* er hat seine Kumpel verpetzt

grass up vt sep *(inform on)* **to grass somebody up (to somebody)** jemanden (bei jemandem) verpfeifen

groovy 1 adj *(cool)* fetzig
  2 interj *(cool)* fetzig!

gross 1 adj *(disgusting)* widerlich [not slang]; **that's gross!** das ist echt widerlich!; **a really gross photo of a human skull full of maggots** ein echt krasses Foto von einem menschlichen Schädel voller Würmer
  2 interj kotzwürg!

gross out vt sep *(disgust)* **the scene where they chopped his head off really grossed me out** bei der Szene, wo sie seinen Kopf abgehackt haben, hat's bei mir echt abgestellt; **he's always grossing out the girls in the class with some disgusting prank or other** er macht immer so ekelhafte Scherze, dass es den Mädchen in der Klasse voll abstellt

grotty adj (a) *(dirty)* dreckig
  (b) *(poor-quality)* grottig

grub n *(food)* Mampfe f; **have we got any grub in?** haben wir was zu futtern da?; **grub's up!** *(the food's ready)* Essen fassen!

gut n *(stomach)* Wampe f; **I've got gut rot** *(stomachache)* ich habe Bauchweh → **cough up**

gutted adj *(very disappointed)* ganz schön down

H

hacked off adj (annoyed) sauer; **I'm really hacked off about what she said** ich bin echt sauer über das, was sie gesagt hat; **she's hacked off with her boyfriend** sie ist sauer auf ihren Freund; **I get really hacked off seeing him sit around doing nothing all day long** es kotzt mich an, wenn ich ihn den ganzen Tag so faul rumsitzen sehe

hag n (a) (ugly woman) **she's a hag** or **an old hag** das ist 'ne echte Nebelkrähe
(b) (nasty woman) **she's an old hag** sie ist eine alte Hexe

hair n **I could do with a hair of the dog** (hangover cure) ich brauch 'nen Schluck gegen den Kater; **keep your hair on!** (calm down) mach mal halblang!; **that'll put hairs on your chest!** Humorous (of strong drink) der hat's in sich!

hairy adj (frightening) haarig; **the emergency landing was pretty hairy** die Notlandung war ziemlich haarig

hang vi (a) (spend time) **he hangs with a bunch of skinheads** der hängt mit ein paar Skinheads ab; **what are you doing? – just** hanging was machst du? – ach, einfach abhängen
(b) **how's it hanging?** (how are you?) alles claro?

hang out vi (a) (spend time) **he hangs out with a bunch of skinheads** der treibt sich mit ein paar Skinheads rum; **what are you doing? – just hanging out** was machst du? – einfach so rumhängen
(b) **just let it all hang out** (relax) bleib ganz locker

hanky-panky n Humorous (sex) Nümmerchen nt; **a bit of** or **some hanky-panky** ein Nümmerchen

happy adj **he was not a happy bunny** or **camper** or **chappy when he found out what I'd done** Humorous (he was upset) er hat sich tierisch aufgeregt, als er rausfand, was ich gemacht hatte; **he's not a happy bunny** or **camper** or **chappy, he hardly ever smiles** Humorous (he's an unhappy person) er ist ein Trauerkloß, er lächelt so gut wie nie

hard-on n (erection) Steifer m; **he got a hard-on** er hat einen Steifen gekriegt; **he had a hard-on** er hatte einen Steifen

hash

hash n (hashish) Hasch nt; **to smoke hash** kiffen

haul vt US **we'll be late if you don't haul ass** (hurry up) wir kommen zu spät, wenn du nicht deinen Arsch bewegst

have vt **(a)** (have sex with) haben; **did you have her?** hast du sie gehabt? **(b)** (beat up) vermöbeln; **I could have you any day** dich schaff' ich locker **(c)** (deceive) **you've been had** da bist du betupst worden **(d)** (phrases) **I think you've had enough, mate** (enough to drink) ich glaub', du hast genug gehabt, mein Freund; **I've just about had it** or **I've had it up to here with you/with this job!** (I'm fed up) ich hab' dich/diesen Job total satt!; **this car has had it** (it's beyond repair) das Auto ist hinüber; **we've really had it now** (we're in trouble) jetzt haben wir den Salat; **I've had it, I can't walk another step** (I'm exhausted) ich bin alle, ich kann keinen Schritt mehr tun; **I'm really going to let them have it when they get home** (tell them off) denen werd' ich was erzählen, wenn sie heimkommen; **I tried to convince her I was innocent, but she wasn't having any of it** (she refused to believe me) ich habe versucht, sie von meiner Unschuld zu überzeugen, sie hat's mir aber nicht abgenommen; **they'd had one or two** or **a couple** (a few drinks) sie hatten ein paar zur Brust genommen

have away vt sep **to have it away with somebody** (have sex) jemanden vernaschen; **they were having it away on the sofa** sie waren dabei, sich auf dem Sofa zu vernaschen

have in vt sep **she has it** or **she's got it in for me** (bears me a grudge) die hat mich auf dem Kieker

have off vt sep **to have it off (with somebody)** (have sex) es (mit jemandem) treiben

have on vt sep (tease) auf den Arm nehmen; **it isn't really true, I was just having you on** das ist nicht wirklich wahr, ich hab' dich nur auf den Arm genommen; **are you having me on?** du nimmst mich wohl auf den Arm?

head n **you should get your head examined** (you must be mad) du solltest dich mal auf deinen Geisteszustand untersuchen lassen; **does she give head?** (fellate) lutscht sie auch?; **he's got his head up his arse** or US **ass** (he's full of himself) das ist ein eingebildeter Arsch mit Ohren; **we laughed our heads off** (laughed a lot) wir haben uns totgelacht; **he was out of his head** (drunk, on drugs) er war voll weg; **he got out of his head** (drunk, on drugs) er ist voll weggetreten; **she's totally off** or **out of her head** (she's mad) die ist nicht ganz dicht; **are you off** or **out of your head?** (are you crazy?) du hast wohl einen Knall? → **do in**

headcase n (a) (*eccentric person*) **she's a headcase** die tickt doch nicht richtig

(b) (*violent person*) Schizo m

heat n US **the heat** (*police*) die Bullerei

hell 1 n **there were a hell of a lot of people there** (*lots*) da waren jede Menge Leute; **it could have been a hell of a lot worse** (*much worse*) es hätt' ein ganzes Ende schlimmer sein können; **they earn a hell of a lot** (*a huge amount*) sie verdienen ein Schweinegeld; **we had a hell of a job doing it** (*it was very difficult*) das war echt schwierig; **we had a hell of a time** (*good*) wir haben uns echt gut amüsiert; (*bad*) es war echt schrecklich; **he put up a hell of a fight** (*resisted strongly*) er hat sich wahnsinnig gewehrt; **he's one** or **a hell of a guy** (*great*) der ist große Klasse; **the waterfall was as big as hell** (*very big*) der Wasserfall war wahnsinnig groß; **it's as cold as hell in here!** (*very cold*) hier drin ist es wahnsinnig kalt!; **they beat** or **kicked** or **knocked the hell out of us** (*beat us up*) die haben Kleinholz aus uns gemacht; (*defeated us heavily*) die haben uns in die Pfanne gehauen; **he bores the hell out of me** (*I find him very boring*) der langweilt mich zu Tode; **get the hell out of here!** (*go away*) mach bloß, dass du hier abhaust!; **the neighbours from hell** (*terrible neighbours*) total nervige Nachbarn; **she gave me hell about it** (*a hard time*) sie hat mich deswegen zur Minna gemacht; **give them hell!** (*expresses encouragement*) gib ihnen Saures!; **go to hell!** (*get stuffed*) geh zur Hölle!; **you lied! – did I hell!** (*I didn't*) du hast gelogen – zum Teufel, hab' ich nicht!; **he's got a new car – has he hell!** (*he doesn't*) er hat ein neues Auto – den Teufel hat er!; **I feel like hell** (*ill*) mir geht's übel; **it hurts like hell** (*a lot*) das tut wahnsinnig weh; **you look like hell** (*terrible*) du siehst grausig aus; **to run like hell** (*run very quickly*) wie verrückt rennen; **he's going out with her – like hell (he is)!** (*expresses disagreement*) er geht mit ihr – den Teufel tut er!; **I'm going to leave now – like hell you are!** (*no you're not*) ich geh' jetzt – den Teufel wirst du tun!; **what/where/when/who/why the hell...?** (*for emphasis*) was/wo/wann/wer/warum zum Teufel ...?; **what the hell, you only live once!** (*I might as well*) was soll's, man lebt schließlich nur einmal!; **to hell with it, let's do something else!** (*expresses frustration*) ist doch egal, machen wir was anderes!; **to hell with what they think!** (*I don't care*) zum Teufel, was die meinen!; **I just hope to hell he leaves soon** (*I really hope*) hoffentlich, hoffentlich haut der bald ab → **bleeding, blinking, bloody, blooming, flaming, flipping, frigging, fucking, sodding**

2 interj (*expresses annoyance*) ach wie blöd!; (*expresses*

surprise) Menschenskind!; **oh hell, we're in trouble now!** *(expresses fear)* o Mist, jetzt gibt's Ärger!; **did you say yes? – hell, no!** *(of course not)* hast du ja gesagt? – zum Teufel, nein!

hick *n esp US (country bumpkin)* Landei *nt*

high 1 *n (from drugs)* **it gave me an amazing high** ich war so high wie nie; **this E is guaranteed to give you your best high ever** von dem Bonbon wirst du garantiert superhigh

2 *adj (on drugs)* **to be high** high sein; **to be high as a kite** total high sein; **to get high (on something)** (von etwas) high werden

hit 1 *n* (a) *(murder)* **he was killed in a Mafia hit** den hat die Mafia kaltgemacht

(b) *(of drug)* *(puff on joint)* Zug *m*; *(injection of heroin, etc)* Schuss *m*; **he took another hit** er hat noch einmal durchgezogen; **this stuff gives you quite a hit** auf den Stoff kannste voll abfahren

2 *vt* (a) *(go to)* **let's hit the clubs** lass uns einen Zug durch die Klubs machen; **we thought we might hit the town tonight** wir haben gedacht, wir machen heute Abend einen Zug durch die Gemeinde; **I think I'm going to hit the road** *(leave)* ich glaub', ich verzieh mich mal; **I'm going to hit the sack now** *(go to bed)* ich geh' jetzt in die Falle

(b) **that whisky really hit the spot** *(was just what I needed)* der

Whisky hat's voll gebracht

hitched *adj (married)* **to get hitched** den Anker werfen

hit on *vt insep US (flirt with)* anbaggern

ho *n esp US Sexist (woman)* Schnalle *f*

hog 1 *n* (a) *(person who eats too much)* Fresssack *m*

(b) *(selfish person)* Egosau *f*

2 *vt (keep for oneself)* **he hogged the computer all afternoon** er hat den ganzen Nachmittag den Computer mit Beschlag belegt

hold → cop

hole *n* (a) *(unpleasant place)* **that bar is a hole** die Kneipe ist ein Loch; **the town is a hole** die Stadt ist ein Kaff

(b) *(anus)* Loch *nt*; **get your hole over here!** *(come here quickly)* beweg deinen Arsch hierher!

(c) *(vagina)* Möse *f*

(d) *Sexist (women)* Schicksen *pl*; **there was some tasty hole in that club last night** gestern Abend waren ein paar geile Schicksen in dem Klub; **look at that bit of hole over there** guck dir mal die Schickse an!

(e) *(sex)* **you look like you haven't been getting your hole recently** du siehst aus, als hättest du schon lange kein Loch mehr von innen gesehen

(f) **I need his help like I need a hole in the head** *(it's the last thing I need)* ich brauch' seine Hilfe so dringend wie Kopfweh

homeboy, homey n US (a) *(friend)* Kumpel m
  (b) *(fellow gang member)* Spezi m

hood n US **the hood** *(neighbourhood)* die Nachbarschaft [*not slang*]; **he's from the hood** er kommt aus der gleichen Ecke wie ich

hooked adj *(addicted)* **to be hooked on heroin** an der Nadel hängen; **I'm hooked on that computer game** ich bin süchtig nach dem Computerspiel

hooker n esp US *(prostitute)* Hure f

hooky, hookey n US **to play hooky** *(play truant)* schwänzen

horn n *(erection)* Ständer m; **to have the horn** *(be sexually aroused)* geil sein; **it really gives me the horn** *(arouses me sexually)* das macht mich total geil

horny adj (a) *(sexually aroused)* geil; **he's a horny bugger** er ist ein geiler Bock; **to be** or **feel horny** geil sein
  (b) *(sexually attractive)* scharf

hot 1 adj (a) *(sexually attractive)* heiß
  (b) *(sexually aroused)* heiß; **I'm so hot for you, baby** ich bin so heiß auf dich, Baby
  (c) *(stolen)* heiß; **some hot goods** heiße Ware; **some hot wheels** *(a stolen vehicle)* ein geklauter Schlitten
  (d) *(radioactive)* verstrahlt [*not slang*]

  (e) *(good)* stark; **the hottest new records** die stärksten neuen Platten; **I'm not very hot on that subject** auf dem Gebiet hab' ich's nicht so drauf; **he's really hot on computers** was Computer betrifft, hat er's wirklich drauf; **she's pretty hot shit when it comes to crosswords** bei Kreuzworträtseln ist sie saugut; **I'm not feeling so hot** *(I'm ill)* ich fühl' mich gar nicht so gut
  (f) *(in good form)* **to be hot** stark drauf sein
  2 npl **to have the hots for somebody** *(be sexually attracted to)* voll auf jemanden abfahren

huff n *(angry mood)* **to be in a huff** stinkig sein; **to get in a huff** stinkig werden; **she went off in a huff** sie war total stinkig und ist abgehauen

humongous adj *(enormous)* riesenmäßig

hump 1 n (a) *(sex)* Nummer f
  (b) *(angry mood)* **he's got the hump** er ist grantig; **what's given you the hump, then?** warum bist du denn so grantig, he?
  2 vt (a) *(have sex with)* **he's humping his girlfriend** er ist gerade dabei, eine Nummer mit seiner Freundin zu schieben
  (b) *(carry)* **we spent the day humping crates of books up the stairs** wir haben den ganzen Tag Bücherkisten die Treppe hoch gewuchtet
  3 vi *(have sex)* eine Nummer schieben

hung *adj* he's hung like a
carthorse *or* mule *Humorous
(has large genitals)* der hat ein
Riesengehänge

hunk *n (attractive man)*
Sahneschnitte *f*

I

in 1 *adj* **it's the in place to go at the moment** *(fashionable)* es liegt gerade voll im Trend, dort hinzugehen; **Mallorca's the in resort this summer** Mallorca liegt diesen Sommer voll im Trend; **you're well in there!** *(you have a good chance of seducing that person)* die/der lässt dich auf jeden Fall ran!

2 *adv* **you're in for it** *(in trouble)* jetzt gibt's Ärger

3 *prep* **get in there, my son!** *(encouraging seduction)* geh ordentlich ran, Alter!

innit *adv (used as a tag)* **I ain't got enough cash, innit?** ich hab' nicht genug Kohle, wa?; **he's the big boss, innit?** er ist der große Boss, wa?

J

jack off vi (masturbate) **she found me jacking off** sie hat mich ertappt, als ich mir gerade einen rubbelte

jammy adj (lucky) **you're so jammy!** du hast ja so ein Schwein!; **you jammy bastard!** du Hund, du glücklicher!

jerk n Insult (stupid man) Stinkstiefel m; **you stupid jerk!** du Stinkstiefel!

jerk around vt sep (waste time of) verarschen; **I'm fed up of being jerked around by this airline** ich hab' die Nase voll, von der Fluggesellschaft verarscht zu werden

jerk off 1 vt sep **he jerked himself off** (masturbated) er hat sich einen gerubbelt

2 vi (masturbate) **she found me jerking off** sie hat mich ertappt, als ich mir gerade einen rubbelte

job n (a) Humorous (piece of excrement) Wurst f; **to do a job** (defecate) eine Sitzung machen

(b) **he was on the job** (having sex) er war gerade dabei

Jock n Racist (Scottish person) Schotte m, Schottin f [not slang]; **oi, Jock, come over here!** he, Schottenrock, komm mal rüber!

ⓘ Die meisten Schotten empfinden die Bezeichnung **Jock** als rassistisch, vor allem, wenn sie abfällig von Engländern benutzt wird und in Verbindung mit **bloody** (Scheiß-) oder **stupid** (blöd) verwendet wird, oder wenn ein Schotte so angeredet wird anstatt mit seinem Vornamen. Trotzdem gibt es Zusammenhänge, in denen das Wort neutraler oder sogar humorvoll benutzt wird und nicht beleidigend für Schotten gemeint ist. Ein Beispiel für einen humorvollen Gebrauch ist journalistischer Jargon wie **Jock-Rock** (Schotten-Rock) für schottische Rockmusik. Trotzdem könnten manche sagen, dass sich auch im harmloseren Gebrauch der angeborene Rassismus von Engländern den Schotten gegenüber widerspiegelt. Nichtmuttersprachler sollten diesen Ausdruck möglichst vermeiden.

jock n US (athlete) **she's going out with a (dumb) jock** sie geht mit so einem (stumpfsinnigen) Kraftpaket aus

john n US (toilet) Klo nt; **I need**

to go to the john ich muss aufs Klo

johnson n US (penis) Gerät nt

joint n (a) (cannabis cigarette) Joint m; **to roll a joint** einen Joint bauen

(b) US (prison) **in the joint** im Knast

(c) US (penis) Schwanz m

jugs npl Sexist (breasts) Möpse pl

junkie, junky n (drug addict) Junkie m; **how long has he been a junkie?** seit wann drückt der?; **she's a biscuit junkie** (loves biscuits) sie ist süchtig nach Keksen; **he's a TV junkie** er ist ein Fernsehjunkie

K

kick vt she kicked my ass esp US (defeated me) sie hat mich in den Sack gesteckt; he kicked my butt esp US (defeated me) der hat mich weggefegt; let's get out there and kick some ass or butt esp US (have a good time) lass uns die Sau rauslassen; he's really going to kick some ass or butt when he finds out esp US (punish) der macht jemanden zur Sau, wenn er das rauskriegt; their new record really kicks ass or butt esp US (it's excellent) ihre neue Platte ist megagut; to kick the bucket Humorous (die) den Löffel abgeben; she kicked it (died) sie ist hopsgegangen → arse, crap, shit, shite

kickin' adj (excellent) hammergeil

kiddie fiddler n (paedophile) Kinderschänder m

kinky adj (perverse) he's into kinky sex er steht auf neckische Spielchen; she was wearing those kinky boots of hers sie hatte diese scharfen Stiefel an; you kinky devil! du Perversling!; ooh, kinky! wie neckisch!

kip 1 n (sleep) Schläfchen nt; you'd better get some kip before we go du haust dich besser mal aufs Ohr, bevor wir gehen; to have a kip 'ne Runde pofen **2** vi (sleep) pofen

kiss vt kiss my arse or US ass! (get stuffed) leck mich am Arsch!; he's always kissing the teacher's arse (being sycophantic towards him) der kriecht immer dem Lehrer in den Arsch; he's always kissing arse (being sycophantic) der ist ja so ein Arschkriecher

kit n she got her kit off in front of everyone (undressed) sie hat vor allen die Hüllen fallen lassen; get your kit off, you horny bastard! runter mit den Klamotten, du scharfer Hengst!

klutz n US (a) Insult (stupid person) Dösel m; you klutz! du Dösel!
(b) Insult (clumsy person) Trampel mf; you klutz! du Trampel!

knacker vt (a) (break) (machine, object) liefern
(b) (injure) I knackered my back playing tennis ich hab' mir beim Tennisspielen den Rücken kaputt gemacht
(c) (ruin) (plan, hopes) kaputt machen

(d) *(exhaust)* fix und fertig machen

knackered *adj* (a) *(exhausted)* kaputt

(b) *(broken)* geliefert; *(worn-out)* abgewrackt

(c) *(injured)* kaputt; **my knee's knackered** ich hab' ein kaputtes Knie

knob 1 *n* (a) *(penis)* Ding *nt*

(b) *(phrases)* **it's like a James Bond movie with knobs on** das ist wie ein James-Bond-Film mit allem Schnickschnack; **you stupid git! – same to you with knobs on!** *(reply to insult)* Blödmann! – selber einer!

2 *vt (have sex with)* pimpern

knock → crap, shit, shite

knockers *npl Sexist (breasts)* Klötze *pl*

knot → tie

kooky *adj esp US (eccentric)* gaga

kraut *Racist* 1 *n* (a) *(German person)* Fritz *m*

(b) *(German language)* Deutsch *nt* [*not slang*]

2 *adj* deutsch [*not slang*]

> ⓘ In manchen Zusammenhängen ist der Ausdruck **kraut** rassistisch, vor allem, wenn er zusammen mit **bloody** (*Scheiß-*) oder **stupid** (*blöd*) verwendet wird. Trotzdem wird der Ausdruck manchmal fast liebevoll oder humorvoll verwendet und soll bei Deutschen keinen Anstoß erregen. Das gilt auch in Bezug auf die deutsche Sprache. Dennoch könnten manche sagen, dass sich auch im harmloseren Gebrauch der angeborene Rassismus von Briten den Deutschen gegenüber widerspiegelt.

L

laid *adj* **did you get laid at the weekend, then?** *(have sex)* hast du es am Wochenende besorgt gekriegt?; **all men are interested in is getting laid** *(having sex)* Männer sind nur daran interessiert, dass es ihnen jemand besorgt

later, later on, laters *interj (goodbye)* see you!, bis denn!

lay *n (sexual partner)* **he's a good lay** er ist gut im Bett; **she's an easy lay** sie ist leicht ins Bett zu kriegen

leak *n* **to take** *or* **have a leak** *(urinate)* für kleine Jungs gehen

leave *vt* **leave it out!** *(stop doing that)* lass es sein!; *(expresses disbelief)* nicht wirklich, eh?

leg **1** *n* **did you get your leg over?** *(have sex)* hast du eine flachgelegt? → **fuck**
 2 *vt* **we legged it** *(ran away)* wir haben uns aus dem Staub gemacht; **we're going to have to leg it** *(hurry)* wir müssen einen Zahn zulegen; **he legged it out of the house** *(ran)* er hat sich verdünnisiert; **leg it boys, the pigs are coming!** bloß weg hier Leute, die Bullen kommen!

legless *adj (drunk)* **to be legless** blau sein; **to get legless** blau werden

lid → **flip**

life *n* **get a life!** *(don't be so boring)* sei nicht so spießig!

load → **cop**

loaded *adj* **to be loaded** *(drunk)* Schlagseite haben; *(on drugs)* breit sein; **he's loaded** *(rich)* er hat Geld wie Heu; **I got loaded** *(drunk)* ich hab' mir den Kanal voll laufen lassen; *(on drugs)* ich hab' mich zugelötet

loaf *n* **use your loaf!** *(use your brain)* schalt mal deine Birne ein!

loony **1** *n* **(a)** *(mentally ill person)* Irrer *m*, Irre *f*; **loony bin** *(mental hospital)* Klapsmühle *f*
 (b) *(eccentric person)* Spinner,-in *m,f*
 2 *adj* **(a)** *(mentally ill)* irre
 (b) *(crazy)* bekloppt; **the loony left** *(in politics)* die Linksextremen

ⓘ In der Bedeutung **(a)** ist die Bezeichnung **loony** *(Irrer)* beleidigend für Menschen, die an einer Geisteskrankheit leiden.

lose → **bottle**

loser *n Insult (useless person)* Lusche *f*

lost *adj* **get lost!** *(go away)* geh zum Kuckuck!; *(expresses refusal)* vergiss es!; *(expresses disbelief)* echt wahr?

lousy *adj* **(a)** *(very bad)* lausig; **we had a lousy time** wir haben uns lausig amüsiert; **they got me a lousy present** sie haben mir ein ganz schäbiges Geschenk gegeben; **to be in a lousy mood** eine lausige Laune haben; **I feel lousy about what I said/did to her** *(remorseful)* ich fühl' mich bescheiden, dass ich das zu ihr gesagt habe/ihr das angetan habe

(b) *(ill)* **I feel lousy** mir geht's lausig

(c) *(expresses contempt)* **he gave me twenty lousy quid** er hat mir zwanzig lausige Pfund gegeben

lucky *adj* **did you get lucky at the weekend?** *(have sex)* warst du am Wochenende erfolgreich?; **are you getting a pay rise too? – I should be so lucky!** *(if only)* kriegst du auch eine Gehaltserhöhung? – schön wär's!

lunchbox *n Humorous (man's genitals)* Paket *nt*

M

make out *vi esp US* to make out (with somebody) *(kiss and canoodle)* (mit jemandem) rummachen

man *interj esp US (form of address)* stop that, man! Mann, lass das!; **hey man, what are you doing?** Mann, was machst du da?; **hey man, that's great!** das ist klasse, Mann!; **man, am I tired!** *(I'm very tired)* Mann, bin ich müde!

man boobs *npl Humorous (large, flabby male pectorals)* Männerbusen *m*

mare *n (difficult thing, nightmare)* it was a mare das war der Hammer

measly *adj (paltry)* poplig; **all we got was a measly ten quid** wir haben nur zehn poplige Pfund gekriegt; **he's a measly git** *(mean)* er ist ein alter Geizkragen

mega 1 *adj (excellent)* echt stark **2** *interj (excellent)* echt stark!

mensch *n US (decent person)* he's a real mensch der ist schwer in Ordnung

mental *adj* (a) *(crazy)* he's mental *(person)* der hat 'ne Meise; things have been pretty

mental at the office *(hectic)* im Büro war die Hölle los; **to go mental** *(get angry)* ausrasten **(b)** *(excellent)* abgefahren

Mickey-Mouse *adj (second-rate)* Pipifax-; **a Mickey-Mouse dictionary** ein Pipifaxwörterbuch

mincer *n Homophobic (homosexual)* Schwulibert *m*

minger *n (ugly person)* potthässliches Teil

minging *adj* (a) *(disgusting)* versifft
(b) *(smelly)* voll stinkig
(c) *(ugly)* potthässlich
(d) *(bad, horrible)* zum Abgewöhnen

missus *n* the missus *(wife)* meine/deine/seine Alte

mo *adv esp US (very)* we're going to be playing some mo phatt sounds today wir spielen heute ein paar echt heiße Sounds

monkey *n* I couldn't *or* don't give a monkey's what they think *(don't care)* was die meinen ist mir doch schnurzegal → **brass**

monty, monte *n* you get to see the full monty *(everything)* da fallen alle Hüllen [*not slang*]; **shall we just paint the**

kitchen, or shall we do the full monty? sollen wir nur die Küche streichen oder ganze Sache machen?

moon *vi (expose one's buttocks)* **to moon at somebody** jemandem den blanken Arsch zeigen

moron *n* Insult *(stupid person)* Schwachkopf *m*; **you (stupid) moron!** du Schwachkopf!

ⓘ Obwohl das Wort **moron** (*Schwachsinniger*) kaum noch verwendet wird, um einen geistig Behinderten zu bezeichnen, ist es, wenn es als Schimpfwort für einen dummen Menschen benutzt wird, dennoch eine Beleidigung für Menschen mit einer geistigen Behinderung.

mother *n* esp US **(a)** *(any man or woman)* **he's a clever mother** der ist ein Superschlauer; **some mother stole my pen** irgend so ein Miststück hat meinen Stift geklaut

(b) *(difficult thing)* **this sum's a real mother** die Rechnung ist sauschwierig; **this door's a mother to open** die Tür geht sauschwer auf

motherfucker *esp US* **1** *n* **(a)** *Insult (contemptible person)* !! Arschficker *m*; **come here, motherfucker!** komm her, du Arschficker!

(b) *(any man or woman)* **he's a clever motherfucker** der ist ein schlaues Stück; **some motherfucker stole my pen** irgend so ein Dreckstück hat

meinen Stift geklaut; **the poor motherfucker broke his leg** der arme Arsch hat sich das Bein gebrochen

(c) *(difficult thing)* **this sum's a real motherfucker** die Rechnung ist scheißschwierig; **this door's a motherfucker to open** die Tür geht scheißschwer auf

2 *interj (expresses annoyance)* !! Scheißdreck!; **you're fired! – motherfucker!** du bist gefeuert! – so 'ne Scheiße!

motor *n (car)* Karre *f*

mouth off *vi (boast)* **he's always mouthing off about what an expensive motor he has** der spuckt immer die großen Töne, was er für eine teure Karre hat

move → arse, ass

muff 1 *n* **(a)** *(vagina)* Muschi *f*
(b) *Sexist (women)* Schnallen *pl*
2 *vt* **(a)** *(drop)* **to muff a catch** den Ball versieben
(b) *(make a mess of)* **to muff a chance** eine Chance versieben

mug *n* **(a)** *(face)* Visage *f*; **mug shot** Verbrecherfoto *nt* [*not slang*]
(b) *(gullible person)* Trottel *m*

munchies *npl* **I've got the munchies** *(I'm peckish)* ich brauch' was zwischen die Zähne

muppet *n* Insult *(stupid person)* Clown *m*; **you muppet!** du Clown!; **I felt a right muppet in my kilt** ich bin mir wie der letzte Heuler vorgekommen in dem Kilt; **stop being such a muppet** stell dich doch nicht so an wie der letzte Heuler

mush n (a) (mouth) Fresse f; I
socked him one in the mush
ich hab' ihm eine in die Fresse
gehauen; **keep your mush shut**
(don't say anything) halt ja die
Fresse → **shut**
  (b) (form of address) oi, mush!
he du Sack!

mutant n (weird person)
Knalltüte f

N

nads npl (testicles) Klöten pl

naff adj (showing poor taste) (film, dress) ätzend; **not inviting her to the party was a really naff thing to do** das war echt uncool, sie nicht zur Party einzuladen

naff off 1 vi (go away) abhauen; **I told him to naff off** ich hab' ihm gesagt, er soll abhauen
2 interj (go away) zieh Leine!; (expresses refusal) is nicht!; (expresses disbelief) ich glaub', ich spinne!

narked adj (annoyed) sauer; **I'm really narked about what she said** ich bin wirklich sauer über das, was sie gesagt hat; **are you narked with me?** bist du sauer auf mich?

neat 1 adj (great) klasse; **that'd be really neat** das wär' klasse
2 interj (great) klasse!

neck → pain

nerd n (socially inept person) Stiesel m; **he's a computer nerd** er ist so ein Computerfuzzi

nick 1 n (a) (prison) Kittchen nt; **in the nick** im Kittchen
(b) (police station) Wache f
(c) (condition) **to be in good/bad nick** gut/nicht gut in Schuss sein
2 vt (a) (arrest) hochnehmen; **she got nicked for shoplifting** sie wurde wegen Ladendiebstahl hochgenommen; **you're nicked!** Sie sind verhaftet! [not slang]
(b) (steal) klauen; **who nicked my pen?** wer hat meinen Stift geklaut?

nifty adj (stylish) klasse

nigger ‼ n Racist (black person) Nigger m

> ⓘ Während **nigger** der schlimmste rassistische Ausdruck ist, wenn er von Weißen benutzt wird, verliert er das Anstößige, wenn er von Schwarzen selbst verwendet wird. Aber selbst dann hat es den Beigeschmack eines armen, gesellschaftlich unterdrückten Schwarzen.

no-no n (thing to be avoided) **turning up late for work is an absolute no-no in our office** Zuspätkommen ist bei uns im Büro absolut nicht drin

nookie n Humorous (sex) **I haven't had any nookie for ages** ich habe schon ewig kein Nümmerchen mehr gemacht; **I**

fancy a bit of nookie ich hätte jetzt Lust, ein Nümmerchen zu machen

nosh n (food) Futterage f; **have we got any nosh in?** haben wir was zu beißen da?

not adv **he's a really nice guy… not!** Humorous (he isn't nice) er ist ein echt netter Kerl… denkste; **I don't fancy her – not much you don't!** (yes you do) ich mach' mir nichts aus ihr – nö, überhaupt nicht!

nuddy n **to be in the nuddy** (naked) splitternackig sein; **they played volleyball in the nuddy** sie haben splitternackig Volleyball gespielt

nuke 1 n (nuclear bomb) Atombombe f [not slang]
2 vt (a) (drop nuclear bomb on) eine Atombombe werfen auf [not slang]
(b) Humorous (microwave) in die Mikrowelle stecken

number n **(to do a) number one** Euphemism (urinate) klein (machen); **(to do a) number two** Euphemism (defecate) groß (machen)

nut 1 n (a) (head) Rübe f; **use your nut!** (use your brain) benutz mal deine Rübe!; **he did his nut when he found out** (was angry) er drehte total ab, als er es rausgefunden hatte; **are you off your nut or something?** (are you crazy?) du hast sie wohl nicht mehr alle?
(b) (crazy person) Wahnsinniger m, Wahnsinnige f

(c) (fan) **she's a Buffy nut** sie ist ein Buffy-Freak
2 vt **I nutted him** (headbutted him) ich hab' ihm 'ne Kopfnuss verpasst; (kicked him in the testicles) ich hab' ihm in die Eier getreten

nutcase n (a) (eccentric person) **she's a nutcase** die hat 'nen Sprung in der Schüssel
(b) (violent person) Schizo m
(c) (mentally ill person) Bekloppter m, Bekloppte f

> ⓘ In der Bedeutung (c) ist die Bezeichnung **nutcase** (Bekloppter) beleidigend für Menschen, die an einer Geisteskrankheit leiden.

nuts 1 npl (testicles) Nüsse pl; **they've got us by the nuts** (in a difficult position) die haben uns am Arsch
2 adj (a) (crazy) behämmert; **that music is driving me nuts** (annoying me) die Musik macht mich ganz kirre; **to go nuts** (go crazy) durchdrehen
(b) (keen) **to be nuts about something/somebody** total verrückt nach etwas/jemandem sein
3 interj **they want us to work at the weekend – nuts to that!** (no way) die wollen, dass wir am Wochenende arbeiten – nie und nimmer!; **nuts to you!** (get stuffed) du kannst mich mal!

nutter n (a) (eccentric person) **she's a nutter** die hat 'nen Sprung in der Schüssel

(b) *(violent person)* Schizo *m*
(c) *(mentally ill person)* Irrer *m*,
Irre *f*

> ⓘ In der Bedeutung **(c)** ist
> die Bezeichnung **nutter** (*Irrer*)
> beleidigend für Menschen, die
> an einer Geisteskrankheit leiden.

O

oats *npl* **he hasn't been getting his oats** *Humorous (having regular sex)* er hätte es mal wieder dringend nötig

OD 1 *n (drug overdose)* goldener Schuss; **he died from a heroin OD** er hat sich einen goldenen Schuss Heroin gesetzt

2 *vi (overdose)* **he OD'd on heroin** er hat sich einen goldenen Schuss Heroin gesetzt; **we OD'd on museums** *(saw lots of museums)* wir haben uns bis zum Pupillenstillstand Museen reingezogen

one 1 *n* **(a)** *(penis)* **he's got a huge one/little one** er hat ein Riesenteil/Miniteil

(b) *(drink)* **to go for a quick** *or* **swift one** einen heben gehen; **to have had one too many** *(be drunk)* einen über den Durst getrunken haben

(c) *(amusing person)* **you are one** *or* **a one!** du bist mir vielleicht einer/eine!

(d) *(blow)* **I socked him one** *(I hit him)* ich hab' ihm eine gescheuert; **I'll give you one if you don't stop it** *(I'll smack you)* wenn du nicht endlich aufhörst, kriegste eine gescheuert

(e) *(phrases)* **he had one off the wrist** *(masturbated)* er hat sich einen aus dem Handgelenk geschüttelt; **he's one of them** *Homophobic (a homosexual)* der ist auch so einer

2 *npl (breasts)* **she's got big/little ones** sie hat viel/wenig; **she's got gorgeous ones** sie hat tolle Dinger → **give**

orgasmic *adj (delicious)* **this cake's orgasmic** der Kuchen ist die Wucht!

out *adv* **(a)** *(in existence)* **this synthesizer is the best one out** dieser Synthesizer ist der beste überhaupt; **he's the jammiest person out** der hat aber auch ein Glück

(b) *(phrases)* **she was out for the count** *(fast asleep)* sie war total weg; **I'm out of here!** *(I'm leaving)* ich mach' dann mal die Fliege; **he was out of it** *(intoxicated)* er war dicht; *(not himself)* er war ziemlich durch den Wind; **one more mistake like that and you'll be out on your arse** *or US* **ass!** *(fired)* noch so ein Fehler, und du kriegst einen Tritt in den Arsch!

P

pack *vt* **to pack a gun** *(be carrying a gun)* 'ne Knarre dabeihaben

pack in *vt sep (stop doing)* **she's packed in her job** sie hat ihren Job geschmissen; **shall we pack it in for the day?** *(stop what we're doing)* sollen wir für heute Feierabend machen?; **just pack it in, will you?** *(stop it)* hör endlich auf damit!

pack up *vi* **(a)** *(machine)* kaputtgehen

(b) *(finish work)* **we pack up for Christmas on the 22nd** über Weihnachten machen wir am 22. den Laden zu

pad *n (house or apartment)* Hütte *f*

Paddy *n Racist (Irish person)* Ire *m*, Irin *f* [*not slang*]; **oi, Paddy, come over here!** he, Kleeblatt, komm mal rüber!

(i) Die meisten Iren empfinden die Bezeichnung **Paddy** als rassistisch, vor allem, wenn sie abwertend von Engländern benutzt wird, zum Beispiel in Verbindung mit **bloody** *(Scheiß-)* oder **stupid** *(blöd)* oder wenn ein Ire so angeredet wird anstatt mit seinem Vornamen. Trotzdem gibt es Zusammenhänge, in denen das Wort neutraler oder sogar humorvoll benutzt wird und nicht beleidigend für Iren gemeint ist. Trotzdem könnten manche sagen, dass sich auch im harmloseren Gebrauch der angeborene Rassismus von Engländern den Iren gegenüber widerspiegelt. Nichtmuttersprachler sollten diesen Ausdruck möglichst vermeiden.

pain *n* **(a)** *(annoying thing)* **to be a pain** nervig sein; **we had to start all over again – what a pain!** wir mussten noch einmal ganz von vorne anfangen – wirklich nervig!; **it's a bit of a pain having to travel such a long way** es ist ein bisschen nervig, immer so weit fahren zu müssen; **to be a pain in the arse** *or US* **ass** *(annoying)* verdammt nerven; **to be a pain in the neck** *or* **backside** *or* **butt** *(annoying)* total nerven

(b) *(annoying person)* Nervensäge *f*; **stop being such a pain!** du bist vielleicht 'ne Nervensäge!; **to be a pain in the arse** *or US* **ass** *(annoying)* obernervig sein; **to be a pain in the neck** *or* **backside** *or* **butt** *(annoying)* total nervig sein

Paki !! 1 n Racist (a) (Pakistani person) Pakistani mf [not slang] (b) (Urdu language) Urdu nt [not slang]

2 adj (Pakistani) pakistanisch [not slang]

> ⓘ Obwohl der rassistische Ausdruck **Paki** ursprünglich für pakistanische Einwanderer gebraucht wurde, wird er heute allgemeiner für Briten mit pakistanischen Eltern oder Großeltern verwendet oder auch für alle Asiaten aus den früheren britischen Kolonien.

Paki shop n Racist (corner shop) Tante-Emma-Laden m

> ⓘ In Großbritannien werden **Paki shops** (Tante-Emma-Läden) von Pakistanern, Indern oder Asiaten betrieben und haben sonntags und bis spätabends geöffnet.

pansy n (a) (effeminate man) Tunte f (b) Homophobic (homosexual) Zarter m

pants 1 npl I wouldn't mind getting into his pants Humorous (having sex with him) dem würde ich gerne an die Wäsche gehen; it bored the pants off me (really bored me) das hat mich zu Tode gelangweilt; he charmed the pants off the boss (totally charmed her) er hat die Chefin voll eingewickelt; the film scared or frightened the pants off me (really scared me) bei dem Film habe ich mir fast ins Hemd gemacht → piss, shit

2 adj the book is pants (very bad) das Buch ist Müll

paralytic adj (very drunk) to be paralytic stockbesoffen sein; I got paralytic ich hab' mir einen angesoffen

party vi (a) (have sex) do you want to party? hast du Lust auf ein bisschen Spaß? (b) (take drugs) I partied all night long ich hab' mich die ganze Nacht zugeknallt

peachy adj US (excellent) spitze; everything's peachy! alles ist bestens!

pecker n (penis) Lümmel m

pede n (paedophile) Kinderschänder m

pee 1 n (a) (urine) Pipi nt (b) (act of urinating) I need a pee ich muss pinkeln; to go for a pee pinkeln gehen; to have a pee pinkeln

2 vt I nearly peed myself or my pants (wet myself) ich hab' mir fast in die Hose gepinkelt; I peed myself (laughing) (laughed a lot) ich habe mich beömmelt

3 vi (urinate) pinkeln

perv n (pervert) Perversling m

peter n US (penis) Pipimann m

phatt adj (good) heiß

pick up vt sep (seduce) abschleppen

piece n (a) esp US (gun) Knarre f (b) (phrases) I wouldn't mind a piece of that! Sexist (I'd like to have sex with her) die würd' ich auch gerne mal vor die Flinte kriegen!; **look at that piece of arse** or US **ass over there!** *Sexist (woman)* guck dir mal die geile Schnitte an!; **it was a piece of cake** *(easy)* das war ein Kinderspiel; **it was a piece of piss** *(easy)* das war total easy; **her brother's a piece of shit** or **shite** *(unpleasant person)* ihr Bruder ist ein Stück Scheiße; **the film was a piece of shit** or **shite** *(very bad)* der Film war totale Scheiße; **he was with a gorgeous piece of skirt** *Sexist (woman)* er hatte 'ne klasse Schnecke dabei

pig 1 *n* **(a)** *(police officer)* Bulle *m*; **the pigs** die Bullen
  (b) *(greedy person)* **he's a (greedy) pig** er ist ein verfressenes Stück
  (c) *(fat person)* **she's a (fat) pig** sie ist 'ne (fette) Qualle
  (d) *(untidy person)* Schwein *nt*
  (e) *(nasty person)* Schwein *nt*; **you pig!** du Schwein!; **he's a sexist pig** er ist ein Machoschwein; **he's a real pig to his sister** er behandelt seine Schwester wie ein Schwein
  (f) *(difficult thing)* **this sum's a real pig** die Rechnung ist echt schwierig; **this door's a pig to open** die Tür geht echt schwer auf
  (g) to be like or **as happy as a pig in shit** *(very happy)* total happy sein
  2 *vt* **we pigged ourselves on biscuits** *(ate a lot)* wir haben Kekse gemampft

pig out *vi* **we pigged out on biscuits** *(ate a lot)* wir haben Kekse gefuttert

pillock *n Insult (stupid man)* Trottel *m*; **you (stupid) pillock!** du Trottel!; **I felt a right pillock in my kilt** ich bin mir in dem Kilt wie der letzte Trottel vorgekommen; **stop being such a pillock** stell dich doch nicht so an wie der letzte Trottel

pinch *vt (steal)* stibitzen; **who pinched my pen?** wer hat meinen Stift stibitzt?

piss 1 *n* **(a)** *(urine)* Pisse *f*; **this beer tastes like piss** *(weak and bad)* das Bier schmeckt wie Pisse
  (b) *(act of urinating)* **I need a piss** ich muss pissen; **to go for a piss** pissen gehen; **to have a piss** pissen
  (c) *(phrases)* **their latest record is piss** *(very bad)* ihre letzte Platte ist Gülle; **to take the piss out of somebody** *(tease)* jemanden verarschen; **I was taking the piss, I wasn't serious** ich habe einen kleinen Scherz gemacht, das war nicht ernst gemeint; **fifty pounds for a two-hour concert? Are they taking the piss?** *(are they serious?)* fünfzig Pfund für ein zweistündiges Konzert? Die wollen uns wohl verarschen; **are you taking the piss, mate? – you're giving it away** *(you're easy to ridicule)* willst du mich verarschen, Mann? – wenn du so blöd bist; **to go (out) on the piss** *(drinking)* die Sause machen → **piece**
  2 *vt* **I nearly pissed myself** or

pissed my pants *(wet myself)* ich hab' mich fast bepisst; **we were pissing our pants** *(scared)* wir haben uns eingepisst; **I pissed myself (laughing)** *(laughed a lot)* ich hab' mich bepisst (vor Lachen)

3 *vi* **(a)** *(urinate)* pissen; **they piss all over us** *(mistreat us)* die behandeln uns wie Scheiße; **we pissed all over them** *(defeated them heavily)* die haben wir platt gemacht; **it was like pissing into the wind** *(a waste of time)* das war gegen den Wind gepisst; **I wouldn't piss on them if they were on fire** *(I couldn't care less about them)* die gehen mir ja so was von am Arsch vorbei

(b) *(rain hard)* **it was pissing with rain** es hat gepisst

4 *adv* *(very)* **it was piss easy** das war pisseinfach

piss about, piss around 1 *vt sep* *(mess about)* **my girlfriend has been pissing me about** meine Freundin hat mich zum Depp gemacht; **the phone company has been pissing me about** die Telefongesellschaft hat mich zum Hugo gemacht; **I'm fed up of being pissed about by this airline** ich hab' die Nase voll, von der Fluggesellschaft so verarscht zu werden

2 *vi* *(mess about)* blöd rummachen

piss artist *n* **he's a piss artist** *(useless person)* er ist die totale Lusche; *(alcoholic)* er ist ein Sumpfhuhn

piss down 1 *vi* **it was pissing down** *(raining hard)* es hat gepisst

2 *vt sep* **it was pissing it down** *(raining hard)* es hat gepisst

pissed *adj* **(a)** *(drunk)* **to be pissed** besoffen sein; **to get pissed** sich besaufen; **I got pissed** ich hab' mich besoffen; **he was as pissed as a newt** *or* **fart** er war voll bis an die Kiemen; **we were pissed out of our heads** *or* **skulls** *or* **tiny minds** wir waren stinkbesoffen

(b) *US (annoyed)* stinksauer; **she's pissed at her boyfriend** sie ist stinksauer auf ihren Freund

pissed off *adj* *(annoyed)* stinksauer; **I'm really pissed off about what she said** ich bin echt stinksauer über das, was sie gesagt hat; **she's pissed off with her boyfriend** sie ist stinksauer auf ihren Freund; **I get really pissed off seeing him sit around doing nothing all day long** es macht mich stinksauer, wenn ich ihn den ganzen Tag so faul rumsitzen sehe; **I'm well pissed off with this whole situation** die ganze Situation kotzt mich an

pisser *n* **(a)** *(unpleasant situation)* **my girlfriend left me – what a pisser!** meine Freundin hat mit mir Schluss gemacht – das is' ja beschissen!; **it's a real pisser having to get up so early** es ist echt beschissen, immer so früh aufstehen zu müssen

(b) *(toilet)* Lokus *m*

pisshead n (alcoholic) Suffkopf m

piss off 1 vt sep (annoy) ankotzen; **do you know what pisses me off the most?** weißt du, was mich am meisten ankotzt?; **I didn't mean to piss you off** ich wollte dich nicht sauer machen

2 vi (go away) **he pissed off halfway through the afternoon** er hat mitten am Nachmittag die Flatter gemacht; **I told him to piss off** ich hab' ihm gesagt, er soll sich verpissen

3 interj (go away, expresses refusal) verpiss dich!; (expresses disbelief) kein Scheiß?

piss-poor adj (very bad) **their latest record is piss-poor** ihre letzte Platte ist Gülle

piss-take n (send-up) Verarsche f; **this is a piss-take, isn't it?** (is it serious?) das ist doch 'ne Verarsche, oder?

piss-up n (party) **I'm organizing a piss-up round at my place** ich veranstalte bei mir 'ne Sauferei; **they couldn't organize a piss-up in a brewery** Humorous (they're useless) die sind doch dümmer als die Polizei erlaubt

(i) Der Ausdruck **they couldn't organize a piss-up in a brewery** (wörtlich: sie könnten nicht mal 'ne Sauferei in einer Brauerei organisieren) ist die geläufigste witzige Wendung, um jemandes völlige Unfähigkeit zu beschreiben, es gibt aber auch Variationen zu diesem Thema, wie zum Beispiel **they couldn't organize an orgy/a fuck in a brothel** (wörtlich: sie könnten nicht mal eine Orgie im Puff organisieren) oder **she couldn't organize a queue at a bus stop** (wörtlich: sie könnte nicht mal 'ne Schlange an der Bushaltestelle organisieren) und **he couldn't get pussy in a cathouse** (wörtlich: der könnte nicht mal 'ne Nutte im Bordell kriegen).

pit 1 n (a) (bed) **I'm off to my pit** ich geh' jetzt ins Nest

(b) (messy place) Schweinestall m

(c) **it's the pits** (terrible) das ist das Allerletzte

2 npl **pits** (armpits) Achselhöhlen pl [not slang]; **her brother's got totally minging pits!** ihr Bruder stinkt voll unter den Armen!

plastered adj (drunk) **to be plastered** sternhagelvoll sein; **I got plastered** ich hab' mir einen angetrunken

plonker n (a) Insult (stupid man) Dösel m; **I felt a right plonker in my kilt** ich bin mir in dem Kilt vorgekommen wie Klein Doofie mit Plüschohren; **not there, you (stupid) plonker!** doch nicht da, du Dösel!

(b) (penis) Gurke f

pom, pommy n Australian (English person) Tommy m; **the poms** die Tommys

ponce n (effeminate man) Weichei nt

pong 1 n (unpleasant smell)
Gestank m

2 vi (smell unpleasant) stinken;
your socks pong deine Socken
stinken; **it pongs in here!** hier
mieft's!

poo 1 n (a) (excrement) Aa nt;
the floor was covered in poo der
Fußboden war voller Aa

(b) (piece of excrement) **a poo**
eine Wurst

(c) (act of defecation) **I need a
poo** ich muss Aa machen; **to do
a poo** (of a person) Aa machen;
(of an animal) einen Haufen
machen; **to go for a poo** Aa
machen gehen; **to have a poo** Aa
machen

2 vi (defecate) (of a person) Aa
machen; (of an animal) einen
Haufen machen

poof n Homophobic (homosexual) Schwuli m; **stop hugging
me, you great poof!** hör auf,
mich zu umarmen, du warmer
Bruder!

poofter n Homophobic
(homosexual) Homo m; **stop
hugging me, you great poofter!**
hör auf, mich zu umarmen, du
warmer Bruder!

poop 1 n US (a) (excrement) **the
floor was covered in poop** der
Fußboden war voller Aa

(b) (piece of excrement) **a poop**
eine Wurst

2 vi US (defecate) (of a person)
Aa machen; (of an animal) einen
Haufen machen

pooped adj esp US (exhausted)
todmüde

Pope n **is she likely to accept?
– is the Pope a Catholic?**
Humorous (of course) wird sie
annehmen? – blöde Frage, ist der
Papst katholisch?

porker n (a) (fat person)
Fettsack m

(b) (lie) Flunkerei f; **to tell
porkers** flunkern

postal adj esp US **to go postal**
(go berserk) ausrasten

pot n (marijuana) Pot m; **to
smoke pot** kiffen

poxy adj (expresses contempt)
beknackt; **you can keep your
poxy money!** du kannst dein
beknacktes Geld behalten!

prat n Insult (contemptible
man) Volltrottel m; **you prat!**
du Volltrottel!; **I felt a right
prat in my kilt** ich bin mir in
dem Kilt wie der letzte Trottel
vorgekommen; **stop being such
a prat** stell dich doch nicht so an
wie der letzte Trottel

prick n (a) Insult (contemptible
man) Saftsack m; **you prick!**
du Saftsack!; **I felt a right prick
in my kilt** ich bin mir in dem
Kilt wie ein Arsch mit Ohren
vorgekommen; **stop being such
a prick!** hör auf, dich wie ein
Saftsack aufzuführen!

(b) (penis) Schwanz m → **spare**

psycho 1 n (violent person)
Psycho m

2 adj **to go psycho** (go berserk)
durchdrehen

pube n (single pubic hair)
Schamhaar nt [not slang]; **I**

shaved my pubes off ich hab'
mir den Pelz rasiert; **he's got
ginger pubes** er hat 'nen
roten Pelz

puke 1 *n (vomit)* Kotze *f*
2 *vi* (a) *(vomit)* kotzen; **this
government makes me puke**
(disgusts me) ich finde diese
Regierung zum Kotzen
(b) *(smell unpleasant)* stinken;
your socks puke deine Socken
stinken; **it pukes in here!** hier ist
ein schrecklicher Mief!
3 *interj (expresses revulsion)*
kotzwürg!

puke up 1 *vt sep (vomit)*
auskotzen; **I puked my guts up**
(vomited violently) ich hab' mir
die Seele aus dem Leib gekotzt
2 *vi (vomit)* kotzen

pull 1 *n* **to be on the pull**
(looking for sexual partner)
jemanden zum Aufreißen suchen
2 *vt* (a) *(seduce)* aufreißen; **he
certainly knows how to pull
the birds** er hat das Weiber-
Aufreißen richtig raus
(b) *(phrases)* **pull the other one!**
(expresses disbelief) wer's glaubt
wird selig!; **they tried to pull a
fast one on us** *(deceive us)* sie
haben versucht, uns aufs Kreuz
zu legen; **pull your finger out!**
(stop being so lazy) reiß dich am
Riemen!
3 *vi (find sexual partner)*
aufreißen

push off 1 *vi (go away)* sich
verkrümeln
2 *interj (go away)* hau ab!

pussy *n* (a) *(vagina)* Pussi *f* → **eat**
(b) *Sexist (sex)* **where's the best
place to get some pussy round
here?** wo kann man denn hier
am besten 'ne Möse aufreißen?;
**he looks like he hasn't had any
pussy for a while** er sieht aus, als
hätte er schon lange keine Möse
mehr aufgerissen
(c) *Sexist (women)* Miezen *pl*

queen *n Homophobic*
(homosexual) Schwuchtel *f*

ⓘ Obwohl **queen** ein
schwulenfeindliches Wort ist,
wenn von Heterosexuellen
in Bezug auf Homosexuelle
benutzt, verliert es jedoch
jeden beleidigenden Zug, wenn
Homosexuelle sich selbst so
bezeichnen.

queer *Homophobic* **1** *n*

(homosexual) Zarter *m*
2 *adj (homosexual)* schwul

ⓘ Obwohl **queer** ein
schwulenfeindliches Wort ist,
wenn von Heterosexuellen
in Bezug auf Homosexuelle
benutzt, verliert es jedoch
jeden beleidigenden Zug, wenn
Homosexuelle sich selbst so
bezeichnen.

quick → one

R

randy *adj (sexually aroused)* scharf; **he's a randy bugger** er ist rattenscharf; **to be** *or* **feel randy** scharf sein

rat 1 *n* **(a)** *(nasty person)* Ratte *f*; **you rat!** du miese Ratte!
(b) *(informer)* Singdrossel *f*
(c) I don't *or* **couldn't give a rat's arse** *or US* **ass what he thinks** *(don't care)* es interessiert mich einen feuchten Scheiß, was der meint
2 *vi (inform) (criminal)* singen; *(pupil)* petzen; **to rat on somebody** *(criminal)* jemanden verpfeifen; *(pupil)* jemanden verpetzen

rat-arsed *adj (drunk)* **to be rat-arsed** fett sein; **I got rat-arsed** ich hab' mir die volle Dröhnung gegeben

ratty *adj (bad-tempered)* **she's really ratty today** sie ist heute echt mies drauf; **he's a ratty old sod** er ist ein miesepetriger alter Knacker

real *adj* **she told us we can't use the phone at work – is she for real?** *(can she be serious?)* sie hat gesagt, wir können vom Arbeitsplatz aus nicht telefonieren – das gibt's ja wohl nicht, oder?; **is that hat for real?** der Hut ist ja wohl der Abschuss!; **go out with you? get real!** *(you must be joking)* ich mit dir ausgehen? hör auf zu träumen!

reefer *n (marijuana cigarette)* Joint *m*

respect *interj (expresses approval, admiration)* meine Achtung!

retard *n* Insult *(stupid person)* Behindi *m*; **you retard!** du Behindi!

> ⓘ Das Schimpfwort **retard** (*Behindi*) wird als eine Beleidigung für geistig Behinderte empfunden.

ring *n (anus)* Loch *nt*

rip off *vt sep (overcharge)* neppen

rip-off *n (case of overcharging)* Nepp *m*; **what a rip-off!** das ist der totale Nepp!

ripped *adj* **he was ripped to the tits** *(drunk)* er war stockvoll; *(on drugs)* er war total bekifft

road *n (way)* **you're in my road** du stehst mir im Weg; **get out of the road!** aus dem Weg! → **hit**

rocker *n* **he's off his rocker** *(crazy)* der hat ein Rad ab

rocks *npl* **to get one's rocks off**
(have orgasm) abspritzen; *(have
sex)* einen wegstecken; **he was
getting his rocks off watching
them suffer** *(enjoying himself)*
er fand es megageil, sie leiden
zu sehen

roger *vt (have sex with)* rammeln
mit; **he rogered me senseless**
(had energetic sex with me) er
hat mich gerammelt, dass mir
Hören und Sehen verging

round *prep* **to be round the
bend** *or* **twist** *(mad)* nicht ganz
richtig im Kopf sein; **to go
round the bend** *or* **twist** *(mad)*
wahnsinnig werden [*not slang*];
have you gone round the bend
or **twist?** tickst du nicht richtig?;
this job is enough to make
any sane person go round the
twist bei dem Job wird ja jeder
normale Mensch wahnsinnig;
**that music is driving me round
the bend** *(annoying me)* die
Musik geht mir auf den Geist

rubber *n esp US (condom)*
Gummi *m*

rumpy-pumpy *n Humorous
(sex)* **I haven't had any rumpy-
pumpy for ages** ich habe schon
ewig kein Nümmerchen mehr
gemacht; **do you fancy (having)
a bit of rumpy-pumpy?** hast du
Lust, mit mir in die Federn zu
hüpfen?

runner *n* **she did a runner**
(left) sie hat sich aus dem Staub
gemacht

S

sack *n* he's good/not much good in the sack *(as a lover)* er bringt's/bringt's nicht; **what's she like in the sack?** wie ist sie im Bett?; **he's a sack of shit** or **shite** *Insult (unpleasant person)* er ist ein Drecksack → **hit**

sad *adj (boring, untrendy)* he spends his afternoons watching soap operas – that's really sad! er guckt nachmittagelang Seifenopern – armer Irrer!; **I think trigonometry is really interesting – you sad bastard!** ich finde Trigonometrie wirklich spannend – armer Irrer!; **Nigel, you sad man, stop playing on the computer!** Nigel, du Irrer, hör endlich auf, am Computer zu spielen!

safe *interj (excellent)* krass

sandwich → **short**

sausage *n* **(a)** *(penis)* Pillermann *m*
   (b) *(foolish person)* **you silly sausage!** du Dummerjan!
   (c) have you heard anything from her? – not a sausage *(nothing)* hast du von ihr gehört? – nicht die Bohne

scab *n (strikebreaker)* Streikbrecher,-in *m,f* [*not slang*]

scare → **shit, shite, shitless**

schlemiel *n US (useless person)* Waschlappen *m*

schmuck *n US Insult (idiot)* Blödmann *m*; **you schmuck!** du Blödmann!

schnozz *n US (nose)* Zinken *m*

scoff *vt (eat)* fressen; **who scoffed all the biscuits?** wer hat all die Kekse gefressen?

scoobie *n* I haven't got a scoobie *(I have no idea)* keinen Blassen!

score **1** *vt (drugs)* beschaffen; **to score some smack** Stoff beschaffen
   2 *vi* **(a)** *(have sex)* einen Stich machen
   (b) *(buy drugs)* Stoff beschaffen

scrap **1** *n (fight)* Prügelei *f*; **to have a scrap (with somebody)** sich (mit jemandem) prügeln; **d'you want a scrap about it?** willst du dich prügeln?
   2 *vi (fight)* sich prügeln

scream *n (funny thing or person)* he's a scream er ist zum Schreien; **their new film's a scream** ihr neuer Film ist zum Schreien; **how was the party? – it was a scream** wie war die Party? – spitzenmäßig

screw 1 n (a) (sex) **d'you fancy a screw?** hast du Lust, 'ne Nummer zu machen?; **to have a screw** 'ne Nummer machen

(b) (sexual partner) **he's/she's a good screw** er ist/sie ist 'ne geile Nummer

(c) (prison officer) Schließer,-in m,f

(d) **he has a screw loose** Humorous (is crazy) bei dem ist 'ne Schraube locker

2 vt (a) (have sex with) 'ne Nummer machen mit; **did you screw him?** hast du mit ihm 'ne Nummer gemacht?; **she screwed the arse** or US **ass off me last night** (had energetic sex with me) sie hat mich letzte Nacht durchgeorgelt, dass mir Hören und Sehen verging

(b) (cheat) **we've been screwed** wir sind abgezockt worden; **the bastards screwed me for £500** die Scheißkerle haben mir 500 Pfund abgezockt

(c) (exploit) **the company is screwing its workforce** die Firma lässt ihre Arbeiter bluten

(d) (phrases) **we're really screwed now** (we've had it) jetzt haben wir die Scheiße; **screw it!** (expresses annoyance) verdammte Scheiße!; (expresses resignation) scheiß drauf!; **they want us to work at the weekend – screw that!** (no way) die wollen, dass wir am Wochenende arbeiten – die haben ja den Arsch offen!; **screw the lot of them!** (they can get stuffed) die können mich alle lecken!; **screw what they say, let's go anyway!**

(ignore it) shitegal, was die sagen, lass uns trotzdem gehen!; **screw you!** (get stuffed) leck mich doch!

3 vi (a) (have sex) 'ne Nummer machen

(b) (mess about) **don't screw with me!** versuch nicht, mich zu verarschen!

screw up 1 vt sep (a) (mess up) vermasseln

(b) (cause psychological harm) **his parents' divorce really screwed him up** seit der Scheidung seiner Eltern hat der echt 'nen Schaden

2 vi (mess things up) **if you screw up again, you're fired!** wenn du's noch mal vermasselst, dann fliegst du!

scum n Insult **they're scum** (contemptible) das ist der letzte Dreck; **you scum!** du Dreckschwein!

scumbag n Insult (nasty person) Dreckschwein nt; **you scumbag!** du Dreckschwein!

search vt **search me!** (I don't know) frag mich was Leichteres!

shack up vi **he's shacked up with his girlfriend** (he's living with her) er lebt mit seiner Freundin zusammen [not slang]; **they're shacked up together** (they live together) sie leben zusammen [not slang]

shades npl (sunglasses) Sonnenbrille f [not slang]

shaft vt (a) (have sex with) **he shafted her** er hat sie gefeilt; **we're really shafted now** (we've *had it)* jetzt haben wir die Kacke

(b) *(cheat)* ausnehmen; **we've been shafted** wir sind ausgenommen worden

shag 1 *n* (a) *(sex)* **d'you fancy a shag?** hast du Lust zu vögeln?; **to have a shag** vögeln

(b) *(sexual partner)* **he's/she's a good shag** er ist/sie ist 'ne geile Nummer

(c) *(boring or annoying task)* **it's a shag having to get up so early** es ist total ätzend, immer so früh aufstehen zu müssen

2 *vt* (a) *(have sex with)* vögeln; **did you shag him?** hast du ihn gevögelt?

(b) *(phrases)* **shag it!** *(expresses annoyance)* verdammter Mist!; *(expresses resignation)* ach, Schitt!

3 *vi (have sex)* vögeln

shagged, **shagged out** *adj* *(exhausted)* **to be shagged** *or* **shagged out** fix und foxy sein

shebang *n* **the whole shebang collapsed in the storm** *(everything)* die ganze Chose ist bei dem Sturm eingekracht

sheila *n Australian (woman)* Tussi *f*

shift → **arse**

shit 1 *n* (a) *(excrement)* Scheiße *f*; **a shit** ein Haufen Scheiße

(b) *(act of defecation)* Schiss *m*; **I need a shit** ich muss scheißen; **to do a shit** scheißen; **to go for a shit** scheißen gehen; **to have a shit** scheißen

(c) *(bad thing)* Scheiße *f*; **the record is a load of shit** die Platte ist totale Scheiße; **you can't expect me to eat that shit** du willst doch nicht etwa, dass ich diese Scheiße esse

(d) *(nonsense)* Kacke *f*; **what she said is complete and utter shit** die hat die totale Kacke erzählt; **you're full of shit!** *(you're a liar)* du erzählst ja so eine Kacke!; **that's a load of shit!** das ist doch die totale Kacke!; **don't give me that shit!** erzähl mir doch nicht so 'ne Kacke!; **to talk shit** Kacke erzählen; **don't start on about that New Age shit!** fang bloß nicht mit der New-Age-Kacke an!

(e) *(stuff)* Scheißzeugs *nt*

(f) *(problems)* Scheiße *f*; **I'm fed up with all this shit, I'm leaving** ich hab' die ganze Scheiße satt, ich gehe; **there's been a lot of shit going on at the office** im Büro ist ziemlich viel Scheiße gelaufen; **I don't need this shit** so 'ne Scheiße muss ich mir nicht geben

(g) *(trouble)* **we're really in the shit now** jetzt sitzen wir in der Scheiße; **you're in big** *or* **deep shit!** jetzt haste die Scheiße!; **he really got in (the) shit for lying to the boss** der hat sich 'nen Scheißärger eingehandelt, weil er den Chef angelogen hat; **she really landed** *or* **dropped us in the shit** sie hat uns da 'ne ganz schöne Scheiße eingebrockt

(h) *(hassle)* **I've had enough shit from you** jetzt reicht mir die Scheiße von dir; **he's always giving me shit about something or other** er scheißt mich dauernd wegen irgendwas zusammen; **I'm not taking any more shit from them** ich lass mich von denen nicht mehr so beschissen behandeln

(i) *Insult (nasty person)* Drecksack m; **you shit!** du Drecksack!; **you little shit!** du gemeines Schwein!; **he's a fucking shit** !! er ist ein alter Sackaffe; **he's a shit to his wife** er ist ein richtiges Arschloch zu seiner Frau

(j) *esp US (anything)* **you don't know shit** du hast ja null Ahnung von nix; **he didn't do shit at the office today** einen Scheiß hat er heut' im Büro getan; **my opinion isn't worth shit round here** kein Schwein interessiert sich hier für meine Meinung

(k) *(heroin)* Braun [*no article*]; *(cannabis)* Shit m

(l) *(phrases)* **we're up shit creek (without a paddle)** *(we've had it)* jetzt haben wir die Scheiße; **they beat** *or* **kicked** *or* **knocked the shit out of us** *(beat us up)* die haben uns zu Klump gehauen; *(defeated us heavily)* die haben uns alle gemacht; **he bores the shit out of me** *(I find him very boring)* der geht mir total auf den Geist; **you lied! – did I shit!** *(I didn't)* du hast gelogen! – Scheiße, hab' ich nicht!; **he's got a new car – has he shit!** *(he doesn't)* er hat ein neues Auto – 'nen Scheiß hat er!; **it's good to meet some other people who actually give a shit about animal rights** *(care)* toll, noch andere Leute zu treffen, denen

der Tierschutz nicht scheißegal ist; **I don't** *or* **couldn't give a shit about it/them** *(don't care)* das ist/die sind mir scheißegal; **he couldn't give a shit** *(doesn't care about anything)* das ist ihm alles scheißegal; **who gives a shit what she thinks?** *(no-one cares)* es interessiert doch kein Schwein, was sie meint; **I got the shits** *(I got diarrhoea)* ich habe Dünnschiss gekriegt; *(I got scared)* ich hatte eine Scheißangst; **prunes give you the shits** *(give you diarrhoea)* von Pflaumen kriegst du Dünnschiss; **spiders give me the shits** *(scare me)* vor Spinnen habe ich den Horror; **to have the shits** *(have diarrhoea)* Dünnschiss haben; **I had the shits** *(I was scared)* ich hatte eine Scheißangst; **then the shit will really hit the fan** *(the trouble will start)* dann ist die Kacke am Dampfen; **I feel like shit** *(ill)* mir geht's beschissen; **it hurts like shit** *(a lot)* das tut brutal weh; **you look like shit** *(terrible)* du siehst aus wie gekotzt; **they treat me like shit** *(badly)* sie behandeln mich wie Scheiße; **he's going out with her – like shit (he is)!** *(expresses disagreement)* er geht mit ihr – 'nen Scheiß tut er!; **I'm going to leave now – like shit you are!** *(no you're not)* ich geh' jetzt – 'nen Scheiß wirst du tun!; **no shit!** *(expresses surprise)* ich krieg' sie nicht mehr alle!; *Ironic (expresses lack of surprise)* Scheiße, echt?; **they really put the shit up us** *(scared us)* die haben uns eine Scheißangst eingejagt; **it scared the shit out of me** *(frightened me to death)* ich hatte total Schiss; **I got shit all help from them** *(none)* einen Scheiß haben sie mir geholfen; **you know shit all about it, so shut your face!** *(you know nothing)* du hast von dem doch keine Scheißahnung, also halt die Klappe!; **shit comes in piles** *(it never rains, it pours)* es kommt immer gleich knüppeldick; **shit floats** *(unpleasant people are successful)* den Arschlöchern gehört die Welt; **shit happens** *(that's life)* was soll's, so was kann mal passieren; **what/where/ when/who/why the shit…?** *(for emphasis)* was/wo/wann/wer/ warum verdammt noch mal …? → **eat, piece, pig, sack, thick, tough**

2 *adj* *(bad)* beschissen; **their music is shit** ihre Musik ist Scheiße; **he's a shit singer** er ist ein beschissener Sänger; **I'm shit at physics** in Physik bin ich beschissen schlecht; **I feel shit** *(ill)* mir geht's beschissen; **we had a shit holiday** das war ein beschissener Urlaub; **this hi-fi sounds shit** die Anlage hört sich beschissen an

3 *vt* **I was shitting bricks** *(scared)* ich hatte die Hosen gestrichen voll; **shit a brick!** *Humorous (expresses surprise)* das is ja 'n Ding!; **I nearly shat myself** *or* **my pants** *(defecated in pants)* ich hab' mir fast in die Hose geschissen; **I was**

shitting myself *or* **my pants** *(was scared)* ich hab' mir in die Hose geschissen

4 *vi* **(a)** *(defecate)* scheißen
(b) *(phrases)* **shit or get off the pot!** *(make your mind up)* mach endlich mal Nägel mit Köpfen!; **I shit on their plan!** *(think it's useless)* ich scheiß' auf ihren Plan!; **you work your guts out for them, and then they just shit on you from a great height** *(treat you badly)* du schuftest dich für die ab, und dann behandeln sie dich wie den letzten Arsch; **they shat on us from a great height** *(defeated us heavily)* die haben uns beschissen alt aussehen lassen

5 *interj* *(expresses annoyance, fear)* Scheiße!; *(expresses surprise)* ach, du Scheiße!; **oh shit, we're in big trouble now!** Scheiße, jetzt gibt's aber Ärger!; **I couldn't find it – shit!** *(expresses disbelief)* ich hab's nicht gefunden – erzähl doch nicht so 'ne Scheiße!

shite 1 *n* **(a)** *(excrement)* Scheiße *f*; **a shite** ein Haufen Scheiße
(b) *(act of defecation)* **I need a shite** ich muss scheißen; **to do a shite** scheißen; **to go for a shite** scheißen gehen; **to have a shite** scheißen
(c) *(bad thing)* Scheiße *f*; **the record is a load of shite** die Platte ist totale Scheiße; **you can't expect me to eat that shite** du willst doch nicht etwa, dass ich diese Scheiße esse
(d) *(nonsense)* Kacke *f*; **what**

she said is complete and utter shite die hat die totale Kacke erzählt; **you're full of shite!** *(you're a liar)* du erzählst ja so eine Kacke!; **that's a load of shite!** das ist doch die totale Kacke!; **don't give me that shite!** erzähl mir doch nicht so 'ne Kacke!; **to talk shite** Kacke erzählen; **don't start on about that New Age shite!** fang bloß nicht mit der New-Age-Kacke an!

(e) *Insult (nasty person)* Drecksack m; **you little shite!** du gemeines Schwein!

(f) *(phrases)* **they beat** or **kicked** or **knocked the shite out of us** *(beat us up)* die haben uns zu Klump gehauen; *(defeated us heavily)* die haben uns alle gemacht; **he bores the shite out of me** *(I find him very boring)* der geht mir total auf den Geist; **it's good to meet some other people who actually give a shite about animal rights** *(care)* toll, noch andere Leute zu treffen, denen der Tierschutz nicht scheißegal ist; **I don't** or **couldn't give a shite about it/them** *(don't care)* das ist/die sind mir scheißegal; **he couldn't give a shite** *(doesn't care about anything)* das ist ihm alles scheißegal; **who gives a shite what she thinks?** *(no-one cares)* es interessiert doch kein Schwein, was sie meint; **I feel like shite** *(ill)* mir geht's beschissen; **it hurts like shite** *(a lot)* das tut brutal weh; **you look like shite** *(terrible)* du siehst aus wie gekotzt; **they treat me like shite** *(badly)* sie behandeln mich wie

Scheiße; **it scared the shite out of me** *(frightened me to death)* ich hatte total Schiss; **what/where/when/who/why the shite…?** *(for emphasis)* was/wo/wann/wer/warum verdammt noch mal …?
→ **piece, sack**

2 *adj (bad)* beschissen; **their music is shite** ihre Musik ist Scheiße; **he's a shite singer** er ist ein beschissener Sänger; **I'm shite at physics** in Physik bin ich beschissen schlecht; **I feel shite** *(ill)* mir geht's beschissen; **we had a shite holiday** das war ein beschissener Urlaub; **this hi-fi sounds shite** die Anlage hört sich beschissen an

3 *vi (defecate)* scheißen

4 *interj (expresses annoyance, fear)* Scheiße!; *(expresses surprise)* ach du Scheiße!; **oh shite, we're in big trouble now!** Scheiße, jetzt gibt's aber Ärger!; **I couldn't find it – shite!** *(expresses disbelief)* ich hab's nicht gefunden – erzähl doch nicht so 'ne Scheiße!

ⓘ Allgemein kann man sagen, dass das Wort **shite** weniger anstößig ist als **shit**. Manchmal klingt **shite** im Gegensatz zu **shit** sogar leicht witzig. Ansonsten gibt es aber keinen Unterschied zwischen den beiden und sie können beliebig gegeneinander ausgetauscht werden. Es gibt allerdings ein paar Wendungen, in denen ausschließlich **shit** gebräuchlich ist.

---

shit-hot *adj (excellent)* saugut;

she's **shit-hot at crosswords** bei Kreuzworträtseln ist sie saugut

shithouse → **brick**

shitless adj (for emphasis) **to be bored shitless** voll angeödet sein; **he bores me shitless** der geht mir total auf den Sack; **to be scared shitless** die Hosen gestrichen voll haben; **he scared me shitless** er hat mir eine Scheißangst eingejagt

shit-scared adj (terrified) **to be shit-scared** eine Scheißangst haben

shitty adj (a) (bad) beschissen; **I don't want to work for your shitty little company** ich will nicht für eure beschissene kleine Firma arbeiten; **she's in a shitty mood** sie hat beschissene Laune; **I feel shitty** (ill) mir geht's beschissen

(b) (nasty) beschissen; **you've been really shitty to me all week** du hast mich die ganze Woche beschissen behandelt; **that was really shitty of you!** das war echt beschissen von dir!

shoot interj US Euphemism [shit] (expresses annoyance) ach du Kacke!; (expresses surprise) Himmel!

shoot up 1 vt sep (drug) drücken; **to shoot up smack** H drücken
2 vi (inject drugs) drücken

shop 1 n **there were toys all over the shop** (everywhere) überall lagen Spielsachen rum; **their defence was all over the shop** (badly organized) ihre

Verteidigung war chaotisch; **I'm all over the shop today** (confused) ich bin heute total durch den Wind
2 vt (inform on) verzinken; **she shopped him to the police** sie hat ihn bei der Polizei verzinkt

short adj **he's one brick short of a load** or **one stick short of a bundle** or **one sandwich short of a picnic** Humorous (slightly insane or stupid) der hat 'nen Hau

(i) Obwohl die drei aufgeführten Wendungen die häufigsten sind, gibt es viele Variationen zum Thema, die mit **short of** gebildet werden, und die verrückt oder dumm bedeuten. So erfinden Menschen neue Möglichkeiten dazu, zum Beispiel **one can short of a six-pack** oder **one egg short of an omelette**. Im Deutschen würde man diese Variationen durch andere Ausdrücke für Hau ausdrücken, wie zum Beispiel einen Vogel, eine Meise, eine Vollmeise, eine Macke, einen Knall, einen Schaden oder einen Haschmich haben.

shove → **arse**, **ass**

shove off 1 vi (go away) **I told him to shove off** ich hab' ihm gesagt, er soll verduften
2 interj (go away) schieb ab!

shut vt **shut your face** or **gob** or **mush** or **trap!** (be quiet) halt die Klappe!; **shut it!** Klappe!

side → bit

silly *adj* **stop playing silly buggers** *(messing about)* hör auf, blöd rumzueiern

skinny-dipping *n (nude bathing)* **we went skinny-dipping** wir waren schwimmen wie Adam und Eva

skint *adj (broke)* pleite

skirt → bit, piece

skive 1 *n* **I took sociology because it's a skive** *(undemanding)* ich hab' Soziologie genommen, weil man sich da keinen abbrechen muss

2 *vi* (a) *(be idle)* Däumchen drehen

(b) *(not go to work)* blau machen; **why isn't she at work today, is she ill? – no, she's just skiving** warum ist sie heute nicht bei der Arbeit, ist sie krank? – nee, die macht nur blau

(c) *(not go to school)* schwänzen

skive off 1 *vt insep* **to skive off work** blau machen; **to skive off school** die Schule schwänzen

2 *vi* (a) *(not go to work)* blau machen

(b) *(not go to school)* schwänzen

skiver *n* (a) *(person who avoids work)* Drückeberger,-in *m,f*

(b) *(person who doesn't go to school)* Schwänzer,-in *m,f*

slag 1 *n* (a) *Insult (promiscuous woman)* Schlampe *f*; **Kelly's a bloody slag!** Kelly ist eine Scheißschlampe!; **you slag!** du Schlampe!

(b) *Insult (contemptible woman)*

Schlampe *f*; **piss off, you stupid slag!** verpiss dich, du alte Schlampe!

2 *vt* (a) *(criticize)* **she's always slagging her brother** sie macht immer ihren Bruder nieder

(b) *(tease)* hochnehmen; **his mates were slagging him about supporting Arsenal** seine Kumpel haben ihn hochgenommen, weil er ein Fan von Arsenal ist

slag off *vt sep* (a) *(criticize)* **he's always slagging me off** er macht mich dauernd nieder

(b) *(tease)* hochnehmen; **his mates were slagging him off for supporting Arsenal** seine Kumpel haben ihn hochgenommen, weil er ein Fan von Arsenal ist

slammer *n (prison)* **in the slammer** hinter schwedischen Gardinen

slapper *n* (a) *Insult (promiscuous woman)* Schickse *f*; **Tracy's a bloody slapper!** Tracy ist eine Scheißschickse!; **you slapper!** du Schickse!

(b) *Sexist (any woman)* Braut *f*

slash *n (act of urinating)* **I need a slash** ich muss eine Stange (Wasser) in die Ecke stellen; **to go for a slash** eine Stange (Wasser) in die Ecke stellen gehen; **to have a slash** eine Stange (Wasser) in die Ecke stellen

sliced bread *n* **she thinks he's the best thing since sliced bread** *(wonderful)* sie meint, er ist der Größte

slob *n* (a) *(lazy person)* **he's a slob** er ist ein fauler Sack; **you**

(lazy) slob! du fauler Sack! **(b)** *(untidy person)* Dreckschwein *nt*; **you (disgusting) slob!** du Dreckschwein! **(c)** *(fat person)* Kloß *m*; **you (fat) slob!** du (fetter) Kloß!

slog 1 *n (hard work)* **preparing for my law exams was a real slog** mich auf mein Juraexamen vorzubereiten war echt ein Schlauch

2 *vt* **I've been slogging my guts out to finish on time** *(working hard)* ich hab' mir einen abgebrochen, um rechtzeitig fertig zu werden

3 *vi (work hard)* **I've been slogging away at this essay all week** ich hab' mir die ganze Woche an diesem Aufsatz einen abgebrochen

sloshed *adj (drunk)* **to be sloshed** einen Affen haben; **I got sloshed** ich hab' mir 'nen Affen angesoffen

slut *n* *Insult (promiscuous woman)* Nutte *f*; **Vicky's a bloody slut!** Vicky ist eine Scheißnutte!; **you slut!** du Nutte!

smack *n (heroin)* H *nt*

ⓘ The German translation **H** is pronounced like the English letter **h**.

smartarse *n (smart aleck)* Klugscheißer,-in *m,f*

smiley *n (LSD tablet)* Mikro *f*

snog 1 *n (kiss)* Schmatz *m*; **go on, give us a snog!** komm schon, gib mir 'nen Schmatz!; **he was having a snog with his girlfriend**

er hat mit seiner Freundin rumgeknutscht

2 *vt (kiss)* abknutschen
3 *vi (kiss)* knutschen

snot *n (mucus)* **a piece of snot** ein Popel; **he had snot running down his nose** der Rotz lief ihm die Nase runter; **a snot rag** *(handkerchief)* eine Rotzfahne

snuff *vt* **she snuffed it** *(died)* sie ist abgenibbelt

s.o.b. *n esp US Insult (unpleasant man)* Sauhund *m*

sod 1 *n* **(a)** *(any man or woman)* **he's a fat sod** das ist ein Kloß; **you cheeky sod!** du freches Stück!; **he's a lazy sod!** das ist ein faules Stück!; **you jammy sod!** du Glückspilz!; **the little sods have eaten all the cake** die Blagen haben den ganzen Kuchen gegessen; **the poor sod broke his leg** das arme Schwein hat sich das Bein gebrochen; **you stupid sod!** du Blödmann!

(b) *Insult (nasty man)* Drecksack *m*; **he's a miserable (old) sod** er ist ein alter Drecksack; **you sod!** du Drecksack!

(c) *(difficult thing)* **this sum's a real sod** die Rechnung ist schweineschwierig; **this door's a sod to open** die Tür geht schweineschwer auf

(d) *(phrases)* **you've done sod all today** *(nothing)* einen Scheißdreck hast du heut' gemacht; **we got sod all help from them** *(none)* einen Scheißdreck haben sie uns geholfen; **I got sod all for**

my efforts (nothing) einen Scheißdreck hab' ich für meine Mühe bekommen; **you know sod all about it, so shut your face!** (you know nothing) einen Scheißdreck weißt du darüber, also halt die Klappe!; **there's sod all else to do, so we might as well watch the film** (nothing else) sonst gibt's verdammt null anderes zu tun, also können wir auch den Film ansehen; **I don't** or **couldn't give a sod what they think!** (don't care) es interessiert mich einen feuchten Mist, was sie meinen

2 vt **(a)** (forget) **sod the consequences, let's just do it** scheißegal, lass es uns einfach machen

(b) (phrases) **sod it!** (expresses annoyance) Mist!; (expresses resignation) Scheiße!; **they want us to work at the weekend – sod that!** (no way) die wollen, dass wir am Wochenende arbeiten – die sind ja nicht ganz sauber!; **sod this for a laugh** or **a lark** (this is a waste of time) das ist doch Scheiße; **sod this for a game of soldiers** (this is a waste of time) das ist doch die totale Scheiße; **I think you're being stupid – well sod you, then!** (get stuffed) du bist blöd! – leck mich doch!

sodding 1 adj (for emphasis) **the sodding car won't start** das Scheißauto springt nicht an; **the sodding bastard wouldn't help me** der Scheißkerl hat mir nicht geholfen; **you sodding idiot!** du saublöder Idiot!; **I can't hear**

a sodding thing ich kann null hören; **it's sodding annoying** das ist scheißärgerlich; **sodding hell** or **heck!** (expresses annoyance) verflucht noch mal!; (expresses surprise) Herr im Himmel!; **who the sodding hell does she think she is?** für wen zum Teufel hält die sich?

2 adv (for emphasis) **the film was sodding awful** der Film war bescheuert; **it's sodding freezing** es ist saukalt; **don't be so sodding stupid** sei nicht so saublöd; Ironic **that's sodding brilliant, now what do we do?** na klasse, und was zum Teufel machen wir jetzt?; **a sodding great lorry** ein saugroßer Lastwagen; **you'd sodding well better do what I say!** verdammt noch mal, tu, was ich dir sage!; **no sodding way am I doing that** einen Scheißdreck werd' ich tun!

sod off 1 vi (go away) **she told me to sod off** sie hat mir gesagt, ich soll mich verkrümeln

2 interj (go away, expresses refusal) verpiss dich!; (expresses disbelief) kein Scheiß?

solid 1 adj (excellent) krass; **their latest single is solid, man** ihre letzte Single ist voll krass, Alter

2 interj (excellent) voll krass!

son n **(a)** (form of address) **all right, my son?** wie geht's, wie steht's?; **go on, my son!** (as encouragement) lass jucken!

(b) (phrases) **son of a bitch** Insult (contemptible man) Saftsack m; **you son of a bitch!** du Saftsack!; **this door's a son**

of a bitch to open *(difficult)* die Tür geht saumäßig schwer auf; **son of a bitch!** *esp US (expresses annoyance)* verdammte Scheiße!; **son of a gun** *esp US Insult (contemptible man)* Schweinepriester *m*; **you son of a gun!** du Schweinepriester!; **son of a gun!** *(expresses surprise)* Mensch Meier!; **how are you, you son of a gun!** *(expresses affection)* wie geht's dir denn, Alter?; **it was an old car, and the son of a gun wouldn't start** *(annoying thing)* es war ein altes Auto, und das blöde Ding wollte einfach nicht anspringen

sorted 1 *adj* **to be sorted** *(in possession of drugs)* was dabei haben
2 *interj (expresses satisfaction)* bingo!

sound 1 *adj (excellent)* geil; **their latest single is sound, man** ihre letzte Single ist voll geil, Mann
2 *interj (excellent)* geil!

space cadet *n (strange person)* Ausgeflippter *m*, Ausgeflippte *f*; **he's nice but he's a bit of a space cadet** er ist nett, aber ein bisschen weggetreten

spaced out *adj* **to be spaced out** *(on drugs)* voll zugedröhnt sein; *(because of tiredness)* abgeschlafft sein; *(because of illness)* angeschlagen sein

spade ‼ *n Racist (black person)* Tintenkopf *m*

spare *adj* **that music is driving me spare** *(annoying me)* die Musik geht mir auf den

Keks; **to go spare** *(get angry)* Zustände kriegen; **she was going spare** *(worried)* sie ist fast durchgedreht; **I felt like a spare prick at a wedding around those two love birds** *Humorous (I felt superfluous)* bei den beiden Turteltauben bin ich mir wie das fünfte Rad am Wagen vorgekommen; **spare tyres** *Humorous (rolls of fat)* Rettungsringe

spastic 1 *n Insult (stupid person)* Spasti *m*; **you spastic!** du Spasti!
2 *adj (stupid)* behindert

> ℹ️ Das Schimpfwort **spastic** *(Spasti)* wird als eine Beleidigung von behinderten Menschen empfunden.

spazzy 1 *n Insult (stupid person)* Spasti *m*; **you spazzy!** du Spasti!
2 *adj (stupid)* behindert

> ℹ️ Das Schimpfwort **spazzy** *(Spasti)* wird als eine Beleidigung von behinderten Menschen empfunden.

speed *n (amphetamine)* Speed *nt*

spew 1 *n (vomit)* Kotze *f*
2 *vt (vomit)* reiern
3 *vi (vomit)* reiern

spew up 1 *vt sep (vomit)* ausreiern; **I spewed my guts up** *(vomited violently)* ich hab' mir fast die Gedärme ausgereiert
2 *vi (vomit)* reiern

spic ‼ *n esp US Racist (Hispanic)* Scheißlatino *m*

spliff n (marijuana cigarette)
Joint m

split vi (inform) petzen; **to
split on somebody** jemanden
verpetzen

spod n (geek) Laschi m

spot → hit

sprog → drop

spunk n (a) (semen) Saft m
(b) (courage) Schneid m; **he
showed real spunk** er hat
wirklich Schneid bewiesen

stark adv **he was stark bollock
naked** (completely naked) er war
splitterfasernackt; **he stripped
stark bollock naked in front of
everyone** er hat sich vor allen
splitterfasernackt ausgezogen;
she's stark raving bonkers (crazy)
sie ist völlig durchgedreht

starkers adj (naked) pudelnackt

steaming 1 adj (drunk) **to be
steaming** total straff sein
2 adv (for emphasis) **a steaming
great hole** ein voll großes Loch

stick 1 npl **she lives in the sticks**
(the middle of nowhere) die
wohnt jwd
2 vt (a) (bear) aushalten [not
slang]; **I can't stick that music/
him** ich kann diese Musik/ihn auf
den Tod nicht ausstehen; **I don't
think I can stick this job much
longer** der Job steht mir ja bis
hier
(b) (stab) abstechen
(c) (phrases) **if you don't like it,
you can stick it!** (too bad) wenn's
dir nicht gefällt, dann steck's
dir doch irgendwohin!; **you can**

stick your job! (forget it) den
Job kannst du dir irgendwohin
schieben!; **stick it up your
jumper!** (get stuffed) steck's
dir doch irgendwo hin!; **stick it
where the sun don't shine!** (get
stuffed) das kannst du dir in den
Arsch schieben!; **he's sticking it
to his neighbour's wife** (having
sex with) er besorgt es der Frau
seines Nachbarn → **arse, short**

ⓘ The translation of **she lives
in the sticks** (die wohnt jwd)
is the abbreviation of ganz
weit draußen pronounced in
Berlin dialect, where ganz is
pronounced janz.

---

stiff n (corpse) Leiche f [not
slang]

stiffy n (erection) Steifer m; **he
got a stiffy** er hat einen Steifen
gekriegt; **he had a stiffy** er hatte
einen Steifen

stoned adj (on drugs) **to be
stoned** stoned sein; **I got stoned**
ich hab' mich zugedröhnt; **I was
stoned out of my brain** or **up
to the eyeballs** Mann, war ich
stoned!

stonking adv (for emphasis) **a
stonking great hole/bruise** ein
Wahnsinnsloch/Wahnsinns blauer
Fleck

stressed out adj (under stress)
**I'm really stressed out about
it** das stresst mich echt; **there's
no need to get stressed out
(about it)** kein Grund, (deshalb)
durchzudrehen

stroppy adj (bad-tempered)

stinkig; **what are you so stroppy about today?** warum bist du denn heute so stinkig?; **my brother's a stroppy old bugger** mein Bruder ist ein alter Stinkstiefel; **there's no need to get stroppy about it** das ist doch kein Grund, gleich so stinkig zu sein; **stop being such a stroppy cow!** ach, nun sei doch nicht gleich stinkig!

strut vt **let's get out there and strut our funky stuff** (dance) lass uns mal ordentlich abhotten

stud n (virile man) Sexprotz m

studmuffin n (attractive man) Traummann m

stuff 1 n **I don't** or **couldn't give a stuff about him** (don't care) er ist mir piepegal → **bit**
2 vt (a) (defeat) fertig machen
(b) (have sex with) nageln
(c) (phrases) **we stuffed our faces (with cake)** (ate a lot) wir haben uns (mit Kuchen) voll gestopft; **stuff it!** (expresses resignation) verdamm mich!; **if you don't like it you can stuff it!** (too bad) wenn's dir nicht gefällt, dann steck's dir doch irgendwohin!; **I told him to stuff it** (go away) ich hab' ihm gesagt, er soll abschweben; **he wants us to come in on Saturday – stuff that!** (no way) er will, dass wir am Samstag arbeiten – der hat sie ja wohl nicht alle!; **you can stuff your job!** (forget it) ich scheiß auf den Job!

tuffed adj (a) (full-up) **I'm stuffed!** ich bin nudelsatt!

(b) (phrases) **get stuffed!** (go away) zieh ab!; (expresses refusal) du kannst mich mal!; **I think she fancies me – get stuffed!** (expresses disbelief) ich glaub', die steht auf mich – spinn weiter!

suck 1 vt esp US **to suck face** (kiss) sich ablutschen
2 vi (be bad) **this album sucks** das Album ist für'n Kübel; **birdwatching sucks, can't we do something more interesting?** (it's boring) Vögel beobachten ist doch für 'n Arsch, können wir nicht was Spannenderes machen?; **we have to get up at six every morning – that sucks!** wir müssen jeden Morgen um sechs aufstehen – das nervt!

suck up vi (be sycophantic) **you're always sucking up to the teacher** du schmeichelst dich immer beim Lehrer ein

suit n (office worker) Krawattenträger m

sun n **she thinks the sun shines out of his arse** (thinks the world of him) sie meint, er ist der Allergrößte

sunshine n **all right, sunshine?** (form of address) wie geht's, mein Bester?; **just watch it, sunshine** (in implicit threats) nimm dich in Acht, Freundchen; **oi, sunshine, what do you think you're doing?** he, Freundchen, was soll das werden?

sussed adj (a) (streetwise) ausgebufft
(b) (worked out) **I still haven't**

got the computer sussed ich blick's bei dem Computer noch immer nicht; **I've got her sussed, she's after his money** ich hab' sie durchschaut, sie ist hinter seinem Geld her; **he's got it sussed, he does almost no work and gets paid a fortune** der hat die Masche raus, er tut fast nichts und verdient ein Vermögen

suss out *vt sep (work out)* **I soon sussed out that she was lying** ich hab' ziemlich schnell rausgekriegt, dass sie gelogen hat; **I haven't sussed out how it works yet** ich hab' noch nicht rausgekriegt, wie das funktioniert; **I decided to suss the place out before booking in there** ich habe beschlossen, mir den Schuppen mal anzugucken, bevor ich gebucht habe; **it took me a while to suss her character out** ich hab' ein Weilchen gebraucht, um rauszufinden, wie sie so tickt

sweat *n* **are you sure you can do it? – no sweat** *(easily)* bist du sicher, dass du das kannst? – kein Problem

sweet → F.A.

swift → **one**

swipe *vt (steal)* mitgehen lassen; **who swiped my pen?** wer hat meinen Stift mitgehen lassen?

swot 1 *n (over-keen student)* Streber,-in *m,f*; **he's a (girlie) swot** er ist ein Streber
  2 *vi (study hard)* **to swot (for an exam)** (für eine Prüfung) pauken

swot up 1 *vt sep (study a lot)* pauken
  2 *vi (study a lot)* **to swot up on something** etwas pauken

T

tab n (of acid) Pille f

tackle n (man's genitals) Gemächt nt

tadger n (penis) Dödel m

tail n US Sexist (women) Schnallen pl; **a piece of tail** 'ne Schnecke

talent n (attractive people) Schönheitspotenzial nt; **check out the talent on this beach!** guck mal das Schönheitspotenzial an diesem Strand an!; **what's the talent like over in Germany?** wie hoch ist denn so das Schönheitspotenzial in Deutschland?

talk vi **he's talking out of his arse** or US **ass** (talking nonsense) er erzählt Stuss

tart n (a) (prostitute) Dirne f (b) Insult (promiscuous woman) Flittchen nt; **Stacy's a bloody tart!** Stacy ist ein Scheißflittchen!; **you tart!** du Flittchen! (c) Sexist (any woman) Braut f; **a tart with a cart** Humorous (air hostess) eine Saftschubse (d) Sexist (girlfriend) Schnepfe f

art up vt sep (make more attractive) (house) aufmotzen; **I need to tart myself up** ich muss mich aufbretzeln

tat n (cheap and nasty goods) Schund m

thick adj (stupid) strohdumm; **he's as thick as two (short) planks** der ist dümmer als die Polizei erlaubt; **he's as thick as shit** der ist dumm wie Schifferscheiße

tie vt **to tie the knot** (get married) den Bund fürs Leben schließen

tight adj (a) (miserly) knausrig; **he's a tight bastard** er ist ein sakrischer Knauser
(b) (drunk) **to be tight** ganz schön getankt haben
(c) (friendly) **to be tight (with somebody)** (mit jemandem) dick befreundet sein

tight-arse n (miserly person) **he's a right tight-arse** er ist ein verdammter Geizhals

tinnies npl esp Australian (cans of beer) Bölkstoff m

tip n (messy place) Schweinestall m; **your bedroom's a tip** in deinem Zimmer sieht's aus wie im Schweinestall

tit n (a) (breast) Titte f; Sexist (get

your) **tits out for the lads!** Brust raus, Mädels!; **that music is really getting on my tits** (annoying me) die Musik geht mir echt auf den Sack → **arse**

(b) Insult (idiot) Schwachkopf m; **I felt (like) a right tit in my kilt** ich kam mir echt beknackt vor in dem Kilt; **not there, you (stupid) tit!** doch nicht da, du Schwachkopf!

tool n (a) (penis) Rohr nt
(b) Insult (contemptible man) Saftsack m

top vt **she topped herself** (committed suicide) sie hat Schluss gemacht

toss n **I don't** or **couldn't give a toss about it/them** (don't care) das interessiert mich/die interessieren mich einen Scheiß; **he couldn't give a toss** (doesn't care about anything) das ist ihm alles scheißegal; **who gives a toss what she thinks?** (no-one cares) das interessiert doch keine Sau, was sie meint; **it's good to meet some other people who actually give a toss about animal rights** (care) toll, noch andere Leute zu treffen, denen der Tierschutz nicht shitegal ist

tosser n Insult (contemptible man) Wichser m; **you stupid tosser!** du blöder Wichser!

toss off 1 vt sep (masturbate) **she tossed him off** sie hat ihm einen runtergeholt; **he tossed himself off** er hat sich einen runtergeholt
2 vi (a) (masturbate) **she found**

me tossing off sie hat mich ertappt, als ich mir gerade einen runterholte
(b) (go away) **tell him to toss off** sag ihm, er soll sich verpissen
3 interj (go away) hau ab, du Arsch!

tottie, totty n (attractive people) Schönheitspotenzial nt; **check out the tottie over there!** guck mal das Schönheitspotenzial da drüben an!; **what's the tottie like over in Germany?** wie hoch ist denn so das Schönheitspotenzial in Deutschland?

tough 1 adj **well, that's just tough, isn't it?** (too bad) Pech gehabt!; **tough shit, mate** (too bad) dein Scheißpech, Alter; **tough titties!** (too bad) so ein Pech aber auch!
2 interj (too bad) **I don't like it – tough!** das gefällt mir nicht – dein Pech!

town → **hit**

toy boy n (young boyfriend) Loverboy m

trap → **shut**

trip 1 n (a) (on drugs) Trip m; **she's on a trip** sie ist auf dem Trip; **she had a bad trip** sie hat 'nen schlechten Trip gehabt; **why does he treat her like that? – it's just an ego trip** (it makes him feel powerful) warum behandelt er sie so? – ach, das ist sein Egotrip; esp US **don't try and lay a guilt trip on me about you failing your exams** versuch bloß nicht, mir einen

Schuldkomplex anzuhängen, weil du durchgefallen bist

(b) *esp US (phrases)* **that guy's a trip!** *(fun, amusing)* der Typ ist der Wahnsinn!; **quantum mechanics classes are a trip** *(weird and wonderful)* Unterricht in Quantenmechanik ist der Wahnsinn

2 *vi (on drugs)* auf dem Trip sein

trolley *n* **he's off his trolley** *(crazy)* der hat 'nen Stich; **a trolley dolly** *Humorous (air hostess)* eine Kaffeeschubse

tub *n* (a) *(fat stomach)* Wanst *m*
(b) *(fat person)* Fettwanst *m*; **he's a great big tub of lard** *(he's fat)* er ist 'ne richtige Walze

turd *n* (a) *(piece of excrement)* Haufen *m*; **a dog turd** ein Hundehaufen
(b) *Insult (contemptible person)* Arschloch *nt*; **piss off, you little turd!** verpiss dich, du Arschloch!

turn off *vt sep* (a) *(sexually)* **that really turned me off** das hat mir total die Lust genommen
(b) *(cause to lose interest)* **her very dry style turns me off** ihr knochentrockener Stil geht mir auf den Geist

turn-off *n* (a) *(sexually)* **that's a real turn-off** da vergeht einem ja total die Lust
(b) *(bore)* **that's such a turn-off** das geht mir echt auf den Geist

turn on *vt sep* (a) *(sexually)* **it really turns me on** das turnt mich total an; **I'm really turned on** ich bin total angeturnt
(b) *(interest)* **the thought**

doesn't exactly turn me on das haut mich nicht gerade vom Hocker; **I find quantum mechanics really fascinating – whatever turns you on, Nigel!** ich finde Quantenmechanik echt faszinierend – naja, Nigel, wenn du dir das geben musst

turn-on *n* (a) *(sexually)* **that's a real turn-on** das ist ein echter Anturner
(b) *(exciting thing)* **it's a real turn-on** das ist echt der Bringer; **it's not exactly a turn-on** das haut mich nicht gerade vom Hocker

twat **1** *n* (a) *(vagina)* Möse *f*
(b) *Insult (contemptible man)* Arschgesicht *nt*; **I felt (like) a right twat in my kilt** ich bin mir in dem Kilt wie der letzte Arsch vorgekommen; **you (stupid) twat!** du (blödes) Arschgesicht!
2 *vt (hit)* dreschen; **I twatted him** ich hab' ihm eine gedroschen; **I twatted the safe with a hammer** ich hab' mit 'nem Hammer auf den Safe eingedroschen; **I twatted my head on the doorframe** ich bin mit dem Kopf gegen den Türrahmen gerumst

twatted *adj (drunk)* **to be twatted** voll fett sein; **I got twatted** ich hab' mich zugezogen

twerp *n Insult (contemptible person)* Hohlkopf *m*; **I felt (like) a right twerp in my kilt** ich bin mir in dem Kilt bekloppt vorgekommen; **you (stupid) twerp!** du Hohlkopf!

twig 1 *vt (understand)* raffen; I
finally twigged what she meant
ich hab's endlich gerafft, was sie
meinte
   2 *vi (catch on)* es checken; I
finally twigged ich hab's endlich
gecheckt

twist → round

twit *n Insult (contemptible
person)* Trottel *m*; I **felt (like) a
right twit in my kilt** ich kam mir
in dem Kilt völlig bescheuert vor;
you (stupid) twit! du Trottel!

U

up 1 *adj* **(a)** *(ready)* **tea's up!**
Essen ist fertig!

(b) *(phrases)* **we're going
canoeing, are you up for it?**
(keen to participate) wir gehen
Kanu fahren, hast du Bock
mitzukommen?; **I'm not really up
for it today** ich hab' heut' keinen
Bock; **her opponent wasn't up
for it** *(prepared to fight)* ihre
Gegnerin hat keinen Kampfgeist
gezeigt; **she was really up for it**
(keen to have sex) sie war echt
heiß

2 *adv* **I'm up to here with
you/this job!** *(fed up)* ich hab'
dich/diesen Job echt über!;
**she hasn't got very much up
top** *(she's stupid)* sie ist etwas
unterbelichtet

3 *prep* **(a)** *(at)* **where's Bill?**
– **up the pub** wo ist Bill? – in der
Kneipe

(b) *(phrases)* **up yours!** *(get
stuffed)* ach, leck mich doch!;
up your bum! *(get stuffed)*
du kannst mich mal!; **up your
arse!** *(get stuffed)* leck mich am
Arsch!; **up yer kilt!** *Humorous
(get stuffed)* du kannst mich
am Abend besuchen!; **he was
right up the boss all afternoon**
(being sycophantic) der ist dem
Chef den ganzen Nachmittag in
den Arsch gekrochen; **the two
of them were up each other the
whole evening** *(flattering each
other)* sie haben sich den ganzen
Abend angeschleimt; **he's totally
up himself** *(full of himself)* der
ist ein eingebildeter Arsch mit
Ohren

V

vibe *n (atmosphere)* **that whole 1970s vibe** das Feeling der Siebzigerjahre; **I get good/bad vibes off that bloke** auf mich kommt der Typ gut rüber/nicht gut rüber; **the house gave me strange vibes** mich hat's gegruselt in dem Haus

virus *n* **he's got the virus** *(he's HIV-positive)* er ist positiv

W

wacko → whacko

waffle 1 *n (verbosity)* **her speech was a load of old waffle** die hat doch nur blödes Zeug gesülzt; **to talk waffle** rumsülzen
 2 *vi (be verbose)* rumsülzen

wally *n Insult (stupid person)* Dussel *m*; **I felt (like) a right wally in my kilt** ich bin mir in dem Kilt wie der letzte Dussel vorgekommen; **not there, you (great) wally!** doch nicht da, du Dussel!

wangle *vt (get hold of)* **I wangled some tickets for the concert** ich habe ein paar Karten für das Konzert aufgetrieben; **I managed to wangle it so that we didn't have to go** ich habe das so getrickst, dass wir nicht mitmussten; **I wangled an extra week's holiday out of the boss** ich habe dem Chef eine Extrawoche Urlaub abgeluchst; **he managed to wangle his way out of doing the washing-up** er hat sich erfolgreich vor dem Abwasch gedrückt

wank 1 *n* **(a)** *(act of masturbation)* Wichsen *nt*; **she found me having a wank** sie hat mich ertappt, als ich mir gerade einen wichste; **a wank mag** *(porn magazine)* ein Wichsblatt
 (b) *(nonsense)* **that's a load of (old) wank!** das ist doch Gülle!
 2 *vi (masturbate)* wichsen

wanker *n Insult (contemptible man)* Wichser *m*; **I felt (like) a right wanker in my kilt** ich bin mir in dem Kilt wie der letzte Arsch vorgekommen; **you stupid wanker!** du blöder Wichser!

way *n* **no way, José!** *(expresses refusal)* kommt nicht in die Tüte!; **way to go!** *US (well done)* echt klasse!

wazz 1 *n (act of urinating)* **I need a wazz** ich muss pieseln; **to go for a wazz** pieseln gehen; **to have a wazz** pieseln
 2 *vi (urinate)* pieseln

wazzed *adj (drunk)* **to be wazzed** dicht sein; **I got wazzed** ich hab' mich zugelötet

wee 1 *n* **(a)** *(urine)* Pipi *nt*
 (b) *(act of urinating)* **I need a wee** ich muss Pipi machen; **to go for a wee** Pipi machen gehen; **to do a wee** Pipi machen; **to have a wee** Pipi machen
 2 *vt* **the baby's weed himself** *(wet himself)* das Baby hat sich voll gepinkelt
 3 *vi (urinate)* Pipi machen

weed n (a) (weak person) Schwächling m
(b) (marijuana) Heu nt; **to smoke weed** kiffen

wee-wee 1 n (a) (urine) Pipi nt
(b) (act of urinating) **I need a wee-wee** ich muss pullern; **to go for a wee-wee** pullern gehen; **to do a wee-wee** pullern; **to have a wee-wee** pullern
2 vi (urinate) pullern

weirdo n (strange person) durchgeknallter Typ

well adv (very) **I was well pleased** das hat mich echt gefreut; **he was well away** (drunk) er hatte einen im Tee; **she was well out of it** (intoxicated) sie war total dicht

wet 1 n (ineffectual person) Waschlappen m
2 adj (ineffectual) schlappschwänzig

whack 1 n (a) (go, attempt) **to have a whack at it** es mal probieren
(b) (amount) **I had to pay the full whack** ich musste voll bezahlen
2 vt (a) esp US (kill) platt machen
(b) (put) **I'll just whack it on my credit card** das zahl' ich mit Plastik
3 adj (bad) mies

whackjob n esp US (a) (eccentric person) durchgeknallter Typ
(b) (mentally ill person) Bekloppter m, Bekloppte f; **the guy's a total whackjob** der Typ ist doch total irre

ⓘ In der Bedeutung (b) ist die Bezeichnung **whackjob** (Bekloppter) beleidigend für Menschen, die an einer Geisteskrankheit leiden.

whacko n esp US (a) (eccentric person) durchgeknallter Typ
(b) (mentally ill person) Bekloppter m, Bekloppte f; **the guy's a total whacko** der Typ ist doch total irre

ⓘ In der Bedeutung (b) ist die Bezeichnung **whacko** (Bekloppter) beleidigend für Menschen, die an einer Geisteskrankheit leiden.

whack off vi (masturbate) **she found me whacking off** sie hat mich ertappt, als ich mir gerade einen streifelte

whassup interj (greeting) alles fit?

wheels npl (car) Blechkiste f; **I need a new set of wheels** ich brauch 'ne neue Blechkiste; **I can't wait till I finally get some wheels** ich kann's kaum erwarten, bis ich endlich 'nen fahrbaren Untersatz habe

whopper n (a) (big thing) Riesenteil m; **the trout I caught was a whopper** die Forelle, die ich gefangen habe, war ein Riesenteil; **that bruise you've got is a whopper** das ist ja ein Riesenteil von blauem Fleck, den du da hast
(b) (lie) faustdicke Lüge

whopping adj (huge)

mordsmäßig; **he had a whopping great bruise on his knee** er hatte einen mordsmäßigen blauen Fleck am Knie

whore *n* (a) *Insult (promiscuous woman)* Nutte *f*; **Janet's a bloody whore!** Janet ist eine Scheißnutte!; **you whore!** du Nutte!

(b) *Insult (contemptible woman)* Nutte *f*; **piss off, you (stupid) whore!** verpiss dich, du blöde Nutte!

wicked 1 *adj* (a) *(excellent)* megageil

(b) **she had her wicked way with him** *Humorous (had sex)* sie hat ihn richtig rangenommen 2 *interj (excellent)* voll geil!

willie, willy *n (penis)* Pieselmann *m*

wimp *n* (a) *(person who is easily scared)* Schisshase *m*; **I'm a wimp when it comes to flying** ich hab' Schiss vorm Fliegen; **don't be such a wimp and ask her to dance** sei nicht so ein Schisshase, nun lad sie schon zum Tanzen ein

(b) *(weak person)* Schwächling *m*

wino *n (drunk)* Alki *m*

wise guy *n (know-all)* Schlaumeier *m*; **stop being such a wise guy** tu doch nicht so verdammt schlau; **OK, wise guy, one more word and I'll blow your brains out** hör her, Schlaumeier, noch ein Wort und ich puste dir das Hirn weg

wobbler, wobbly *n* **to throw a wobbler** *or* **wobbly** *(get angry)* einen Aufstand machen; *(panic)* durchdrehen

wog ‼ *n Racist (black person)* Bimbo *m*

wop ‼ *n Racist (Italian)* Spaghettifresser *m*; *(any southern European)* Kanake *m*

wrist → **one**

Yank *n (American)* Ami *m*

Yid *n Racist (Jew)* Jude *m*, Jüdin *f* [*not slang*]

yo *interj (greeting)* na, Alter!; *(to attract attention)* he du!; **yo, I did it!** *(expresses approval)* yes, ich hab's gemacht!

Z → cop

zilch 1 *n (nothing)* **there's zilch on TV tonight** heute Abend gibt's null im Fernsehen; **how much food is left? – zilch** wie viel Essen ist noch da? – null; **you don't know zilch about it** du hast davon ja null Ahnung

  2 *adj (no)* **I got zilch help from her** ich habe null Hilfe von ihr bekommen

zip, zippo *n US (nothing)* **we won six to zip(po)** wir haben sechs zu null gewonnen [*not slang*]; **how much food is left? – zip(po)** wie viel Essen ist noch da? – null; **you don't know zip(po) about that subject** du hast davon ja null Ahnung

A

Aa *nt (Kot)* poo; **Aa machen** *(Darm entleeren)* to do a poo

abchecken *vt (überprüfen)* to check [*nicht Slang*]; **ich muss das erst mit meinen Eltern abchecken** I'll have to OK that with my parents first

abdüsen *vi (weggehen)* to take off; **die Party war langweilig, da bin ich ziemlich früh abgedüst** the party was boring so I took off pretty early

Abflug *m* **den** *oder* **einen Abflug machen** *(sterben)* to kick it; *(weggehen, fliehen)* to leg it; **also Leute, ich mach' jetzt den Abflug, ich muss morgen früh raus** right, guys, I'm out of here, I've got an early start tomorrow

abgefahren *adj (großartig)* mental; **die Band macht voll abgefahrene Musik** that band's music is totally mental

abgefuckt *adj (in üblem Zustand)* fucked up

abgehen *vi (a) (sich erregen)* **Mann, ich bin gestern voll abgegangen** I got totally wired yesterday, man

  (b) *(unterhaltsam sein)* **was willst du denn da? Da geht doch nichts ab** what d'you want to go there for? The place is totally dead; **in der Disko geht immer was ab** the crack's always pretty good down the disco; **jetzt geht die Party ab** the party's really rocking now; **was geht ab?** *(was ist los?)* what's the crack?

  (c) ihm ist einer abgegangen *(er hat ejakuliert)* he came; **das ist so geil, da geht mir einer ab** *(ich finde das hervorragend)* it's so totally awesome, I'm just creaming myself

abhängen *vi (herumsitzen)* to hang; **was machst 'n du heute? – Einfach abhängen** what are you up to today? – Just hanging

abhauen *vi (sich entfernen)* to leg it; **ich hau ab** I'm off; **hau ab!** get lost!; **ich hab' ihm gesagt, er soll abhauen** I told him to get lost

abhotten *vi (tanzen)* to shake one's booty

abkacken *vi (Darm entleeren)* to have a shit

abkauen *vt* **sie hat mir einen abgekaut** *(hat mich fellationiert)* she sucked me off

abkotzen *vi (sich ärgern)* to be pissed off; **ich kotz' ab, Mensch!** Christ, what a bloody shag!

abkratzen *vi (sterben)* to croak

ablachen *reflexiv* **sich einen ablachen** *(herzlich lachen)* to crack up; **ich hab' mir einen abgelacht** I cracked up

abmatten *vi* **(a)** *(schlafen)* to crash
   (b) *(ausruhen)* to chill
   (c) *(herumhängen)* to chill

abmurksen *vt (töten)* **jemanden abmurksen** to bump somebody off

abnehmen *vt (glauben)* to buy; **das nimmt dir nie jemand ab!** nobody's ever going to buy that!; **Uwe hat erzählt, dass er gestern 10 km gerannt ist. Das nehme ich ihm nicht ab** Uwe said he ran 10 km yesterday, but I'm not buying it

abnibbeln *vi (sterben)* to snuff it

abrotzen *vi (ejakulieren)* to shoot one's load

abschlabbern **1** *vt (küssen)* **der Oli hat den ganzen Abend auf dem Sofa gesessen und die Tanja abgeschlabbert** Oli just sat on the sofa sucking face with Tanja all evening
   2 *reflexiv* **sich abschlabbern** to suck face; **jetzt schlabbern die sich schon wieder ab!** God, they're sucking face again!

abschleppen *vt (einen Sexualpartner mitnehmen)* **jemanden abschleppen** to get off with somebody

abschnallen *vi* **(a)** *(fassungslos sein)* to be gobsmacked; **ich hab' gedacht, ich schnall' ab** I was gobsmacked; **ich hab' im Lotto gewonnen, da schnallste ab, was!** get a load of this, I won the lottery!
   (b) *(nicht mehr folgen können)* **als er mir die Quantentheorie erklären wollte, hab' ich voll abgeschnallt** I hadn't got a scoobie what he was on about when he tried to explain quantum theory to me; **ich schnall' ab, das begreift doch keine Sau!** you've lost me there, mate, you can't expect anyone to understand that!

abspritzen *vi (ejakulieren)* to come

abwürfeln *vi (erbrechen)* to blow chunks

abzischen *vi (weggehen)* to take off; **he Leute, ich zisch' ab** I'm out of here, guys!; **zisch ab, du störst hier!** see ya, you're not wanted here!

abzocken *vt (übermäßig viel berechnen)* **jemanden abzocken** to rip somebody off

Affe *m* **(a)** *beleidigend (Idiot)* gobshite; **du blöder Affe!** you stupid gobshite!; **er ist ein eingebildeter Affe** he's totally up himself
   (b) *(Redewendungen)* **einen Affen haben** *(betrunken sein)* to be sloshed; **ich hab' mir 'nen Affen angesoffen** I got sloshed; **einen Affen schieben** *(auf Entzug sein)* to go through cold turkey; **ich saß da drauf wie ein Affe auf dem Schleifstein** *(ungeschickt, lächerlich)* I

looked a right plonker sitting there; **sich zum Affen machen** *(sich blamieren)* to make a tit of oneself; **du bist wohl vom wilden Affen gebissen?** *(du bist wohl verrückt?)* are you completely off your block?; **mich laust der Affe!** *(ich bin hocherstaunt)* well, blow me!

Affenarsch *m beleidigend (lächerliche Person)* bell-end

Alki *m, f (Alkoholiker)* alkie

alle *adj* **alle sein** *(erschöpft sein)* to be knacked

Alte *f* (a) *(Ehefrau)* missus; **meine/deine/seine Alte** the missus; **ich fahr' mal zum Bahnhof, meine Alte abholen** I'm off to the station to pick up the missus
(b) *(Chefin)* boss
(c) *sexistisch (Frau)* bitch; **die Alte ist mir doch voll an die Eier gegangen** the mad bitch tried to grab me by the balls

Alten *npl (Eltern)* **meine Alten** my mum and dad

Alter *m* (a) *(Kumpel)* mate; **willst du Ärger, Alter?** d'you want some, mate?; **mein Alter** mate; **na mein Alter, wie steht's?** how's it going, mate?
(b) *(Ehemann)* old man
(c) *(Chef)* boss

Ami *m (Amerikaner)* Yank; **die Amis** the Yanks

anbaggern *vt (mit sexuellen Motiven ansprechen)* **jemanden anbaggern** to chat somebody up

andersrum *adj homophob (homosexuell)* bent

andrehen *vt (verkaufen)* **jemandem etwas andrehen** to palm something off on somebody; **was haben sie dir denn da angedreht?** what have you gone and got conned into buying now?

anfixen *vt* **jemanden anfixen** *(zum ersten Mal Heroin spritzen lassen)* to fix somebody up for the first time

angearscht *adj* **angearscht sein** *(in schlechter Lage sein)* to be in big shit

angefickt *adj* **angefickt sein** *(in schlechter Lage sein)* to be fucked

angeschissen *adj* **angeschissen sein** *(in schlechter Lage sein)* to be in the shit

Angsthase *m (ängstliche Person)* scaredy-cat

ankacken *vi* **gegen jemanden nicht ankacken können** *(sich nicht messen können)* not to be in the same fucking league as somebody; **gegen den kannst du sowieso nicht ankacken** you're not in the same fucking league as him

anknallen *vt sexistisch (schwängern)* to knock up; **der hat die schon mit sechzehn angeknallt** he knocked her up when she was just sixteen

ankotzen *vt* (a) *(ärgern)* to piss off; **der Job kotzt mich an!** I'm pissed off with this job!; **du kotzt mich an mit deinem ewigen Gejammer!** you really piss me off

anlabern

with your constant moaning!
(b) *(anwidern)* **du kotzt mich einfach an!** you're totally gross!

anlabern vt *(verbal belästigen)* **jemanden anlabern** to come on to somebody

anlachen reflexiv **sich jemanden anlachen** *(mit sexuellen Motiven ansprechen)* to pick somebody up; **ich habe ihn mir angelacht** I picked him up

Anmache f *(Taktik, jemanden mit sexuellen Motiven anzusprechen)* chat-up line

anmachen vt (a) *(mit sexuellen Motiven ansprechen)* to chat up
(b) *(provozieren)* to wind up

ansaufen reflexiv **ich hab' mir einen angesoffen** I got paralytic

anschaffen vi *(sich prostituieren)* to turn tricks; **seit wann geht die anschaffen?** how long has she been turning tricks?; **jemanden anschaffen schicken** to pimp somebody out

anscheißen vt (a) *(verraten)* **jemanden (bei jemandem) anscheißen** to dump somebody in the shit (with somebody)
(b) *(kritisieren)* **jemanden anscheißen** to give somebody a bollocking; **wie lange muss ich mich denn noch von meinem idiotischen Chef anscheißen lassen?** how much longer am I going to have to take this shit from that idiot boss of mine?
(c) *(ärgern)* **jemanden anscheißen** to fuck somebody off; **der Job scheißt mich voll an** I'm totally fucked off with this job

anschmieren 1 vt *(verraten)* **jemanden (bei jemandem) anschmieren** to dump somebody in it (with somebody)
2 reflexiv **sich anschmieren** to end up looking like a twit; **na, da habe ich mich ja schön angeschmiert!** I ended up looking like a right twit!

antatschen vt *(berühren)* to grope; **tatsch mich nicht an, du Schwein!** get your filthy paws off me, you pig!

Äpfel npl, **Äpfelchen** npl scherzhaft *(Brüste)* titties

Arm m **Arme wie Bindfäden oder Schweißerdrähte haben** *(ein Schwächling sein)* to be a weed; **jemanden auf den Arm nehmen** *(veralbern)* to have somebody on; **du willst mich wohl auf den Arm nehmen?** are you having me on?; **da haben sie dich auf den Arm genommen** they were having you on

arm → **fressen**

Armleuchter m beleidigend, euphemistisch [Arschloch] *(dummer Mensch)* wazzock; **du Armleuchter!** you wazzock!

Arsch m (a) *(Gesäß)* arse; **die hat 'nen Arsch wie ein Brauereipferd** she's got a fat arse
(b) beleidigend *(nichtswürdige Person)* arse; **du Arsch!** you stupid arse!; **sich zum Arsch machen** to make an arse of oneself
(c) *(Redewendungen)* **ein Arsch mit Ohren** *(lächerliche Person)* a prick; **mit der Frisur**

sehe ich aus wie ein Arsch mit Ohren I look like a right prick with this haircut; **du Arsch mit Ohren!** you prick!; **ich habe mir den Arsch abgefroren** *(ich habe sehr gefroren)* I froze my bollocks off; **am Arsch der Welt** *(sehr abgelegen)* in the middle of bloody nowhere; **ich hab' mir den Arsch aufgerissen, das rechtzeitig fertig zu kriegen** *(ich habe mich sehr angestrengt)* I've been busting my balls to finish it on time; **na los, beweg deinen Arsch!** *(beweg dich)* come on, shift your arse!; **na los, komm aus dem Arsch!** *(beweg dich)* come on, get your arse into gear!; **auf den Arsch fallen** *(Misserfolg haben)* to make a cock-up; **mit dem Projekt sind wir mordsmäßig auf den Arsch gefallen** we made a right cock-up of the project; **wenn das ein Lied ist, dann ist mein Arsch 'ne Himbeere** *(das ist ein miserables Lied)* if that's a song then I'm a flipping banana; **den Arsch hochreißen** *(kaputtgehen)* to get fucked; **einen kalten Arsch kriegen** *(sterben)* to buy it; **den Arsch zukneifen** *(sterben)* to go for a burton; **einen im Arsch haben** *(betrunken sein)* to be arseholed; **im Arsch sein** *(kaputt sein)* to be fucked; **mein Bein ist im Arsch** my leg's fucked; **Lothars Ehe ist im Arsch** Lothar's marriage is fucked; **in den Arsch gehen** *(kaputtgehen)* to get fucked; **der Fernseher ist in den Arsch gegangen** the telly's fucked; **etwas in Arsch**

kriegen *(kaputtmachen)* to fuck something; **der kriegt den Arsch nicht hoch** *(er ist träge)* he just sits around on his arse all day; **mach dich endlich an die Arbeit, oder kriegst du mal wieder den Arsch nicht hoch?** come on, do some work for once, or are you just going to sit around on your arse all day long again?; **der kriecht doch jedem in den Arsch** *(er ist ein Kriecher)* he's a real arse-licker; **den Arsch offen haben** *(nicht bei Verstand sein)* to be out of one's fucking mind; **die haben doch alle den Arsch offen** they're all out of their fucking minds; **mir platzt der Arsch** *(ich bin wütend)* I've fucking well had it; **die haben mich wegen den Graffiti an den Arsch gekriegt** *(sie haben mich dafür verantwortlich gemacht)* I got in the shit because of the graffiti; **wenn du nicht sofort mit dem Gebrüll aufhörst, kriegst du den Arsch voll!** *(du wirst verprügelt)* stop that racket at once or I'll slap your arse till it's raw!; **der hat von seinem Vater den Arsch voll gekriegt** *(er wurde verprügelt)* his dad beat the crap out of him; **den Arsch voll kriegen** *(verlieren)* to get one's arse kicked; **unsere Mannschaft hat auswärts den Arsch voll gekriegt** we got our arses kicked in the away match; **leck mich am Arsch!** *(lass mich in Ruhe)* kiss my arse!; **ich könnte mich** *oder* **mir in den Arsch beißen!** *(ich ärgere mich)* I could bloody kill myself!; **jemandem**

den Arsch retten *(jemanden retten)* to save somebody's arse; **ich habe ihnen den Arsch gerettet** I saved their arses; **mein Auto willst du? Das kannst du dir in den Arsch stecken!** *(das kannst du vergessen)* lend you my car? No fucking way!; **den Job kannst du dir in den Arsch schieben!** you can stick your job up your arse!; **jemanden in den Arsch treten** *(körperliche Gewalt zufügen)* to kick somebody up the arse; *(jemanden antreiben)* to give somebody a kick up the arse; **sie hat ihm einen Tritt in den Arsch gegeben** *(sie hat sich von ihm getrennt)* she gave him the fucking boot; **noch so ein Fehler, und du kriegst einen Tritt in den Arsch!** *(du wirst entlassen)* one more mistake like that and you'll be out on your arse!; **das geht mir ja so am Arsch vorbei** *(das ist mir egal)* I couldn't give a fuck; **was er von mir denkt geht mir ja so am Arsch vorbei** I couldn't give a fuck what he thinks of me; **das geht mir zehn Meter am Arsch vorbei** *(das ist mir egal)* I couldn't give a flying fuck

Arschbacke *f* (a) *(Pobacke)* bum cheek; **was, nur zwei Jahre Knast? Die sitz' ich doch auf einer Arschbacke ab!** *(mit Leichtigkeit)* two years in the nick? That's a piece of piss!
(b) *beleidigend (lächerliche Person)* dickbrain; **du Arschbacke!** you dickbrain!; **he, du Arschbacke, du willst wohl** Streit? oi, dickbrain, d'you want some?

Arschficker !! *m* (a) *homophob (Homosexueller)* bumfucker
(b) *beleidigend (nichtswürdige Person)* fucking arsehole; **du Arschficker!** you fucking arsehole!

Arschgeige *f beleidigend (Dummkopf)* pillock; **du Arschgeige!** you pillock!

Arschgesicht *nt beleidigend (nichtswürdige Person)* twat; **du Arschgesicht!** you twat!

Arschkarte *f* **die Arschkarte ziehen** *(der Benachteiligte sein)* to be out of fucking luck; **alle haben eine Beförderung bekommen, nur ich hab' mal wieder die Arschkarte gezogen** everyone got promoted, I was the only one who was out of fucking luck again

Arschkriecher *m*, **Arschkriecherin** *f (unterwürfiger Mensch)* arse-licker

Arschloch *nt* (a) *(After)* arsehole
(b) *beleidigend (nichtswürdige Person)* arsehole; **du blödes Arschloch!** you stupid arsehole!; **du dreckiges Arschloch!** you bloody arsehole!

Arschtritt *m* **jemandem einen Arschtritt geben** *(körperliche Gewalt zufügen)* to give somebody a kick up the arse; *(entlassen, verlassen)* to give somebody the fucking boot; **einen Arschtritt kriegen** *(entlassen oder verlassen*

werden) to get the fucking
boot

Assi m, **Asi** m beleidigend
(Asozialer) crusty

Ast m sich einen Ast lachen
(herzlich lachen) to laugh like a
drain; ich hab' mir bei dem Film
einen Ast gelacht I laughed like
a drain during the film

ätzend adj (a) (furchtbar) die
machen ätzende Musik their
music blows; ein ätzender Lehrer
a teacher who blows; ich finde
Mathe ätzend maths blows
  (b) (uncool) (Film, Kleidung)
naff
  (c) (langweilig) jetzt erzählt der
wieder seine ätzenden Witze
yawn! He's telling his boring
jokes again; die Schule ist ätzend
school's a yawn

aufbrezeln reflexiv sich aufbrezeln (sich auffällig zurecht-
machen) to tart oneself up

aufgabeln vt (kennen lernen)
wo hast du denn die Tussi
aufgegabelt? where did you dig
her up?; die habe ich gestern in
der Disko aufgegabelt I ran into
her at the disco yesterday

aufgeilen reflexiv sich an etwas
aufgeilen (erregt werden) to get
off on something

aufklatschen vt jemanden
aufklatschen (zusammen-
schlagen) to kick the shit out of
somebody

aufkreuzen vi (auftauchen) to
show up

aufmischen vt (aggressiv

beeinflussen) Neonazis haben
die Demo aufgemischt a bunch
of neonazis were causing aggro
on the demo

aufreißen vt (a) (mit sexuellen
Motiven ansprechen) to chat up
  (b) (sexuell erfolgreich sein mit)
to pull

Aufreißer m (sexuell aktiver
Mann) womanizer [nicht Slang];
das ist ein richtiger Aufreißer
he's always chasing after the
birds

Aufriss m (a) (Aufregung)
(wegen einer Sache) einen
Aufriss machen to make a
hoohah (about something)
  (b) (Person, mit der man Sex
haben will) was ist denn mit
deinem Aufriss von letzter Nacht
geworden? what happened with
that bird you pulled last night,
then?

aufschlagen vi (ankommen) to
swing round; ich werde so gegen
sieben bei euch aufschlagen I'll
swing round your place around
seven

Aufstand m (Aufregung)
(wegen einer Sache) einen
Aufstand machen to throw a
wobbler (because of something)

aufziehen vt (necken, provozieren) to bug

ausflippen vi (a) (wütend
werden) to flip (out)
  (b) (verrückt werden) to flip
(out)
  (c) (ängstlich sein) to freak out

ausgeflippt adj (a) (unkon-

ventionell) freaky; **seine neue Freundin ist ziemlich ausgeflippt** his new girlfriend's a bit of a freak

(b) *(nicht Herr seiner Sinne)* out of it; **dort hängen völlig ausgeflippte Typen rum** you get some totally tripped out dudes hanging out round there

Ausgeflippter *m,* **Ausgeflippte** *f* (a) *(unkonventionelle Person)* freak

(b) *(Person, die nicht Herr ihrer Sinne ist)* space cadet

ausgekotzt *adj* **du siehst mal wieder aus wie ausgekotzt** *(du siehst schlecht aus)* you look like shit; **ich fühle mich wie ausgekotzt** *(mir ist schlecht)* I feel like shit

auskotzen *vt (erbrechen)* **etwas auskotzen** to puke something up

auspacken *vi* (a) *meist sexistisch (gebären)* to drop a sprog

(b) *(Geheimnis verraten)* to talk; **na los, Freundchen, pack aus, wenn dir dein Leben lieb ist** you'd better start talking now, pal, if you know what's good for you

ausrasten *vi (wütend werden)* to go mental; **als ich ihm sagte, dass ich schwul bin, da hat es bei ihm ausgerastet** *(er wurde wütend)* he went mental when I told him I'm gay; **bei dem hat's ausgerastet, und da ist er Amok gelaufen** *(er ist durchgedreht)* he totally freaked out and ran amok

ausspucken *vt (Geld)* to fork out; **was, deine Eltern haben dir nichts dazu gegeben? Na, die könnten auch mal ein bisschen was ausspucken!** what, your parents didn't give you anything towards it? I'd have thought they'd have forked out something!

B

baggern vi *(mit sexuellen Motiven bereden)* **guck mal, wie der Kevin bei der baggert** look at Kevin trying to chat her up; **wenn der Oli baggert, wird jede Frau schwach** Oli's got such smooth chat-up lines that no woman could resist him; **ich hab' mich totgelacht, als der Typ anfing, wie wild zu baggern** I cracked up when he started trying to chat me up with every line he knew

ballern vt **jemandem eine ballern** *(jemanden schlagen)* to sock somebody one; **sag mal, ich soll dir wohl mal eine ballern oder was?** d'you want some?

Banane f **sich zur Banane machen** *(sich blamieren)* to make a tit of oneself

ⓘ There are several German phrases that mean *to make a fool of oneself* and follow the same construction as **sich zur Banane machen** *(to make a tit of oneself)* but use different images, for example: **sich zum Elch** (literally, an elk) **machen**, **sich zum Ei** (an egg) **machen**, **sich zur Feile** (a file) **machen**, and **sich zum Affen** (a monkey) **machen**.

Bär m *meist sexistisch (weibliches Geschlechtsorgan)* beaver

Bart m **jemandem um den Bart gehen** *(jemandem schmeicheln)* to suck up to somebody

barzen vt **einen barzen** *(Haschisch oder Marihuana rauchen)* to smoke some blow

Bastard m *beleidigend (nichtswürdiger Mann)* tosser

Bau m **(a)** *(Gefängnis)* **im Bau** in the clink
(b) *(Gefängnisstrafe)* **dafür gibt's zehn Tage Bau** you get ten days in the clink for that

Baum → **ficken**

behumsen vt *(betrügen)* to diddle

beißen → **Gras**

bekloppt adj *(verrückt)* **bekloppt sein** to be a nutcase; **ich bin mir bekloppt vorgekommen** I felt like a twerp; **wie kann man nur so bekloppt fragen?** what a daft question!; **das war eine völlig bekloppte Situation** it was a total pain

Bekloppter m, **Bekloppte** f
(a) *(lächerliche Person)* twerp
(b) *(geisteskranke Person)* nutcase

i In sense (b), the term **Bekloppter** (*nutcase*) is offensive to people with a mental disability.

beknackt 1 *adj* (a) *(verrückt)* nuts; **du bist wohl beknackt?** are you nuts?

(b) *(ärgerlich)* **das ist ja eine beknackte Situation!** what a pain!

(c) *(blöd)* poxy; **du kannst dein beknacktes Geld behalten!** you can keep your poxy money!; **so eine beknackte Frage!** what a flipping stupid question!; **ich kam mir echt beknackt vor** I felt (like) a right tit

2 *adv (dumm)* **er hat sich total beknackt verhalten** he behaved like a right tit; **frag nicht so beknackt!** what a flipping stupid question!

bekotzen *reflexiv* **sich bekotzen** *(sich erbrechen und Kleidung usw. beschmutzen)* to puke all over oneself

beömeln *reflexiv* **ich hab' mich total beömelt** *(habe mich amüsiert)* I totally cracked up

bepissen *reflexiv* **ich hab' mich bepisst (vor Lachen)** *(habe mich amüsiert)* I pissed myself (laughing)

Berg *m* Kindersprache *(Kothaufen)* poo-poo; **einen Berg machen** *(Darm entleeren)* to do a poo-poo

besaufen *reflexiv* **sich besaufen** to get pissed; **ich hab' mich sinnlos besoffen** I got pissed out of my tiny mind

bescheiden *euphemistisch* [*beschissen*] 1 *adj (sehr schlecht)* crummy; **das Wetter war echt bescheiden** the weather was really crummy

2 *adv (sehr schlecht)* **mir geht's bescheiden** I feel pretty crummy

bescheißen 1 *vt (betrügen)* to con

2 *vi (betrügen)* **heh, nicht bescheißen!** oi, stop trying to con me!

bescheuert 1 *adj* (a) *(verrückt)* bonkers

(b) *(blöd)* effing stupid; **so eine bescheuerte Frage!** what an effing stupid question!

(c) *(abwertend)* effing; **das bescheuerte Auto springt nicht an** the effing car won't start; **du bescheuerter Idiot!** you effing idiot!; **der Film war bescheuert** the film was effing terrible; **ich kam mir bescheuert vor** I felt like an effing idiot

2 *adv (dumm)* **bescheuert fragen** to ask an effing stupid question; **bescheuert aussehen** to look effing stupid; **wie bescheuert arbeiten** to work like crazy

Beschiss *m* **das ist Beschiss** *(Betrug)* it's a con; **Beschiss machen** *(betrügen)* to cheat [*nicht Slang*]; **der macht beim Kartenspielen immer Beschiss** the crafty bugger always cheats at cards

beschissen 1 *adj* (a) *(sehr schlecht)* shit; **die machen beschissene Musik** their music is shit; **ich will nicht für eure**

beschissene kleine Firma arbeiten I don't want to work for your shitty little company; **ich fühl' mich beschissen, dass ich das zu ihr gesagt habe** I feel shit about saying that to her; **das beschissene Auto springt nicht an** the bloody car won't start; **das is' ja beschissen!** what a pisser!; **es ist echt beschissen, immer so früh aufstehen zu müssen** it's totally shit always having to get up so early

(b) *(unanständig, unmoralisch)* shitty; **das war echt beschissen, was du da gemacht hast!** that was a really shitty thing to do!

2 *adv* (a) *(sehr schlecht)* **mir geht's beschissen** *(ich bin krank)* I feel like shit; **jemanden beschissen behandeln** to treat somebody like shit; **in Physik bin ich beschissen schlecht** I'm shit at physics; **das ist ziemlich beschissen gelaufen** it was a bloody disaster

(b) *(unanständig, unmoralisch)* **sie behandelt ihn echt beschissen** she treats him like shit

Besen → fressen

besoffen *adj (betrunken)* pissed

besorgen *vt* **es jemandem besorgen** *(koitieren mit)* to give somebody one; **ich hab's ihr besorgt** I gave her one; **es besorgt kriegen** *(koitieren)* to get laid; **hast du es besorgt gekriegt?** did you get laid?

Besuch *m* **ich habe Besuch** *euphemistisch (ich menstruiere)* I've got the decorators in

Bettkante *f* **die würde ich nicht von der Bettkante schubsen** *oder* **stoßen** *(ich finde sie attraktiv)* I wouldn't kick her out of bed

betütert *adj (betrunken)* woozy

Bienenstiche *npl sexistisch (sehr kleine weibliche Brüste)* fried eggs

Biest *nt* (a) *(launische Frau)* moody cow

(b) *beleidigend (unmoralische Frau)* tart; **du Biest!** you tart!

Bimbo !! *m rassistisch (Schwarzer)* coon

Bindfäden → Arm

Birne *f (Kopf)* nut; **schalt mal deine Birne ein!** use your loaf!; **sie hat nicht viel in der Birne** she's a bit of an airhead; **als ich die Kellertreppe runterging, habe ich mir voll die Birne angerammt** I nutted myself when I was going down the stairs into the cellar; **du kriegst gleich ein paar vor die Birne!** I'll knock your block off if you don't watch it!; **ich hab' ein paar vor die Birne bekommen** *(ich wurde geschlagen)* I copped a couple; **wir haben uns am Sonnabend die Birne ausgeleitert** *(wir haben uns betrunken)* we got out of our faces on Saturday → Scheiße

blasen *vt* **sie hat mir einen geblasen** *(sie hat mich fellationiert)* she gave me a blow job

blau *adj (betrunken)* **blau sein** to be legless; **blau werden** to get legless

blaumachen vi (nicht zur Arbeit gehen) to skive (off work)

blöd 1 adj (a) (dumm) dumb; **so eine blöde Frage!** what a dumb question!; **der ist eben ein bisschen blöd, so was begreift der nicht** he'll never understand that, he's a bit thick; **für Chemie bin ich zu blöd** I'm flipping useless at chemistry; **du bist blöd!** stuff you!; **der ist so blöd wie ein Sack Holz voll Nüsse** he's as thick as two (short) planks → **Rind**

(b) (unangenehm) **so ein blödes Wetter!** bleeding weather!; **das war eine blöde Situation** it was a pain; **jetzt hast du mich in eine ganz schön blöde Lage gebracht** you've really gone and dumped me in it now; **ich habe das blöde Gefühl, dass ich was vergessen habe** I've got this nagging feeling I've forgotten something; **das ist schon ein blödes Gefühl, wenn man vor all den Leuten steht und seinen Text nicht mehr kann** you feel like a right twit when you're standing in front of all those people and can't remember your lines; **das Blöde daran ist, dass ich dazu kein Geld habe** it's a pain cos I haven't got enough money for it; **mir ist heute was Blödes passiert, ich habe mich aus der Wohnung ausgesperrt** I locked myself out of the flat today, it was a real pain; **is ja blöd!** what a pain!

(c) (schwachsinnig) mental

2 adv (dumm) **frag nicht so blöd!** what a dumb question!; **ich kam mir blöd vor** I felt like a twit; **er hat sich ihr gegenüber echt blöd verhalten** he behaved like a right twit towards her; **ich hab' nur blöd rumgestanden** I just stood there like a twit

Blödsinn 1 m (a) (Unsinn) garbage; **er hat die ganze Zeit nur Blödsinn geredet** he just talked garbage the whole time; **der hat ja so einen Blödsinn erzählt** what he said was complete and utter garbage

(b) (Minderwertiges) garbage; **für so einen Blödsinn zahle ich doch keine 50 Euro!** I'm not paying 50 euros for that garbage!

(c) (alberne Streiche) **was haben wir in den Ferien für 'n Blödsinn gemacht** we got up to all sorts of nonsense in the holidays; **die Kinder machen wieder Blödsinn** the kids are acting up again; **Onkel Franz macht mit den Kindern immer Blödsinn** Uncle Franz is always clowning around with the kids

2 interj (Ausdruck des Widersprechens) nonsense!

blond adj (dumm) **blond sein** to be an airhead

Blondine f (dumme Frau) airhead

Boah eh interj (Ausruf der Überraschung) far out!; (Ausruf der Anerkennung) yo!; **Boah eh, geiles Handy!** yo, that's one wicked mobile!

Bock m (a) (Mann) **er ist ein**

geiler Bock he's a horny bugger
  (b) **ich hab' null Bock** *(ich habe keine Lust)* I can't be arsed; **die junge Generation hat doch null Bock auf nichts** young people today just can't be arsed; **hast du Bock mitzukommen?** are you up for coming?

Bockmist *m* (a) *(Unsinn)* balls; **das ist doch Bockmist!** that's (a load of) balls!; **Bockmist reden/verzapfen** to talk/spout (a load of) balls
  (b) **Bockmist bauen** *(etwas schlecht ausführen)* to screw up; **Mann, da habt ihr aber Bockmist gebaut!** Christ, you've really gone and screwed it up, haven't you?

bockstark *adj (toll)* awesome

Bohnenstroh → **dumm**

Bonbon *m oder nt (Ecstasy-tablette)* (tab of) E; **einen Bonbon einwerfen** to drop an E *oder* to drop a tab of E

Braten *m* **sie hat 'nen Braten in der Röhre** *scherzhaft (sie ist schwanger)* she's up the duff

Bratpfanne *f* **die hat ein Gesicht wie 'ne Bratpfanne** *(sie ist hässlich)* she has a face like the back end of a bus

Brauereipferd → **Arsch**

Braut *f sexistisch (Frau, Freundin)* ho

breit *adj (voll)* **breit sein** *(mit Drogen)* to be loaded; *(mit Alkohol)* to be hammered

Brett *nt (flache weibliche Brust)*

die ist doch wie 'n Brett she's flat as a pancake

Brikett !! *nt rassistisch (Farbiger)* shade

Brötchen *nt scherzhaft* (a) *(weibliches Geschlechtsorgan)* muff; **wie ein Brötchen aussehen** *(lächerlich aussehen)* to look a right state; *(hässlich aussehen)* to have a face like the back end of a bus
  (b) *(Geschlechtsverkehr)* **du brauchst wohl mal wieder ein Brötchen?** you look like you could do with a bit of muff

Brust *f* **Brust raus!** *sexistisch* (get your) tits out for the lads!

brutal *adv (sehr)* frigging; **das tut brutal weh** that's frigging painful; **ein brutal großes Auto** a frigging enormous car

Büchse *f meist sexistisch (weibliches Geschlechtsorgan)* fanny

Buchstabe *m* **meine/seine vier Buchstaben** *euphemistisch (Gesäß)* my/your bottie

ⓘ The **vier Buchstaben** *(four letters)* referred to in this expression are **A-S-C-H**, which is a euphemism for the German word **Arsch** *(arse)*.

Bude *f (Wohnung, Haus)* place; **ich habe ein paar Freunde zu mir auf die Bude eingeladen** I've invited a couple of friends round to my place; **sturmfreie Bude haben** *(in der Lage sein, unbehindert Besuch zu empfangen)* to have the place to oneself; **am Wochenende habe ich sturmfreie Bude** I've got the place to myself at the weekend

Büffelhüfte f *sexistisch, beleidigend (hässliche, dicke Frau)* fat old hag

Bulle m (a) *(Polizist)* pig; **die Bullen** the pigs
(b) *(sexuell hochaktiver Mann)* stud

Bullensau f *beleidigend (Polizist)* bloody pig

Bullenschaukel f *(Polizeiauto)* pig wagon

Bullerei f *beleidigend (Polizei)* **die Bullerei** the filth

Bums m *(Tanzveranstaltung)* bop; **wir gehen am Wochenende zum Bums** we're going to the bop at the weekend

bumsen 1 *vi* (a) *(koitieren)* to bonk; **hast du Lust zu bumsen?** d'you fancy a bonk?; **die haben im Auto gebumst** they had a bonk in the car
(b) *(heftig aufschlagen)* **er ist mit dem Kopf gegen den Balken gebumst** he bashed his head on the beam; **die bumst ständig irgendwo dagegen** she's always bashing into things
2 *vt (koitieren mit)* to bonk

Bunter !! m *rassistisch (nichtweißer Ausländer)* wog

Busengrapscher m *(Mann, der Frauen unsittlich berührt)* groper; **wir haben so einen Busengrapscher in der Firma** there's this bloke at the company who can't keep his filthy paws to himself

Buslenker → rund

C

checken vt (a) (überprüfen) to check out; **ich muss die Bremsen checken lassen** I need to get the brakes checked out

(b) (verstehen) to twig; **sag das noch mal. Ich hab's noch nicht gecheckt** say that again, I didn't get it

(c) (geistig auf Draht sein) **Onkel Hanno wird auch langsam senil, der checkt das einfach nicht mehr** Uncle Hanno's getting a bit senile, the lights are on but nobody's home; **meine Mutter ist zwar gebrechlich, aber checkt's noch voll** my mum's a bit frail, but she's still got all her marbles

chillen vi (relaxen) to chill out; **he Mann, chill mal ein bisschen!** (sei ruhig) hey, chill out, man!

chillig adj (gemütlich) chilled-out

clean adj (nicht mehr abhängig) clean; **clean werden** to get clean

Computerfuzzi m (Computer-fanatiker) computer geek

cool 1 adj (a) (toll) cool; **das Coolste waren die Clowns** the clowns were the coolest bit

(b) (abgeklärt) cool; **Felix ist voll der coole Typ** Felix is such a cool dude

2 adv (a) (toll) **Jenny hat ziemlich cool getanzt** Jenny's dancing was pretty cool

(b) (abgeklärt) **tu nicht immer so cool!** why d'you always have to be so cool about everything?

3 interj cool!

D

Dachschaden *m* einen
Dachschaden haben *(nicht
bei Verstand sein)* to need
to get one's head examined;
(geistesgestört sein) not to be
right in the head; **ich in Frieder
verliebt sein, du hast wohl
'nen Dachschaden!** me, in love
with Frieder? You need to get
your head examined!; **seit
seinem Nervenzusammenbruch
hat er einen Dachschaden** he
hasn't been quite right in the
head since he had his nervous
breakdown

Dämlack *m beleidigend
(dummer Mensch)* silly moo

dämlich 1 *adj (dumm)* daft
2 *adv* **dämlich fragen** to ask a
daft question; **der hat vielleicht
dämlich geguckt** he stood there
gawping like an idiot

dicht *adj* **(a)** *(voll)* **dicht sein** *(mit
Drogen)* to be well out of it; *(mit
Alkohol)* to be wazzed
(b) *(Redewendungen)* **nicht
ganz dicht sein** *(nicht bei
Verstand sein)* to be out of one's
head; **ich soll dir Geld leihen?
Du bist ja wohl nicht ganz dicht!**
lend you some money? Are you
out of your head or something?

dick *adj* **das Schwein hat
meine Tochter dick gemacht**
(geschwängert) the bastard
knocked my daughter up; **ich
habe dicke Eier** *(ich bin sexuell
bedürftig)* my balls are bursting

Dicker *m*, **Dicke** *f* **(a)** *(korpulenter Mensch)* fatty
(b) *(Anredeform für Freund)* **na,
mein Dicker?** all right, me old
mucker?
(c) *(Anredeform für Partner)*
my little pudding; **na Dicke, wie
wär's mit 'nem Nümmerchen?**
any chance of a quickie, my little
pudding?

Ding *nt (Penis)* thing

Doc *m (Arzt)* doc

Dödel *m* **(a)** *beleidigend
(dummer Mensch)* plonker; **du
Dödel!** you plonker!
(b) *(Penis)* plonker

Doktor *m (Mensch mit
intellektuellem Habitus)* pointy
head

doof 1 *adj* **(a)** *(dumm)* dumb;
so eine doofe Frage! what a
dumb question!; **der ist eben ein
bisschen doof, so was begreift
der nicht** he'll never understand
that, he's a bit thick; **für Chemie
bin ich zu doof** I'm flipping

useless at chemistry; **du bist doof!** stuff you!

(b) *(unangenehm)* **so ein doofes Wetter!** bleeding weather!; **das war eine doofe Situation** it was a pain; **ich habe das doofe Gefühl, dass ich was vergessen habe** I've got this nagging feeling I've forgotten something; **is ja doof!** what a pain!

2 adv *(dumm)* **frag nicht so doof!** what a dumb question!; **ich kam mir doof vor** I felt like a twit; **er hat sich ihr gegenüber echt doof verhalten** he behaved like a right twit towards her; **ich hab' nur doof rumgestanden** I just stood there like a twit

Doofi m, **Doofie** m beleidigend *(dummer Mensch)* div; **du Doofie!** you div!; **in dem Kleid sehe ich aus wie Klein Doofi (mit Plüschohren)** *(lächerlich)* I look like a (right) div in that dress

Doofkopp m beleidigend *(dummer Mensch)* stupid bugger; **du Doofkopp!** you stupid bugger!

Doofmann m (a) beleidigend *(dummer Mensch)* dope; **du Doofmann!** you dope!
(b) *(Spielverderber)* misery-guts

Dope nt *(Haschisch)* dope; **hast du Dope dabei?** have you got any dope on you?

Dose f meist sexistisch *(weibliches Geschlechtsorgan)* box

drauf adv (a) **drauf sein** *(auf Drogen sein)* to be tripping
(b) **wie bist'n du heute drauf?** *(was ist denn mit dir los?)* what's

got into you today?; **ich bin heut' gut drauf** I feel up for anything today; **ich bin heut' schlecht drauf** I'm feeling crabby today

draufgehen vi *(sterben)* to snuff it

Dreck m **einen Dreck werd' ich tun** *(das werde ich nicht tun)* no bleeding way am I doing that; **einen Dreck hab' ich bekommen** *(ich habe nichts bekommen)* I got F.A.; **einen feuchten Dreck hab' ich bekommen** scherzhaft *(ich habe nichts bekommen)* I got sweet Fanny Adams; **sie kümmert sich einen feuchten Dreck um ihn** scherzhaft *(überhaupt nicht)* she couldn't give a rat's arse about him; **das geht dich einen feuchten Dreck an** scherzhaft *(geht dich nichts an)* that's got sweet F.A. to do with you; **jemanden wie den letzten Dreck behandeln** *(sehr schlecht)* to treat somebody like shit; **das ist der letzte Dreck** *(sie sind Abschaum)* they're scum

Dreckloch nt *(schlechter Wohnort)* shithole

Drecksack m beleidigend *(nichtswürdige Person)* shit; **du Drecksack!** you shit!

Dreckschwein nt beleidigend (a) *(nichtswürdige Person)* scumbag; **du Dreckschwein!** you scumbag!
(b) *(unhygienische Person)* filthy slob
(c) *(schlüpfrige Person)* filthy pig

Dresche f *(Prügel)* der hat erst aufgehört, als ich ihm Dresche

angedroht habe he only stopped when I threatened to do his head in; **du kriegst gleich Dresche!** d'you want me to do your head in?; **ich habe gestern von meinem Vater Dresche gekriegt** my dad beat the crap out of me yesterday

dröhnen vi (high machen) to give you a high; **geiler Stoff, Mann, der dröhnt echt gut** this is awesome stuff, man, it gives you one hell of a high

Dröhnung f (Rauschzustand) **ich hab' mir die volle Dröhnung gegeben** I got totally out of my face; **dann haben wir Bong geraucht, und ab ging die Dröhnung** then we smoked a bong and got out of our faces

drüberrutschen vi (schnellen Sex haben) to have a quickie

drücken 1 vt (injizieren) to shoot up; **H drücken** to shoot up smack

2 vi (Drogen spritzen) to shoot up; **seit wann drückt die Jenny?** how long has Jenny been a junkie?

3 reflexiv **sich drücken** (einer Aufgabe ausweichen) to wangle one's way out of it; **sich vor etwas drücken** to wangle one's way out of something; **du willst dich doch bloß wieder vor dem Abwasch drücken** you're just trying to get out of doing the washing-up again

druff adj **druff sein** (auf Drogen sein) to be tripping

Druffi m (jemand, der regelmäßig Drogen nimmt) stoner

dumm adj **dumm wie Bohnenstroh** oder **wie ein Sack Holz voll Nüsse sein** (von sehr schwacher Intelligenz sein) to be as thick as two (short) planks; **mach mich nicht dumm!** (verwirre mich nicht) don't mess with my head!; **die Frau Schweikart kann Grammatik überhaupt nicht erklären, die macht mich total dumm** Mrs Schweikart is useless at teaching grammar, she totally does my head in → **Ochse, Ziege**

Dummfick m beleidigend (dummer Mensch) dumbfuck; **du Dummfick!** you dumbfuck!

Dummquatscher m, **Dummschwätzer** m beleidigend (dummer, geschwätziger Mensch) **er ist ja so ein Dummquatscher!** he talks such a load of guff!

Dumpfbacke f beleidigend (dummer, langweiliger Mensch) boring fart; **du alte Dumpfbacke!** you boring old fart!

Dünnpfiff m (Durchfall) the runs pl; **Dünnpfiff haben/kriegen** to have/get the runs

Dünnschiss m (Durchfall) the shits pl; **Dünnschiss haben/kriegen** to have/get the shits; **geistiger Dünnschiss** (Unsinn) verbal diarrhoea

durchdrehen vi (verrückt sein) to be bonkers; (verrückt werden) to go bonkers; **ich dreh' durch,**

Mensch! Christ, this is driving me bonkers!

durchgeknallt *adj (verrückt)* freaky; **durchgeknallt sein** *(eine Person)* to be a freak; **ein durchgeknallter Typ** a freak; **wir haben letzte Woche einen total durchgeknallten Film gesehen** we saw this totally freaky film last week

Dussel *m beleidigend (begriffsstutziger, ungeschickter Mensch)* wally; **du Dussel!** you wally!; **und ich Dussel hab' ihm geglaubt!** and I believed him like a wally!

E

E *nt (Ecstasy)* E; **E schmeißen** to do E; **hast du E?** have you got any E on you?

echt *adv (intensivierend)* dead; **das ist echt blöd** this is really stupid; **das hast du echt gut gemacht** you did dead well; **der hatte echt ätzende Klamotten an** he was wearing dead naff clothes

Effenberg *m (beleidigende Geste)* **der Schiri hat sich tierisch über seinen Effenberg aufgeregt** the ref had a real paddy when he gave him the finger → **Vogel**

Ei *nt* (a) *(Hoden)* ball; **Eier** balls; **sie hat ihm in die Eier getreten** she kicked him in the balls (b) *(Redewendungen)* **ein Ei legen** *(Darm entleeren)* to have a dump; **sich zum Ei machen** *(sich blamieren)* to make a tit of oneself; **ach du dickes Ei!** *(Ausruf der Überraschung)* fuck a duck! → **dick**

Eichhörnchen → **ficken**

Eimer *m* **aussehen wie ein Eimer** *oder* **ein Gesicht wie ein Eimer haben** *(hässlich aussehen)* to have a face like the back end of a bus; **für'n Eimer** *(kaputt)* duff; **das Auto ist im Eimer** *(kaputt)* the car's had it

eine → **geben**

einen *art* **einen Kurzen/Langen haben** *(einen kurzen oder langen Penis haben)* to have a little one/ big one → **fahren**

einfahren *vi (stark wirken)* to be potent; **Mann, das Zeug fährt tierisch ein!** this is totally potent stuff, man!

einpennen *vi (schlafen)* to crash out

einpissen *reflexiv* **sich einpissen** *(ängstlich sein)* to piss oneself; **piss dich nicht ein, das wird sie schon nicht merken!** *(sei kein Angsthase)* there's nothing to worry about, you great poof, she won't notice!; **ich hab' mir** *oder* **mich fast eingepisst vor Lachen** *(ich habe herzlich gelacht)* I pissed myself (laughing); **ich hab' mir** *oder* **mich fast eingepisst vor Angst** *(ich hatte große Angst)* I was pissing myself

einscheißen *reflexiv* **sich einscheißen** (a) *(Darm in die Kleidung entleeren)* to shit oneself; **ich hab' mich direkt vor der Klotür eingeschissen** I shat myself right in the bog doorway (b) *(große Angst haben)* to shit

oneself; **ich hab' mich vor Angst
fast eingeschissen!** I was shitting
myself!

einschiffen *reflexiv* **sich
einschiffen** *(ängstlich sein)* to
piss oneself; **schiff dich nicht ein,
das wird sie schon nicht merken!**
(sei kein Angsthase) there's
nothing to worry about, you
great poof, she won't notice!;
ich hab' mir *oder* **mich fast
eingeschifft vor Lachen** *(ich habe
herzlich gelacht)* I pissed myself
(laughing); **ich hab' mir** *oder*
mich fast eingeschifft vor Angst
(ich hatte große Angst) I was
pissing myself

einschleimen *reflexiv* **sich
bei jemandem einschleimen**
(sich einschmeicheln) to creep
up to somebody; **du versuchst
dich immer, beim Lehrer
einzuschleimen** you're always
creeping up to the teacher

einwerfen *vt (Tablette)* to
swallow; **ein E einwerfen** to drop
an E

Ekelbatzen *m,* **Ekelpaket** *nt*
(a) *(fieser Mensch)* creep
(b) *(ekliger Mensch)* **in der
Straßenbahn saß so ein
Ekelpaket neben mir, der hat
vielleicht gestunken** this really
gross bloke sat next to me on the
tram, he totally stank

Elch *m* **sich zum Elch machen**
(sich blamieren) to make a tit

of oneself; **du und Schönheits-
königin? Ich glaub', mich
knutscht ein Elch!** *scherzhaft (das
ist unglaublich)* a beauty queen,
you? Get out of here!

Emma *f* **sie hat ihre Emma**
*euphemistisch, scherzhaft (sie
menstruiert)* it's her time of the
month

Ende *nt* **da gab's Sekt und
Kaviar ohne Ende** *(sehr viel)*
there was loads of champagne
and caviar; **der hat Schulden
ohne Ende** *(sehr viele)* he's up
to his neck in debt; **wir haben
geschuftet ohne Ende** *(sehr)*
we slogged our guts out; **es
hat geregnet ohne Ende** *(sehr)*
it rained non-stop; **der hat
gebaggert ohne Ende, konnte
aber doch nicht bei ihr landen**
he kept trying to chat her up but
didn't manage to get off with
her

Entsafter *m* **auf den Entsafter
müssen** *sexistisch (sexuell
bedürftig sein)* to be gagging for
some hole

es *pron* **es (mit jemandem)
machen** *oder* **tun** *(koitieren)* to
do it (with somebody)

Esel *m* **den hat der Esel im
Galopp verloren** *(er hat unklare
Elternschaft)* nobody's quite sure
about his parentage [*nicht Slang*]

Eurone *f* euro [*nicht Slang*]

F

fahrbar → Untersatz

fahren *vi* **einen fahren lassen** *(Wind abgehen lassen)* to let one rip; **darauf kannst du einen fahren lassen!** *(das ist ganz sicher)* too bloody right!

Falle *f (Bett)* pit; **ist der Felix immer noch in der Falle?** is Felix still in his pit?; **ich haue mich in die Falle** *(ich gehe ins Bett)* I'm going to hit the sack

faseln **1** *vi (viel und wirr reden)* to spout nonsense; **er hat nur gefaselt** he just spouted nonsense **2** *vt (viel und wirr reden)* to spout; **Unsinn faseln** to spout nonsense

Faust *f* **das Gesicht zur Faust geballt** *(mit einem grimmigen Gesicht)* with a face like thunder

Feile *f* **sich zur Feile machen** *(sich blamieren)* to make a twat of oneself

Felltierchen *nt (weibliches Geschlechtsorgan)* furry front bottom

fertig *adj* **(a)** *(erschöpft)* shattered **(b)** *(völlig betrunken)* out of it; **der ist ja so was von fertig** he's totally out of it **(c)** **mit den Nerven fertig sein** *(einem Nervenzusammenbruch* nahe sein*)* to be a nervous wreck **(d)** *(überrascht)* stunned; **da bin ich fertig!** well, blow me!

fertig machen *vt* **(a)** *(verprügeln)* **jemanden fertig machen** to do somebody in **(b)** *(töten)* **jemanden fertig machen** to do somebody in **(c)** *(rügen)* **jemanden fertig machen** to have a go at somebody **(d)** *(erschöpfen)* **jemanden fertig machen** to do somebody in

fett **1** *adj* **(a)** *(korpulent)* fat [*nicht Slang*]; **fettes Schwein** *(korpulente Person)* fat pig; **fette Sau** *(korpulente Person)* fat git **(b)** **fett sein** *(betrunken sein)* to be twatted **2** *adv (intensivierend)* **da hab' ich fett verdient** I earned a freaking fortune; **die Party ging fett ab** it was a freaking brilliant party

Fettsack *m beleidigend (korpulenter Mensch)* porker

fetzig **1** *adj (großartig)* groovy **2** *adv (großartig)* **auf der Party ging's fetzig ab** it was a groovy party; **die Band hat fetzig gespielt** the band was groovy

feucht → Dreck

Feuerstein → Furz

Fick !! *m (Geschlechtsverkehr)* fuck; **er/sie ist ein guter Fick** he's/she's a good fuck

ficken !! **1** *vt* (a) *meist sexistisch (koitieren mit)* to fuck; **der fickt doch alles, was bei drei nicht auf dem Baum ist** he'll fuck anything on two legs; **da guckste wie 'n frisch geficktes Eichhörnchen** *scherzhaft (du guckst erstaunt oder dumm)* there's no need to stand there looking like a bloody lemon!

(b) *(verprügeln)* **jemanden ficken** to kick the fuck out of somebody

(c) *(fertig machen)* **jemanden ficken** to fuck somebody over **2** *vi (koitieren)* to fuck; **mit jemandem ficken** to fuck somebody; **Mann, hab' ich eine Lust zu ficken** Christ, I really fancy a fuck; **die haben im Auto gefickt** they had a fuck in the car

Ficker !! *m* (a) *(jemand, der häufig Geschlechtsverkehr hat)* **der ist der totale Ficker** he fucks around big time

(b) *beleidigend (nichtswürdiger Mann)* fucker; **du Ficker!** you fucker!

Fidschi !! *m rassistisch (Asiate)* slope

Film *m* **auf dem** *oder* **einem Film sein** *(unter LSD stehen)* to be on an acid trip; **Film schieben** *(unter LSD stehen)* to see Lucy in the sky with diamonds; **ich habe gedacht, ich bin im falschen Film** *(ich war verwundert)* I was totally gobsmacked

Finger *m* **den Finger rausziehen** *(sich beeilen)* to shift one's butt; **also, wenn du noch rechtzeitig dort sein willst, dann ziehst du jetzt besser den Finger raus** you're going to have to shift your butt if you want to get there on time; **jemandem den Finger zeigen** *(eine beleidigende Geste machen)* to give somebody the finger → **Vogel**

Fisch *m* **den Fisch machen** *(weggehen, fliehen)* to leg it; **es ist schon spät, ich mach' jetzt den Fisch** it's getting late, I'm gonna head

Fischkopp *m rassistisch (Norddeutscher)* Northern German [*nicht Slang*]; **der Neue aus der Verwaltung ist doch ein Fischkopp** the new guy in admin's a thick, dour northerner

> ⓘ The racial stereotype of northern Germans is of people who are rather slow, stupid and dour. Although originally a demeaning term, **Fischkopp** is now rarely offensive and is often used jokily by northern Germans about themselves.

fix *adj* **fix und foxy** *oder* **alle sein** *(erschöpft sein)* to be shagged out; **nach seiner Scheidung war er fix und foxy** he was a total wreck after his divorce

fixen *vi (Heroin spritzen)* to shoot up; **seit wann fixt der?** how long has he been a smackhead?

Fixer *m*, **Fixerin** *f (jemand, der Heroin spritzt)* smackhead

flapsig *adj (unernst)* eine

flapsige Bemerkung a wisecrack; **sei nicht immer so flapsig** stop being such a wise guy

Flatter f **die** oder **eine Flatter machen** (kaputtgehen, sterben) to conk out; (weggehen, fliehen) to leg it; **ich mach' jetzt die Flatter, ich muss morgen früh raus** I'm gonna take off, I've got an early start tomorrow

Flitzer m (Exhibitionist) streaker

Fluppe f (Zigarette) ciggy

Fotze !! f (a) sexistisch (weibliches Geschlechtsorgan) cunt
(b) sexistisch (Frau) bit of cunt; **er ist nur hinter den Fotzen her** all he's interested in is chasing after pussy
(c) sexistisch, beleidigend (nichtswürdige Frau) fucking bitch; **du blöde Fotze!** you fucking bitch!
(d) (etwas Minderwertiges) pile of fucking crap; **das soll ein Auto sein? Das is' 'ne Fotze!** call that a car? It's a pile of fucking crap!; **du siehst aus wie Fotze früh um vier** (du siehst schlecht aus) you look like fucking shit

ⓘ **Fotze** is by far the most offensive word in the German language. While it is an extremely sexist term when used by men to refer to a woman or the female genitals, it has been reclaimed by some younger women and no longer has this sexist connotation when used by them.

foxy → **fix**

Frauenversteher m sexistisch (langweiliger Mann) girlie wuss

Fresse f (Mund) mush; **die große Fresse haben** (prahlen) to mouth off; **jemandem eins in die Fresse geben** (jemanden schlagen) to sock somebody one in the mush; **halt die Fresse!** (sei ruhig) shut your mush!; **(ach, du) meine Fresse!** (Ausruf der Verwunderung) bugger me!; (Ausruf der Frustration) bugger it!

fressen 1 vt (a) (gierig essen) to scoff; **du frisst mich ja arm!** oder **du frisst mir ja die Haare vom Kopf!** (du isst viel) you're going to eat me out of house and home!
(b) (verstehen) **etwas fressen** to get something into one's thick skull; **das ist jetzt das fünfte Mal, dass ich ihm das erkläre, ich hoffe, dass er's jetzt endlich gefressen hat** that's the fifth time I've explained it to him, I hope he's finally got it into his thick skull
(c) (Redewendungen) **ich könnte dich fressen!** (habe dich sehr gern) I could just eat you up!; **sie hat an ihm einen Narren** oder **Affen gefressen** (hat ihn sehr gern) she thinks he's the best thing since sliced bread; **Mann, die habe ich gefressen!** (ich mag sie nicht) Christ, I hate her guts!; **keine Angst, ich fress' dich schon nicht** (tue dir nichts) don't worry, I don't bite; **ich fress' 'nen Besen, wenn...!** (das wäre überraschend) I'll

eat my hat if...!; **in der Not frisst der Teufel Fliegen** (wenn man sich einschränkt, kommt man immer zurecht) beggars can't be choosers; **der meint wohl, er hätte die Weisheit mit Löffeln gefressen** (er ist besserwisserisch) he's such a wise guy

2 vi (a) (viel oder gierig essen) to stuff one's face; **friss nicht so viel, arbeite lieber!** stop stuffing your face and do some work!; **Harold frisst wie ein Schwein!** Harold's always stuffing his face like a pig!

(b) (Redewendungen) **der frisst ihr aus der Hand** (sie kontrolliert ihn) she's got him eating out of the palm of her hand; **ich habe sie zum Fressen gern** (sehr gern) I could just eat her up

Frommser m (Kondom) johnnie

Froschfresser m rassistisch (Franzose) Froggie

frühstücken vi **rückwärts frühstücken** scherzhaft (erbrechen) to do a technicolour yawn

fuck interj (Ausruf des Ärgers oder der Überraschung) shagging hell!; (Ausruf des Schmerzes) shag it!

Fummel m (a) (Kleid) rags pl; **in dem Fummel kannst du aber nicht zu der Party gehen** you can't go to the party in those rags; **schicker Fummel, ist der neu?** that's a cool dress, is it new?

(b) (von Mann getragenes Frauenkleid) **im Fummel** in drag; **'nen Fummel anhaben** to be in drag

fummeln vi (schmusen) **wir haben nur ein bisschen gefummelt, sonst war nichts** we just had a bit of a feel, but it didn't go any further

Furz m (a) (Darmwind) fart; **einen Furz lassen** to do a fart

(b) (Redewendungen) **jeder Furz** (Kleinigkeit) the slightest bloody thing; **sie rennt wegen jedem Furz gleich zum Arzt** the slightest bloody thing and she immediately runs to the doctor; **und für nur zwei Tage Zelten hat meine Alte die Kanarienvögel eingepackt und den Fön und das gute Geschirr und Furz und Feuerstein!** (alles Mögliche) we were only going camping for a couple of days, but the missus still took the canaries and her hairdryer and the best crockery and Christ alone knows what else!; **sie kennt wirklich Furz und Feuerstein** (alles Mögliche) she knows all sorts of shit

furzen vi (Wind abgehen lassen) to fart

Furzer m (a) (Person, die viel furzt) fartypants; **eh, haltet euch die Nasen zu, da kommt wieder der Furzer!** hold your noses folks, here comes Mr Fartypants!

(b) beleidigend (lächerlicher Mensch) piss artist

Furzknoten m beleidigend (lächerlicher Mensch) little squirt

Fut f meist sexistisch (weibliches Geschlechtsorgan) pussy

G

gaga *adj* (a) *(verrückt)* kooky
(b) *(blöd)* **bei der Arbeit muss man ja gaga werden** that job must do your head in; **du machst mich ganz gaga mit deinen ewigen Fragen** you're doing my head in with all your questions
(c) *(senil)* gaga; **gaga werden** to go gaga

Gardine *f* **hinter schwedischen Gardinen** *(im Gefängnis)* in the slammer

Gebaumel *nt scherzhaft (männliche Geschlechtsorgane)* wedding tackle *pl*

geben *vt* **jemandem eine geben** *(jemanden schlagen)* to give somebody one; **komm' Achim, gib ihm eine!** *(in Schlägerei)* come on, Achim, let him have it!

Gedöns *nt (Aufsehen)* **(wegen einer Sache) ein Gedöns machen** to make a hoohah (about something)

gefickt *adj (erschöpft)* fucked

Gehänge *nt scherzhaft (männliche Geschlechtsorgane)* crown jewels *pl*; **der hat ein Riesengehänge** he's hung like a carthorse

gehen *vi* (a) **mit jemandem gehen** *(befreundet sein)* to go out with somebody
(b) *(Redewendungen)* **was geht?** *(was gibt es?)* whassup!; **na Alter, was geht?** whassup, man!; **geht's noch?** *(bist du verrückt?)* er, hello!; **he, geht's noch? lass die Pfoten von meiner Freundin** er, hello! Get your paws off my girlfriend

Gehirn *nt* **es hat mir das Gehirn weggeblasen** *oder* **weggepustet** *(es hat mich stark beeindruckt)* it blew my mind → **scheißen**

Geier *m* **weiß der Geier!** *(ich habe keine Ahnung)* fuck knows!

geil 1 *adj* (a) *(sexuell erregt)* horny; **die Blonde gestern auf der Disko war total geil** that blonde at the disco yesterday was totally horny; **der ist total geil auf sie** *(sexuell an ihr interessiert)* he's totally got the horn for her; **geil wie ein Puma** *(sexuell sehr erregt)* absolutely gagging for it; **geil wie Pumascheiße** *(sexuell äußerst erregt)* bloody gagging for it
(b) *(begehrenswert)* horny
(c) *(toll)* awesome
2 *adv (sexuell erregt)* **der hat sie die ganze Zeit total geil angeguckt** he was leering at her

the whole time
3 *interj* awesome!

Geist *m* **den Geist aufgeben**
(sterben, kaputtgehen) to give
up the ghost; **jemandem auf den
Geist gehen** *(nerven)* to get on
somebody's wick

Gelber !! *m*, **Gelbe** *f*
rassistisch (Chinese) chink

Gemächt *nt scherzhaft
(männliche Geschlechtsorgane)*
tackle

geplättet *adj* **(a)** *(überrascht)*
gobsmacked
(b) *(müde)* jiggered

gequirlt → **Scheiße**

Gerät *nt (Penis)* chopper

gesengt → **Sau**

Gesicht → **Bratpfanne, Eimer,
Faust**

Gesichtselfmeter *interj (was
für eine hässliche Person!)* what
a minger!

Gesichtslähmung *f* **die
totale Gesichtslähmung haben**
(betrunken sein) to be out of
one's face; **wir haben gesoffen
bis zur totalen Gesichtslähmung**
we got out of our faces

Glocken *npl* **(a)** *sexistisch
(Brüste)* jugs
(b) *(Hoden)* knackers; **sie hat
ihm ein paar auf die Glocken
gegeben** she kicked him in the
knackers

gluckern *vi (Alkohol trinken)* to
booze; **die gluckert auch ganz
schön** she's fond of a bevvy or
two

göbeln *vi (erbrechen)* to barf

golden → **Schuss**

Gras *nt* **(a)** *(Marihuana)* grass
(b) ins Gras beißen *(sterben)* to
cop it

Griffel *m (Finger)* finger [*nicht
Slang*]; **nimmst du mal ganz
schnell deine Griffel da weg?** get
your filthy mitts off there this
minute!

groß *adj* **groß machen** *(Darm
entleeren)* to do a number two;
musst du groß oder klein? do
you need to do a number two or
a number one?

grottenschlecht 1 *adj (sehr
schlecht)* woeful
2 *adv (sehr schlecht)* **die hat
grottenschlecht gesungen** her
singing was woeful; **das hast du
grottenschlecht gemacht** that's a
woeful effort

grunzen *vi (schlafen)* to be
sawing logs; **kann ich mal den
Max sprechen? – Nö, der grunzt
schon** can I speak to Max?
– Sorry, mate, he's already hit
the sack

Gülle *f (Unsinn)* wank; **das ist
doch Gülle!** that's a load of (old)
wank!; **Gülle reden/verzapfen** to
talk/spout (a load of) wank

Gummi *m (Kondom)* rubber

Gusche *f (Gesicht)* face [*nicht
Slang*]; **halt die Gusche!** *(halt
den Mund)* shut your mush!; **du
kriegst gleich ein paar vor die
Gusche!** *(Ohrfeigen)* I'm going to
sock you one in the mush if you
don't watch it!

H

H *nt (Heroin)* smack; **H drücken** to shoot up smack

> ⓘ The German term **H** is pronounced like the English letter **h** when it refers to heroin, and not "ha" as is usually the case.

Haare → fressen

haben *vt* **sie nicht mehr alle haben** *(nicht bei Verstand sein)* to be out of one's tiny mind; **ich soll dir mein Auto leihen? Du hast sie ja wohl nicht alle!** lend you my car? Are you out of your tiny mind?

hacke, hackedicht, hackenstramm *adj (betrunken)* wasted

Hackfleisch *nt* **aus dir mach' ich Hackfleisch!** *(Gewaltandrohung)* I'll have your guts for garters!

Hals → Scheiße

Hammer *m* **das ist ja der Hammer!** *(nicht zu fassen)* get a load of that!; **das war der Hammer** *(es war schwierig)* it was a mare

hammergeil *adj (sehr gut)* wicked

Hamster *m* **der wollte doch einen Hunderter von mir, ich glaub', mein Hamster bohnert!** *scherzhaft (das ist unerhört)* he wanted me to give him a hundred euros, is he for real?; **was, ich soll den Ede zu meiner Party einladen, ich glaub', mein Hamster bohnert!** ask Ede to my party? Get real!

Hand → fressen

Harter *m (Erektion)* **einen Harten haben/kriegen** to have/get a hard-on; **mach' dir deswegen mal keinen Harten** *(mach dir keine Sorgen)* don't get your bloody knickers in a twist about it

Hasch *nt (Haschisch)* hash

Haschmich *m* **einen Haschmich haben** *(nicht bei Verstand sein)* to be crackers; *(leicht geistesgestört sein)* not to be all there; **du hast wohl 'nen Haschmich** you must be crackers; **seit seinem Nervenzusammenbruch hat er einen Haschmich** he hasn't been all there since he had his nervous breakdown

Häuschen *nt* **(a)** *meist scherzhaft (Toilette)* little boys' room **(b) ganz aus dem Häuschen sein**

(aufgeregt sein) to be bouncing off the walls

Heckmeck *m* **(a)** *(dummes Gerede)* codswallop; **erzähl doch nicht so einen Heckmeck!** stop talking codswallop!

(b) *(dumme Streiche)* **Mensch, haben wir so allerlei Heckmeck gemacht!** boy, did we get up to some larks!; **he, mach keinen Heckmeck!** *(mach keine Dummheiten)* hey, stop larking around!

(c) *(Umstände)* kerfuffle; **der ganze Heckmeck mit der Hochzeit macht mich noch wahnsinnig** the whole kerfuffle about the wedding is driving me crazy; **einen Heckmeck machen** *(Umstände machen)* to get in a flap

heiß *adj* **(a)** *(sexuell erregt)* hot; **heiß auf jemanden sein** to be hot for somebody

(b) *(begehrenswert)* hot; **ist die heiß!** she's a hottie!

(c) *(toll)* hot

(d) *(illegal)* hot; **Vorsicht, das ist heiße Ware!** careful, those are hot goods!

(e) *(gefährlich)* hairy; **das mache ich nicht mit, das ist mir zu heiß** count me out, it looks too hairy to me

heizen *vi (schnell fahren)* to bomb along

herumballern *vi (Pistole abfeuern oder Explosivkörper zünden)* **die Nachbarn haben die ganze Nacht herumgeballert** the neighbours were letting off bangers all night; **in den Staaten kommt es immer wieder vor, dass irgend so ein Amokschütze wie wild herumballert** in the States there's always someone or other running amok, taking a pot at anything that moves

herumfaseln *vi (wirr reden)* to spout drivel

herumnölen *vi (sich beklagen)* to whinge

herumsülzen *vi (viel Dummes reden)* to blether on

Hete *f (heterosexueller Mensch)* het

Hetero 1 *m (heterosexueller Mann)* straight man; **der ist doch nicht schwul, das ist ein echter Hetero** he's not gay, he's as straight as they come

2 *f (heterosexuelle Frau)* straight woman

high *adj (im Rauschzustand)* **high sein** to be high; **(von etwas) high werden** to get high (on something)

Himbeere → **Arsch**

hin *adv* **(a)** *(von etwas)* **hin und weg sein** *(begeistert sein)* to be blown away (by something)

(b) **hin sein** *(kaputt sein)* to have had it

(c) **hin sein** *(erschöpft sein)* to be shattered

(d) **hin sein** *(tot sein)* to be a gonner

(e) *(nicht mehr vorhanden)* **jetzt ist mein ganzes Geld hin** that's all my money down the drain; **da war die Ruhe hin** that did for the peace and quiet

hinterhersteigen vi jemandem hinterhersteigen *(sexuelles Interesse an jemandem haben)* to be trying to get into somebody's pants; **der steigt Jasmin doch schon lange hinterher** he's been trying to get into Jasmin's pants for ages

Hinterlader m *homophob (Homosexueller)* turd burglar

Hintern m *(Gesäß)* bum; **komm' mit dem Hintern hoch!** *(beweg dich)* shift your butt!

Hinterteil nt *euphemistisch (Gesäß)* backside; **setz dich jetzt auf dein Hinterteil und mach die Aufgaben!** sit your backside down and do your homework!

hochkriegen vt **er kriegt ihn nicht hoch** *(er bekommt keine Erektion)* he can't get it up → **Arsch**

hochnehmen vt (a) *(aufgreifen und verhaften)* to nick; **der ist hochgenommen worden** he got nicked

(b) *(veralbern)* **jemanden hochnehmen** to wind somebody up

hochziehen vt *(aufgreifen und verhaften)* to nab; **sie haben ihn bei einem Einbruch hochgezogen** he got nabbed while attempting a break-in

hohl adj (a) *(dumm)* **der hat vielleicht hohles Zeug geredet** he was talking total garbage; **das ist ja richtig hohl, was der da gemacht hat** that was a whack thing to do

(b) *(unintelligent und ein-gebildet)* **hohl sein** to be an airhead

Holz nt **viel Holz vor der Hütte haben** *scherzhaft (große Brüste haben)* to be a big girl

Homo m *homophob (Homosexueller)* homo

Honk m *beleidigend (dumme, ungeschickte Person)* clod

hopsgehen vi *(sterben)* to kick it

Hornochse m *beleidigend (dumme Person)* clot; **du Hornochse!** you clot!; **und ich Hornochse habe ihm geglaubt!** and I believed him like a clot!

Hose f **(sich) in die Hose scheißen** *(Darm in die Kleidung entleeren)* to shit oneself; *(große Angst haben)* to crap oneself; **ich hab' mir direkt vor der Klotür in die Hose geschissen** I shat myself right in the bog doorway; **ich hab' mir fast in die Hose geschissen!** I was crapping myself!; **der scheißt (sich) doch schon in die Hosen, wenn ihn seine Frau mal streng anguckt** he's such a wimp, all it takes is for his wife to give him a stern look and he's already crapping himself; **scheiß dir nicht gleich in die Hosen, du wirst schon nicht durchfallen!** *(sei kein Angsthase)* don't worry, you bloody great poof, you won't fail!; **die Hosen (gestrichen) voll haben** *(Angst haben)* to be scared shitless; **das sollte eine Überraschung werden, die ist aber gewaltig in die Hose gegangen** *(war ein Misserfolg)* it was meant to be a surprise but the whole thing went pear-shaped; **der Witz ist in die Hose gegangen** the joke went down like a lead balloon; **meine Prüfung ist in die Hose gegangen** my test was a total disaster; **tote Hose sein** *(langweilig)* to be snoresville; **wie war die Party? – Tote Hose!** how was the party? – It was snoresville!

Hosenscheißer *m* (a) *(ängstliche Person)* bloody wimp (b) *(junge, unerfahrene Person)* bloody little kid; **was weiß denn der Hosenscheißer schon vom richtigen Leben?** he's just a bloody little kid who's barely out of nappies, what does he know about what life's really like? (c) *beleidigend (lächerliche Person)* little squirt

Hucke *f* **sich die Hucke voll laufen lassen** *(sich betrinken)* to have a skinful

Hüfte *f East German* **aus der**

Hüfte kommen *(etwas zustande bringen)* to get it sorted

Huhn *nt beleidigend (weibliche Person)* bint; **sie ist ein verrücktes/dummes Huhn** she's a crazy/stupid bint

Hund *m* (a) *beleidigend (Mann)* bastard; **du dummer/gemeiner Hund!** you stupid/miserable bastard! (b) **vor die Hunde gehen** *(sterben)* to cash in one's chips → **scheißen**

Hunni *m (hundert Euro)* hundred euros *pl [nicht Slang]*; **wie viel hat denn die Reparatur gekostet? – 'n Hunni** how much did the repair cost? – a hundred

Hütte *f (Wohnung, Haus)* place; **was habt ihr denn für eure Hütte bezahlt?** how much did you pay for your place?; **am Wochenende ist die Hütte voll, da haben wir nämlich Besuch** we've got visitors at the weekend so we're going to have a full house → **Holz**

I

Inselaffen *npl rassistisch (Briten)*
die Inselaffen the parochial
bloody Brits

> (i) The term **Inselaffen** was
> coined fairly recently as an
> expression of contempt for
> what Germans see as the
> excessive neoliberalism of British
> economic policy. It is now used
> more widely to refer to the
> German stereotype of British
> people who are considered to
> have an island mentality and
> to be parochial, arrogant and
> socially rather inept.

irre *adj* **(a)** *(toll)* wild; **ist ja irre!**
wild!
  (b) *(verrückt)* loony

Ische *f sexistisch (Frau)* ho

Itaker *m rassistisch (Italiener)*
eyetie

Iwan *m rassistisch (Russe)* rusky;
**du machst doch alles falsch, du
Iwan!** you can't do anything
right, you stupid bloody
rusky!

Iwanischer *m*, **Iwanische** *f*
rassistisch (Russe) rusky

J

Joint *m (Zigarette aus Marihuana)* joint; **einen Joint bauen** to roll a joint

Jordan *m* **über den Jordan gehen** *(sterben)* to cash in one's chips

juckig *adj (sexuell bedürftig)* **juckig sein** to have hot pants; **die Alte ist doch juckig!** *sexistisch* that bitch is on heat, man!

Jugo *m rassistisch (Mensch aus Ex-Jugoslawien)* fucking Yugoslavian

> ℹ The racist term **Jugo** refers to immigrants from any part of the former Yugoslavia, such as Bosnians, Serbs, etc.

Junkie *m (Drogenabhängiger)* junkie; **er ist ein Fernsehjunkie** he's a TV junkie

K

Kacke 1 *f* **(a)** *(Kot)* shit; **ich glaube, ich bin in Kacke getreten** I think I've trodden in some shit; **pass auf, da ist Kacke auf dem Bürgersteig** look out, there's a turd on the pavement

(b) *(Minderwertiges)* shite; **das Album ist Kacke** that album's (a load of) shite; **du meinst doch wohl nicht, dass ich so 'ne Kacke esse** surely you're not expecting me to eat that shite?

(c) *(Unsinn)* shite; **Kacke erzählen** to talk shite; **die hat die totale Kacke erzählt** what she said is complete and utter shite; **du erzählst ja so eine Kacke!** you're full of shite!; **das ist doch die totale Kacke!** that's a load of shite!

(d) *(Fehler)* **bei den Reisevorbereitungen hat's Kacke gegeben** there was a fuck-up over the travel arrangements; **so eine Kacke!** what a fuck-up!; **Kacke bauen** *(etwas schlecht ausführen)* to fuck up

(e) *(Redewendungen)* **dann ist die Kacke am Dampfen!** *(dann wird es Unannehmlichkeiten geben)* then the shit will really hit the fan!; **wenn du noch einmal mein Auto nimmst, ohne Bescheid zu sagen, dann ist die Kacke am Dampfen!** if you take my car again without telling me, you're really going to be in the shit!; **so 'ne Kacke!** *oder* **ach, du Kacke!** *(Ausruf des Ärgers)* shite!; **seine Frau hat ihn verlassen – was** *oder* **so 'ne Kacke!** *(wie ärgerlich)* his wife left him – what a bastard!; **es ist total Kacke, immer so früh aufstehen zu müssen** *(es ist sehr ärgerlich)* it's a real bastard always having to get up so early; **jetzt haben wir die Kacke** *(Ärger)* we're in the shit now; **verfluchte Kacke!** *(Ausruf des Ärgers)* fucking shite!

2 *interj (Ausruf des Ärgers)* shite!; **Kacke, jetzt muss ich alles noch mal machen!** shite, I've got to do it all over again now!

> ⓘ **Kacke** is generally considered to be slightly milder in register than **Scheiße**, and thus usually corresponds more closely to the English term *shite* than it does to *shit*. Nevertheless, there are some usages of **Kacke** that are more idiomatically translated using *shit*.

kacken *vi (Darm entleeren)* to have a crap; **sie muss mal kacken**

she needs a crap; **ich muss mal übelst kacken** I'm busting for a crap

Kackmist interj (Ausruf von Ärgernis) buggeration!

Kaff nt (langweiliger Wohnort) snoresville; **das ist hier wirklich ein Kaff!** this place really is snoresville!

kalt → kotzen

Kampflesbe f beleidigend (sehr männlich wirkende Lesbierin) bull dyke

Kampftrinken nt (exzessives Trinken) **wenn das deine Vorstellung von Urlaub ist, jeden Abend Kampftrinken, na dann ohne mich** if all you want from a holiday is to get totally slaughtered every night, then count me out; **Partys bei Manne enden doch meistens im Kampftrinken** Manne's parties usually end up with everyone getting totally slaughtered

Kanake m rassistisch (Ausländer) bloody foreigner

ⓘ While **Kanake** is now used as a racist slur for all foreigners, it was initially directed mainly towards Turks or people of Turkish descent. However, **Kanake** has now been widely reclaimed by second and third generation Turks in Germany as a term of pride, particularly in the hip hop and rap scene. It is, however, best avoided by people outside this scene.

Kanakensprache f, **Kanakspraak** f rassistisch (Ausländerdeutsch) pidgin German

ⓘ **Kanakensprache** is the pidgin German spoken by many Turkish immigrants or immigrants from the former Yugoslavia. It has become well-established, and there are now even comedy TV programmes in **Kanakensprache**, as well as humorous dictionaries and grammars. An example of **Kanakensprache** would be a taxi driver from one of the above ethnic communities asking his fare *wo du wolle?* instead of the standard German *wohin wollen Sie?*

Kante f **sich die Kante geben** (sich betrinken) to get hammered

Kanten m (gepresstes Haschisch) block of hash

kaputt adj (erschöpft) knackered

kaputtlachen reflexiv **sich kaputtlachen** (herzlich lachen) to laugh one's head off; **Franz und Eva heiraten, ich lach' mich kaputt!** Franz and Eva getting married, that's a good one!

kaputtmachen 1 vt (a) (ruinieren) to knacker (b) (erschöpfen) to knacker **2** reflexiv **sich kaputtmachen** (sich überanstrengen) to knacker oneself

Karre f (Auto) motor

Käse m (Smegma) cock cheese

Keks m jemandem auf den Keks gehen *(ärgern, nerven)* to get on somebody's wick

ℹ️ There are a number of other similar constructions in German, all of which mean to annoy somebody, from the very mild **jemandem auf die Nerven gehen** *(to get on somebody's nerves)* to the somewhat stronger expression **jemandem auf den Sack gehen** *(to get on somebody's tits)*.

Kerl m *(Mann)* guy

kicken vi (a) *(schnelle und starke Wirkung haben)* to have a kick
(b) *(Fußball spielen)* to play footie

Kies m *(Geld)* dough

kiffen vi *(Haschisch oder Marihuana rauchen)* to smoke pot; **der kifft** he's a pothead

Kiffer m, **Kifferin** f pothead

killen vt *(streng rügen)* **der killt mich, wenn er das erfährt** I'm dead if he finds out; **was, du hast sein Auto geschrottet? Der killt dich** what, you wrote off his car? You're dead!

Kimme f *(Gesäßspalte)* crack

Kippe f *(Zigarette)* fag

kirre adj *(verwirrt)* nuts; **bei dem Lärm wird man ja ganz kirre** that noise is driving me nuts; **jemanden kirre machen** *(verwirren)* to drive somebody nuts; **das Durcheinander hat mich so kirre gemacht, dass ich gar nichts mehr wusste** it was

total chaos and I got in a real tizz and didn't know whether I was coming or going

Kiste f (a) *meist scherzhaft (weibliche Brust)* bristols pl; **Mann, hat die 'ne Kiste!** Christ, look at the bristols on her!
(b) *(Auto)* old banger
(c) *(Liebesbeziehung)* **der hat mal wieder Ärger mit der Kiste** his bird's giving him grief again; **na wie läuft deine Kiste mit Jenny?** how's your thing with Jenny going, then?

Klamotten npl *(Kleider)* clothes [*nicht Slang*]; **Hannes hat immer die coolen Klamotten an** Hannes is always wearing cool gear

Klampfe f *(akustische Gitarre)* guitar [*nicht Slang*]; *(elektrische Gitarre)* axe

Klappe f (a) *(Mund)* gob; **der macht immer an der falschen Stelle die Klappe auf** he's always opening his big gob at the wrong moment; **die große Klappe haben** *oder* **schwingen** *(prahlen)* to shoot one's mouth off; **die Klappe aufreißen** *(angeben)* to mouth off; *(nicht schweigen können)* to open one's trap; **halt die Klappe!** *(sei ruhig)* shut your gob!; **Kinder, haltet jetzt mal die Klappe dahinten im Auto!** belt up in the back there, children!; **Klappe!** *(sei ruhig)* shut it!; **ich geb dir gleich ein paar auf die Klappe!** *oder* **du kriegst gleich paar auf die Klappe!** *(ich schlage dich)* I'm gonna punch your lights out!

(b) *(Bett)* pit; **ist der Felix immer noch in der Klappe?** is Felix still in his pit?; **ich haue mich mal in die Klappe** *(ich gehe ins Bett)* I'm going to hit the sack

(c) *(öffentliche Toilette als Schwulentreff)* cottage

klatschen *vt* (a) **jemandem eine klatschen** *(jemanden schlagen)* to deck somebody one; **ich klatsch' dir gleich eine!** d'you want a punch in the gob?

(b) *(zusammenschlagen)* **jemanden klatschen** to kick the shit out of somebody

(c) *(werfen)* to whang; **etwas gegen etwas klatschen** to whang something against something

klauen 1 *vt (stehlen)* to nick; **jemandem etwas klauen** to nick something off somebody

2 *vi (stehlen)* to nick stuff; **die Silke klaut** Silke's always nicking stuff

klein *adj* **klein machen** *(urinieren)* to do a number one; **musst du groß oder klein?** do you need to do a number two or a number one?

klemmen *vt (stehlen)* to pinch; **jemandem etwas klemmen** to pinch something off somebody

Klo *nt (Toilette)* loo; **auf dem Klo sein** to be on the loo; **ich muss aufs Klo** I need (to go to) the loo

kloppen *reflexiv* **ich habe mir einen gekloppt** *(ich habe masturbiert)* I whacked myself off

Kloß *m beleidigend (dicke Person)* fat slob

Klöten *npl (Hoden)* rocks; **musst du dir ständig an den Klöten rumspielen?** could you stop playing pocket billiards for five minutes?

Klugscheißer *m,* **Klugscheißerin** *f (Klugredner)* smartarse; **hör zu, du Klugscheißer** look here, smartarse

Knacker *m* **(alter) Knacker** *(alter Mann)* old codger

Knacki *m* (a) *(Häftling)* con (b) *(ehemaliger Häftling)* ex-con

knallen 1 *vt* (a) *meist sexistisch (koitieren mit)* to do; **hast du sie geknallt?** did you do her?

(b) **jemandem eine knallen** *(jemanden schlagen)* to sock somebody one

2 *vi* **gegen etwas knallen** *(heftig aufschlagen)* to smash into something; **er ist mit dem Auto gegen einen Baum geknallt** he smashed his car into a tree; **sie knallt doch gegen jede Kante!** she's always clattering into things!

Knast *m* (a) *(Gefängnis)* nick; **im Knast sein** to be in the nick

(b) *(Gefängnisstrafe)* **dafür gibt's zehn Tage Knast** you get ten days in the nick for that

(c) *(Hunger)* **Knast haben/ kriegen** to have/get the munchies

knausrig *adj (geizig)* tight; **Mann, dein Vater ist aber knausrig!** Christ, your dad's a tight git!

kneifen

kneifen *vi (sich aus Angst vor etwas drücken)* to chicken out; **vor etwas kneifen** to chicken out of something

Knete *f (Geld)* brass; **aus der Knete kommen** *(etwas zustande bringen)* to get it sorted

knülle *adj* **knülle sein** *(betrunken sein)* to be steaming

knutschen *vi (sich küssen)* to snog; **mit jemandem knutschen** to snog somebody

Knutschfleck *m (blauer Fleck vom Küssen)* love bite

Koffer *m* **einen Koffer stehen lassen** *(Wind abgehen lassen)* to guff; **du kriegst gleich paar vor 'n Koffer!** *(Drohung)* you're gonna get a bunch of fives!

Kohle *f* (a) *(Geld)* dosh
(b) *rassistisch (Farbiger)* **!!** darkie

Koks *m (Kokain)* coke

koksen *vi (Kokain nehmen)* to do coke

Kokser *m*, **Kokserin** *f* coke-head

kommen *vi (einen Orgasmus haben)* to come

Kotzbrocken *m* beleidigend (a) *(nichtswürdige, lästige Person)* jerk
(b) *(launische Person)* moody old sod

Kotze *f (Erbrochenes)* puke

kotzen 1 *vi* (a) *(erbrechen)* to puke; **du bist zum Kotzen!** *(ekelst mich an)* you're gross!; **du bist zum Kotzen, kannst du nicht einmal pünktlich sein?** *(du ärgerst mich sehr)* you're bloody unbelievable, why can't you be on time for once?; **das ist ja zum Kotzen!** *(ärgerlich)* it's bloody disgusting!; **wie du dich deiner Frau gegenüber benimmst, das ist einfach zum Kotzen!** it's bloody disgusting the way you treat your wife!; **ich finde diese Regierung zum Kotzen** this government makes me puke; **da kann man das kalte Kotzen kriegen!** *(ärgerlich werden)* it really makes me puke!
(b) *(sich ärgern)* to be pissed off; **ich habe dem das Bier weggeklaut. Der hat vielleicht gekotzt!** I nicked his beer off him and he was well pissed off!
2 *vt* **ich habe mir fast die Seele aus dem Leib gekotzt** *(ich musste stark erbrechen)* I puked my guts up

kotzübel *adj* **mir ist kotzübel** *(mir ist furchtbar schlecht)* I feel bloody terrible; **wie du deine Freundin behandelst, da wird mir kotzübel!** I think it's bloody terrible the way you treat your girlfriend!

Krähe *f sexistisch (hässliche Frau)* dog

krass 1 *adj (großartig)* fierce
2 *interj (großartig)* fierce! → **voll**

krepieren *vi (sterben)* to buy it

Kronjuwelen *npl scherzhaft (männliche Geschlechtsorgane)* crown jewels

Kuh *f beleidigend (dumme,*

ärgerliche Frau) cow; **du dumme Kuh!** you stupid cow!; **ach lass sie doch, die alte Kuh!** don't take any notice of the (stupid) old cow!

Kuhdorf *nt*, **Kuhnest** *nt* *(kleines, abgelegenes Dorf)* little village out in the sticks

Kumpel *m (Freund)* mate; **willst du Ärger, Kumpel?** d'you want some, mate?

Kurve *f* **die Kurve kratzen** *(sterben)* to check out; *(verschwinden)* to hop it; **ich kratz' mal die Kurve, ich muss morgen früh raus** I'm gonna hit the road, I've got an early start tomorrow; **erst hat er sie dick gemacht, und dann hat er die Kurve gekratzt** once he'd knocked her up you couldn't see his arse for dust

kurz → **einen**

L

labern 1 vi *(viel, unintelligent reden)* to witter on
 2 vt *(dumm reden)* to spout; **die hat nur Schwachsinn gelabert** she just spouted a load of nonsense

Laden m *(Geschäft, Firma)* **er will jetzt seinen eigenen Laden aufmachen** he wants to set up his own business; **der ganze Laden hat mir gestunken, drum habe ich gekündigt** I was sick of the bloody place so I handed in my notice

Lage → schmeißen

lang → einen

langen vt **jemandem eine langen** *(jemanden schlagen)* to belt somebody one; **eine gelangt bekommen** *(geschlagen werden)* to get belted

Langer m *(großer, meist dünner Mann)* lanky; **na Langer, wie geht's?** how's it going, lanky?; **der Lange ist im Urlaub** lanky's on holiday

Lappen m (a) *(Fahrerlaubnis)* licence
 (b) *(Geldschein)* note; **rück mal 'n paar Lappen raus!** come on, you can spare a couple of notes!

Larve f *(Gesicht)* face [*nicht Slang*]; **der Typ hatte dermaßen eine hässliche Larve!** that guy had such an ugly mug!

Laschi m *(langweiliger Mann)* spod

Latte f *(Erektion)* boner; **eine Latte haben/kriegen** to have/get a boner; **sag mal hast du Latte?** *(bist du verrückt?)* are you off your bloody nut or something?

lattenstramm adj *(betrunken)* twatted

laufen → voll

Laufpass m **jemandem den Laufpass geben** *(sich von jemandem trennen)* to dump somebody

lausen → Affe

lausig 1 adj *(sehr schlecht)* lousy; **eine lausige Laune haben** to be in a lousy mood; **er hat mir vierzig lausige Euros gegeben** he gave me forty lousy euros
 2 adv *(sehr schlecht)* **wir haben uns lausig amüsiert** we had a lousy time; **die hat lausig gesungen** her singing was lousy

lecken vt (a) **leck mich doch!** *(lass mich in Ruhe)* screw you!
 (b) **eine Frau lecken** *(Cunnilingus machen)* to go down on a woman → **Arsch**

Leine f zieh Leine! (hau ab) bugger off!

Lesbe f homophob (lesbische Frau) dyke; **die mit den kurzen Haaren und der Brille ist doch bestimmt 'ne Lesbe** that woman with the short hair and the glasses has got to be a dyke; **wir müssen uns mehr für die Rechte von Schwulen und Lesben einsetzen** we need to do more for gay and lesbian rights; **ich kenne viele Lesben** I know lots of gay women

ⓘ **Lesbe** can be used offensively by homophobic people to denote a lesbian, in which case the most appropriate translation is *dyke*. However, when it is used by lesbians to describe themselves, or by heterosexuals in a non-offensive way, then the best translation is *gay woman* or *lesbian*. The examples above show this difference in usage.

Linie f eine Linie ziehen (Kokain nehmen) to snort a line

Loch nt (a) sexistisch (weibliches Geschlechtsorgan) hole
(b) (heruntergekommener Ort) hole

locker → Maul

Löffel m den Löffel abgeben oder wegschmeißen (sterben) to kick the bucket

Lokus m scherzhaft (Toilette) lav; **auf dem Lokus sein** to be on the lav; **ich muss auf den Lokus** I need (to go to) the lav

lose → Maul

Lover m (Liebhaber) fancy man

Luder nt (a) (launische Frau) moody bitch
(b) beleidigend (unmoralische Frau) slapper; **du Luder!** you slapper!
(c) (Kosewort) honeybunch

Lümmel m (a) (Mann mit schlechten Manieren) lout
(b) (Penis) pecker

Lusche f (unfähiger Mensch) useless git

M

machen → es, groß, klein

Mary *f sexistisch (Frau, Freundin)*
little woman; **meine Mary** the
oder my little woman

-mäßig *suffix* –wise; **wetter-
mäßig war der Urlaub Spitze** the
holiday was great weather-wise;
jobmäßig sieht es nicht gut aus
things aren't looking too good
on the job front; **was machen
wir getränkemäßig?** *(wie
organisieren wir die Getränke?)*
what are we going to do about
the drinks?

Matratze *f* **('ne Runde)
Matratze horchen** to catch some
Zs

Maul *nt (Mund)* gob; **du kriegst
gleich ein paar aufs Maul!**
(Drohung) you're gonna get a
smack in the gob!; **es gibt gleich
paar vors Maul!** d'you want a
smack in the gob or something?;
das große Maul haben *(prahlen)*
to shoot one's mouth off; **halt's
Maul!** *(sei ruhig)* shut your face!;
**Mensch, der immer mit seiner
Politik, der kann einfach nicht
das Maul halten** Christ, him and
his politics, he just can't keep
his gob shut about it; **der hat
ein loses** *oder* **lockeres Maul**

(er ist frech, schwatzhaft) he
can't keep his gob shut; **nimm
mal das Maul nicht so voll!** *(gib
nicht an, behaupte nicht zu viel)*
don't be so bloody cocky!; **die
nimmt das Maul ganz schön
voll** *(gibt an, behauptet sehr
viel)* she's just mouthing off; **der
reißt das Maul ziemlich weit auf**
(gibt an, übernimmt sich) he's
just mouthing off; **dem müssen
wir das Maul stopfen!** *(ihn zum
Schweigen bringen)* we need to
make him keep his gob shut!;
jemandem übers Maul fahren
(rüde unterbrechen) to butt in
on somebody; **der hat sich ganz
schön das Maul verbrannt** *(hat
sich in eine unangenehme Lage
gebracht)* he's really landed
himself in it by speaking his
mind; **sich über etwas das Maul
zerreißen** *(klatschen)* to have a
good bitch about something

Maulkorb *m (Redeverbot)*
**jemandem einen Maulkorb
verordnen** to have somebody
gagged

Maulsperre *f* **(a)** *(beim Essen)*
**nimm' nicht so viel auf einmal
in den Mund! Du kriegst ja die
Maulsperre!** *(wirst unfähig zu
sprechen und zu kauen)* don't

stuff your face like that, you'll choke yourself to death!
 (b) *(höchstes Erstaunen)* **er konnte das gar nicht fassen. Er stand nur da mit Maulsperre** he couldn't believe it. He just stood there with his jaw on the floor

Mäuschen *nt* (a) *(weibliches Geschlechtsorgan)* front bottom
 (b) *(Freundin)* bit of fluff
 (c) *(Anrede)* honey; **na, mein Mäuschen, wollen wir mal?** how about it, honey?

Mäuse *npl (Geld)* bread *sing;* **wo hast du die Mäuse versteckt?** where have you hidden the bread?

mega- *präfix* **megageil** *(großartig)* wicked; **ein Mega-Ereignis** a massive event; **mega-günstige Notebooks** ultra-cheap notebooks; **bei Schlemmer kaufen Sie megagünstig ein!** shop at Schlemmer for ultra-low prices!; **megagut** top; **das war ein megaguter Film** that was a top film; **das hat megagut geschmeckt** that was orgasmic; **die Band hat megagut gespielt** the band were awesome; **mega-cool** totally cool; **wie war das Konzert? – Megacool!** what was the concert like? – Totally cool!

Meise *f* **eine Meise haben** *(nicht bei Verstand oder geistesgestört sein)* to be doo-lally; **ich in Frieder verliebt sein, du hast wohl eine Meise!** me, in love with Frieder? Are you completely doo-lally?; **seit seinem Nerven-zusammenbruch hat er eine Meise** he's been a bit doo-lally since he had his nervous breakdown

Memme *f (verwöhnte, feige Person)* wuss

mies *adj (schlecht)* crummy; **ich fühl' mich richtig mies** I feel pretty crummy; **eine miese Laune haben** to be ratty

Miese *npl (Schulden)* **ich habe 300 Miese auf dem Konto** I'm 300 euros in the red

Mieze *f sexistisch (Frau)* bird

Minna *f* **jemanden zur Minna machen** *(streng rügen)* to give somebody a row

Mische *f* **Mische machen** *(Haschisch-Mischung fertig machen oder Haschisch mischen)* to mix up some hash and tobacco

Mist **1** *m* (a) *(Minderwertiges)* garbage; **für so einen Mist zahle ich doch keine 100 Euro!** I'm not paying 100 euros for that garbage!; **du meinst doch nicht, dass ich so einen Mist esse** surely you're not expecting me to eat that garbage?; **das Album ist Mist** that album's a load of garbage
 (b) *(Unsinn)* garbage; **er hat die ganze Zeit nur Mist geredet** he just talked garbage the whole time; **Mist erzählen** to talk garbage; **der hat ja so einen Mist erzählt** what he said was complete and utter garbage; **du erzählst ja so einen Mist** that's a load of garbage; **Mist verzapfen** to spout garbage
 (c) *(Panne, ärgerlicher Zustand)*

jetzt haben wir den Mist! we've really had it now!; **das ist ganz großer Mist!** oh, hell!

(d) *(kritikwürdige Handlung)* **was soll der Mist?** what the hell do you think you're doing?; **eh, macht mal keinen Mist!** oi, what the hell do you think you're doing?; **mach bloß keinen Mist!** stop playing silly buggers!; **in meiner Jugend habe ich so allerlei Mist gemacht** I was a real hellraiser when I was young; **Mist bauen** to muck up; **der hat am Arbeitsplatz Mist gebaut, dann haben sie ihn fristlos entlassen** he mucked up at work and was sacked on the spot; **da haben wir mal wieder Mist gebaut** we've gone and mucked it up again; **du baust nur Mist, weißt du das?** you're flipping unbelievable, you are!

(e) *(Schmutz, Abfall)* rubbish; **du solltest mal den ganzen Mist aus dem Keller räumen** you should clear all the rubbish out of the cellar

(f) *(Herkunft, Urheberschaft)* **das ist doch nicht auf deinem Mist gewachsen, oder?** you never came up with that yourself, did you?

(g) *(Redewendungen)* **Mist verdammter!** *oder* **verdammter Mist!** *(Ausdruck des Ärgers)* flipping hell!; **schöner Mist!** *(Ausdruck der unangenehmen Überraschung)* flipping hell!; **so ein Mist!** *(Ausdruck des Ärgers)* damn it!

2 *interj (Ausdruck des Ärgers)* damn it!

Mistkerl *m beleidigend (nichtswürdiger, gemeiner Mann)* pig; **du Mistkerl!** you pig!

Miststück *nt beleidigend* (a) *(Frau)* bitch

(b) *(unmoralische Frau)* bloody whore; **du Miststück!** you bloody whore!

mitgehen *vi* **etwas mitgehen lassen** *(stehlen)* to swipe something; **wer hat meinen Stift mitgehen lassen?** who swiped my pen?

mitkriegen *vt* (a) *(verstehen, hören)* to get; **der hat den Witz nicht mitgekriegt** he didn't get the joke; **es ist schon traurig, wie wenig Max im Englischunterricht mitkriegt** it's tragic how little Max picks up from his English classes

(b) *(herausfinden)* to know [*nicht Slang*]; **wie hat Karin bloß mitgekriegt, dass ich 'ne Party mache?** how come Karin knows I'm having a party?

Moos *nt (Geld)* lolly

Möpse *npl sexistisch, scherzhaft (weibliche Brüste)* jugs

Möse *f meist sexistisch (weibliches Geschlechtsorgan)* twat

Motherfucker *m beleidigend (nichtswürdiger Mann)* mother

Muff *m sexistisch (weibliches Geschlechtsorgan)* beaver

Mugge *f (musikalische Gelegenheitstätigkeit)* gig

Mumu *f (weibliches Geschlechtsorgan)* front bottom

Murmel *f (Kopf)* bonce

Muschi *f (weibliches Geschlechts-organ)* front bottom

Muttersöhnchen *nt*
(verwöhnter Junge oder Mann)
mummy's boy

N

Nadel f an der Nadel hängen *(heroinsüchtig sein)* to be on the needle; **sich die Nadel setzen** *(Heroin spritzen)* to shoot up

Nagel m etwas an den Nagel hängen *(etwas aufgeben)* to pack something in

nageln vt sexistisch jemanden nageln *(koitieren mit)* to give somebody one; **die Alte dort würde ich auch mal gern nageln** I'd give her one

Narr → fressen

nass adj (a) *(attraktiv)* fuckable (b) *(sexuell bedürftig)* horny

Nasse npl East German *(Schulden)* ich habe 800 Nasse I'm 800 euros in the red

neben präp neben sich stehen *(nicht bei klarem Verstand sein)* to be out of it

Neger m rassistisch einen Neger abseilen *(Darm entleeren)* to park a darkie

Nerven npl jemandem auf die Nerven gehen *(ärgern)* to get on somebody's nerves; **Mann, das Gequatsche geht mir auf die Nerven** God, their chattering is really getting on my nerves; **musst du denn immer den Mädchen auf die Nerven gehen?** why are you always winding the girls up?; **meine Nerven!** *(Ausruf der Verwunderung)* flipping heck!

nerven 1 vi *(ärgern)* to be a pain; **das nervt echt** it's a real pain
  2 vt *(ärgern)* jemanden nerven to get on somebody's nerves

Nest nt *(Bett)* die Susie geht doch mit jedem ins Nest Susie will jump into bed with just about anyone; **liegt der immer noch im Nest?** is he still in his pit?; **raus aus dem Nest!** rise and shine!; **ich haue mich ins Nest** I'm going to hit the sack

Nigger ⚠️ m rassistisch *(Schwarzer)* nigger

nölen vi *(sich beklagen)* to whinge

Not → fressen

Notstand m sexuellen Notstand haben scherzhaft *(sexuelles Bedürfnis)* to be gagging for it; **bei ihm ist der Notstand ausgebrochen** scherzhaft *(er hat ein starkes sexuelles Bedürfnis)* he's gagging for it

Nummer f *(Geschlechtsverkehr)* hump; **eine (kleine) Nummer schieben** *(koitieren)* to hump;

wollen wir 'ne kleine Nummer schieben? d'you fancy (having) a hump?; **eine Nummer mit jemandem schieben** to hump somebody

Nüsse *npl (Hoden)* nuts; **Vorsicht, sonst gibt's ein paar auf die Nüsse!** watch it or I'll kick you in the nuts!

Nutte *f* **(a)** *(Prostituierte)* slut **(b)** *beleidigend (unmoralische Frau)* slut; **du Nutte!** you slut! **(c)** *sexistisch beleidigend (nichtswürdige Frau)* whore

O

Oberkante *f* mir steht's **Oberkante Unterlippe** *(ich kann es nicht mehr ertragen)* I've totally had it; *(mir ist übel nach zu viel Alkoholkonsum)* I'm a bit the worse for wear

Ochse *m* **dummer Ochse** *beleidigend (dummer Mensch)* blockhead; **du dummer Ochse!** you blockhead!

Ofen *m (Motorrad)* **ein heißer Ofen** a cool pair of wheels

Ohr *nt* **(a)** *(Brust)* **Ohren** knockers **(b)** *(Redewendungen)* **die Ohren anklappen** *(staunen)* to be totally gobsmacked; **als ich das gesehen habe, habe ich nur die Ohren angeklappt** I was totally gobsmacked when I saw it; **da klappst du die Ohren an, Mensch!** it's totally gobsmacking, man!; **jemanden übers Ohr hauen** *(betrügen)* to take somebody for a ride → **Arsch**

Oldies *npl (Eltern)* **meine Oldies** my mum and dad

Ossi *m rassistisch (Bewohner der neuen Bundesländer)* bloody East German; **die Ossis sind eben mal dumm und faul** those bloody East Germans are all stupid and lazy; **das ist unser Ossi im Büro** this is our eastern German colleague

ⓘ **Ossi** can be used offensively by West Germans to denote a person from the former East Germany, in which case the most appropriate translation is *bloody East German*. However, when it is used by East Germans to describe themselves, or by West Germans in a non-offensive way, then the best translation is *eastern German*. The examples above show this difference in usage.

P

Pampa *f* mitten in der Pampa *(weit abgelegen)* in the sticks

Pappe *f* (a) *(Ausweis)* ID card (b) *(auf Papier geträufelte Einzeldosis LSD)* wrap

Pappnase *f (unwichtige Person)* non-entity

Patengeschenk *nt scherzhaft (männliche Genitalien)* tackle

pennen *vi (schlafen)* to crash

Penner *m*, **Pennerin** *f (Obdachloser)* dosser

Pep *nt (Speed)* pep pills *pl*; **hast du Pep dabei?** have you got any pep pills on you?

Pfanne *f* jemanden in die Pfanne hauen *(jemanden verraten)* to land somebody in it; *(jemanden besiegen)* to beat the hell out of somebody

Pfeife *f* (a) *(Penis)* cock (b) *(unfähige Person)* useless git

Pflaume *f* (a) *sexistisch (weibliches Geschlechtsorgan)* minge (b) *(Schwächling, Versager)* wimp

picheln *vi (viel trinken)* to booze; **wusstest du nicht, dass der pichelt?** didn't you know he's an alkie?; **und abends pichelt sie**

dann wieder and in the evening she hits the bottle again

piepegal *adj* das ist mir piepegal *(das ist mir vollkommen egal)* I couldn't give a stuff; **die Schule ist ihm piepegal** he couldn't give a stuff about his schoolwork; **seine Meinung ist mir piepegal** I couldn't give a stuff what he thinks; **das ist ihm alles piepegal** he couldn't give a stuff (about anything)

Pieselmann *m Kindersprache (Penis)* willy

pieseln *vi (urinieren)* to wee-wee; **Johannes, hast du gepieselt?** Johannes, have you had a wee-wee?; **ich muss pieseln** I need a wee-wee; **pieseln gehen** to go for a wee-wee

Pillen *npl (Ecstasy)* tabs; **Pillen schlucken** to drop some tabs; **hast du Pillen dabei?** have you got any tabs on you?

Pimmel *m (Penis)* cock

ⓘ The term **Pimmel** was originally a mild term used by, and of, children and would have been translated by the English term *willy*. However, it has recently become widely used in pornography and is thus now almost never used in its original context.

pinkeln vi (urinieren) to pee; **hast du gepinkelt?** have you had a pee?; **ich muss pinkeln** I need a pee; **pinkeln gehen** to go for a pee

Pisse f (Urin) piss; **das Bier schmeckt wie Pisse** (schmeckt nicht) this beer tastes like piss

pissen vi (a) (urinieren) to piss; **hast du gepisst?** have you had a piss?; **ich muss pissen** I need a piss; **pissen gehen** to go for a piss
(b) (regnen) to piss down; **es pisst!** it's pissing down!

Pisser m beleidigend (lächerliche Person) fuckwit; **du kleiner Pisser!** you little fuckwit!

Pisspott m (a) (Nachttopf) pisspot
(b) beleidigend (unangenehmer Mensch) pisspot

pisswarm adj (unangenehm lauwarm) piss-warm

Platte → Scheiße

Po m (Gesäß) bottom

Polacke m, **Polackin** f rassistisch (Pole) Polack

Polente f (Polizei) **die Polente** the cops

poofen vi (schlafen) to get some shuteye; **ich geh jetzt poofen!** I'm going to go and get some shuteye; **der pooft schon** he's already hit the sack

Popel m (a) (Stück Nasenschleim) bogey

(b) (unwichtige Person) Joe Public

poppen 1 vt (koitieren mit) **jemanden poppen** to have it off with somebody
2 vi (koitieren) to have it off

Pott m (a) (Kochtopf) pot [nicht Slang]
(b) (Nachttopf) potty
(c) (Toilette) crapper
(d) **zu Potte kommen** (etwas zustande bringen) to get oneself sorted; **er kommt mit seinem Leben nicht zu Potte** he can't seem to get his life sorted

potthässlich adj (hässlich) minging; **ein potthässliches Teil** a minger

Proletenschwein nt beleidigend (a) (Arbeiter) working-class scum; **er ist ein Proletenschwein** he's working-class scum; **in der Kneipe hängen nur Proletenschweine ab** that pub's where all the working-class scum hang out
(b) (kulturloser oder dummer Mensch) ignorant git
(c) (schlecht gekleideter Mensch) chav

Prollo m, **Prolo** m, **Proll** m beleidigend (a) (Arbeiter) working-class scum; **er ist ein Prollo** he's working-class scum; **in der Kneipe hängen nur Prollos ab** that pub's where all the working-class scum hang out
(b) (kulturloser oder dummer Mensch) ignorant git
(c) (schlecht gekleideter Mensch) chav

Puff m (Bordell) whorehouse

Puffmutter f (Besitzerin eines Bordells) madame

Puffnutte f (Prostituierte) scrubber

Puller m (Penis) tadger; **ich habe mir eine auf den Puller gesteckt** sexistisch (ich habe mit einer Frau koitiert) I dipped my wick

Pullermann m, **Pullermatz** m Kindersprache (Penis) willy

pullern vi Kindersprache (urinieren) to wee-wee; **Kevin, hast du gepullert?** Kevin, have you had a wee-wee?; **ich muss pullern** I need a wee-wee;

pullern gehen to go for a wee-wee

Puma, Pumascheiße → geil

Pumpe f East German (Schluss) **als ich sie mit dem anderen erwischt habe, war natürlich Pumpe** of course, when I found her with another man, that was it

Puppe f sexistisch (Frau, Freundin) bird

pupsen vi (Wind abgehen lassen) to trump

pushen vi (Heroin spritzen) to shoot up scag; **seit wann pusht der?** how long has he been on the scag?

Q

quaken 1 *vi (Unsinn reden)* to talk guff

2 *vt* to spout; **was quakt der wieder für einen Stuss?** what bollocks is he spouting now?

Qualle *f beleidigend (dicke Person)* fat pig

quarzen *vt* **einen quarzen** *(Haschisch oder Marihuana rauchen)* to smoke some blow

Quatsch 1 *m* (a) *(Unsinn)* garbage; **er hat die ganze Zeit nur Quatsch geredet** he just talked garbage the whole time; **der hat ja so einen Quatsch erzählt** what he said was complete and utter garbage

(b) *(Unsinniges)* garbage; **für so einen Quatsch zahle ich doch keine 50 Euro!** I'm not paying 50 euros for that garbage!

(c) *(kritikwürdige Handlung)* **was soll der Quatsch?** what the hell do you think you're doing?; **eh, macht mal keinen Quatsch!** oi, what the hell do you think you're doing?; **mach bloß keinen Quatsch!** stop mucking around!

(d) *(alberne Streiche)* **was haben wir in den Ferien für 'n Quatsch gemacht** we got up to all sorts of nonsense in the holidays; **die Kinder machen wieder Quatsch** the kids are acting up again; **Onkel Franz macht mit den Kindern immer Quatsch** Uncle Franz is always clowning around with the kids

2 *interj (Ausdruck des Widersprechens)* nonsense!

quatschen 1 *vi* (a) *(plaudern)* to natter; **komm doch bei mir vorbei, dann können wir ungestört quatschen** come round my place so we can have a quiet natter

(b) *(etwas verraten)* to grass

2 *vt (dummes Zeug reden)* to spout; **der hat nur dummes Zeug gequatscht** he just spouted a load of nonsense

R

Rad *nt* ein *oder* das Rad abhaben *(verrückt sein)* to be off one's rocker; **am Rad drehen** *(sich ärgern)* to go ballistic

Radieschen *nt* die Radieschen von unten besehen *(tot sein)* to be pushing up the daisies

raffen *vt (verstehen)* to twig; **na, hast du's endlich gerafft, dass er nichts von dir wissen will?** well, have you finally twigged that he doesn't want anything to do with you?; **Mathe raff' ich einfach nicht** I'm totally clueless at maths; **du raffst aber auch gar nichts!** you're totally clueless, you are!

rallig *adj (sexuell bedürftig)* gagging for it; **die Alte ist doch rallig!** *sexistisch* that bitch is on heat!; **bo, der Typ da drüben sieht vielleicht klasse aus, der macht mich ganz rallig** fwoar, that's one fit guy over there, he's giving me the hots

rammeln 1 *vi (koitieren)* to go at it; **die haben die ganze Nacht gerammelt!** they were going at it all night!; **mit jemandem rammeln** to roger somebody **2** *vt (koitieren mit)* to roger; **er hat mich gerammelt, dass mir**

Hören und Sehen verging he rogered me senseless

ramschen *vi (sich übermäßig bereichern)* to get filthy stinking rich

ranschmeißen *reflexiv* sich an jemanden ranschmeißen *(sich aufreizend anbieten)* to throw oneself at somebody

Ratte *f (hinterlistiger, charakterloser Mensch)* rat

ratzen *vi (schlafen)* to doss

regeln *vt* etwas geregelt kriegen *(etwas zustande bringen)* to get something sorted; **hast du das mit deiner Freundin jetzt geregelt gekriegt?** have you got things sorted with your girlfriend?; **Max kriegt in der Schule gerade gar nichts geregelt** Max is a disaster at school

reihern *vi (erbrechen)* to spew up

relaxen *vi (ruhig sein)* to chill; **bei ein bisschen Musik relaxen** to chill to some music

Rettungsringe *npl (dicker Bauch oder Fett auf den Hüften)* spare tyres

Riecher *m* **(a)** *(Nase)* hooter

(b) *(Gespür)* nose; **der hat einen guten Riecher für Geschäfte** he's got a good nose for business

Rille *f (Gesäßspalte)* bum crack; **ich hasse es, wenn der Schlüpfer in der Rille sitzt!** I hate it when your knickers ride up your bum crack!

Rind *nt* **blödes Rind** *beleidigend (dumme Person)* silly b; **du blödes Rind, wie konntest du nur!** how could you do a thing like that, you silly b!

Rindvieh *nt beleidigend (dumme Person)* stupid bugger; **du Rindvieh!** you stupid bugger!; **ich Rindvieh hab' ihm das geglaubt** and I believed him like a stupid bugger

Ritze *f* **(a)** *(Gesäßspalte)* bum crack; **ich hasse es, wenn der Schlüpfer in der Ritze sitzt!** I hate it when your knickers ride up your bum crack!
 (b) *sexistisch (weibliches Geschlechtsorgan)* slit

Rohr *nt (Penis)* dong; **der hatte voll das Rohr** *(großer erigierter Penis)* he had a massive hard-on

Rosette *f (After)* ring; **dir platzt gleich die Rosette!** *(Gewaltandrohung)* you're dead!

rot *adj* **die hat gerade ihre rote Woche** *sexistisch (sie menstruiert)* she's on the rag

Roter *m*, **Rote** *f (Kommunist, Sozialist oder Sozialdemokrat)* red; **die Roten** the reds

Rotz *m (Nasenschleim)* snot

Rotzbengel *m* **(a)** *(Junge)*

snotty-nosed brat
 (b) *(unerfahrener junger Mann)* **er ist ein richtiger Rotzbengel** he's pretty wet behind the ears

Rotze *f (Nasenschleim)* snot

rotzen *vi* **(a)** *(spucken)* to gob
 (b) *(schniefen)* to sniff snot up one's nose
 (c) *(ejakulieren)* to blow one's load

Rotzer *m*, **Rotzjunge** *m* **(a)** *(Junge)* snotty-nosed brat
 (b) *(unerfahrener junger Mann)* **er ist ein richtiger Rotzer** *oder* **Rotzjunge** he's pretty wet behind the ears

Rübe *f (Kopf)* nut; **benutz mal deine Rübe!** use your nut!; **du hast nichts in der Rübe!** *(du bist dumm)* you've got nothing but sawdust between your ears! → **Scheiße**

rückwärts → **frühstücken**

rumgammeln *vi (herumalbern)* to fart around

rumknutschen *vi (sich küssen)* to snog; **mit jemandem rumknutschen** to snog somebody

rummachen *vi (schmusen)* to canoodle

rumschmieren *vi (schmusen)* to make out

rumzicken *vi (schwierig sein)* to act up

rund *adj* **rund sein** *(betrunken sein)* to be wasted; **rund wie ein Buslenker** *(sehr betrunken)* totally wasted

rundlaufen *vi (geistig normal*

sein) **die läuft nicht richtig rund**
she's not quite right in the head

runterholen *vt* **ich habe mir
einen runtergeholt** *(ich habe
masturbiert)* I tossed myself off;

sie hat ihm einen runtergeholt
she tossed him off

runterkommen *vi (langsam
vom Trip runterkommen)* to
come down

S

sabbern *vi (viel reden)* to blether on

Sack *m* **(a)** *(Person)* bastard; **er ist ein schlauer Sack** he's a clever bastard; **irgend so'n Sack hat meinen Stift geklaut** some bastard nicked my pen; **was für 'n blöder Sack!** what a stupid bastard!; **he, du Sack!** oi, mush!
  (b) *(Hodensack)* bag
  (c) *(Redewendugen)* **jemandem auf den Sack gehen** *(ärgern)* to get on somebody's tits; **Mann, das Gequatsche geht mir auf den Sack** God, their chattering is really getting on my tits; **hör endlich auf, mir mit deinem Scheißumweltschutz auf den Sack zu gehen!** can't you stop banging on about your bloody environmentalism for once, it's getting on my tits!; **jemanden in den Sack stecken** *(besiegen)* to kick the crap out of somebody → **blöd, dumm**

Sackgesicht *nt beleidigend (nichtswürdige Person)* wazzock; **du Sackgesicht!** you wazzock!

Sackratten *npl (Geschlechtskrankheit)* **die Sackratten haben** to have the clap

Saft *m (Sperma)* spunk

Saftsack *m beleidigend (nichtswürdige Person)* prick; **du Saftsack!** you prick!

Sargnagel *m (Zigarette)* cancer stick

Sau *f* **(a)** *beleidigend (nichtswürdige Person)* git; **sie ist eine blöde Sau** *(sie ist dumm)* she's a stupid git
  (b) *sexistisch (weibliche Person)* bitch; **sie ist 'ne geile Sau** she's a horny bitch
  (c) *sexistisch (attraktive Frau)* tasty bit of arse
  (d) *sexistisch (sexuell überaktive Frau)* **das ist 'ne richtige Sau** she's a fucking nympho
  (e) *(unhygienische Person)* pig; **wäscht du dich eigentlich nie, du Sau?** when's the last time you had a bath, you filthy pig?
  (f) *(unanständige Person)* filthy pig; **du Sau!** you filthy pig!
  (g) *(Redewendungen)* **der fährt wie eine gesengte Sau!** *(fährt wild und rücksichtslos)* he drives like a bloody maniac!; **das interessiert doch keine Sau!** *(interessiert niemanden)* nobody gives a toss about that!; **zu der Lesung kam keine Sau** *(kam niemand)* there was hardly a bloody soul at the reading; **die**

säuisch

Sau rauslassen *(wild feiern)*
to have a totally wild time;
das ist unter aller Sau! *(ist
unzumutbar)* this is the pits!; **das
juckt wie Sau!** *(juckt heftig)* it
itches like shit!; **ihre Wohnung
sah aus wie Sau** her flat was
bloody filthy; **jemanden zur Sau
machen** *(scharf rügen)* to bust
somebody's balls

sau- *präfix (sehr)* bloody; **er ist
saudumm** he's bloody stupid;
er ist saublöd *(sehr dumm)* he's
bloody stupid; *(nicht nett)* he's
a bloody idiot; **das Auto war
saubillig** the car was bloody
cheap; **der Film war saugut** the
film was bloody good; **wir haben
uns saugut amüsiert** we had a
bloody marvellous time; **ich fühle
mich heute sauwohl** I feel bloody
brilliant today

sauber *adj* **der ist ja nicht
ganz sauber!** *(Ausdruck der
Empörung)* is he having a laugh?

sauer *adj* **auf jemanden/über
etwas sauer sein** *(sich ärgern)* to
be brassed off with somebody/
about something

Sauerei *f* (a) *(Skandal)* bloody
scandal; **das ist eine Sauerei,
was die mit den Steuergeldern
machen** it's a bloody scandal
what they get up to with taxpayers' money
  (b) *(unmoralische Handlung)*
**die machen doch nur Sauereien
in dem Film!** that film's full of
nothing but bloody filth!
  (c) *(unanständige Geschichte)*
filthy story; *(unanständiger

Witz) filthy joke; **erzählst du
schon wieder Sauereien?** are you
telling your bloody filthy little
stories again?
  (d) *(unhygienischer Zustand)*
bloody filthy mess; **was ist das
denn für eine Sauerei in deinem
Zimmer?** what's this bloody filthy
mess in your room?; **ich finde,
das ist eine Sauerei, dass die
Hunde da überall hinscheißen!** I
think it's bloody disgusting that
the dogs shit all over the place!

saufen 1 *vt (trinken)* **komm, wir
gehen einen saufen** come on,
let's go for a bevvy; **er hat schon
drei Bier gesoffen** he's already
had three beers
  2 *vi (viel trinken)* to booze; **seit
wann säuft dein Mann?** how
long has your husband been on
the booze?; **das kommt vom
Saufen, dass deine Hände so
zittern** your hands shake like
that because of all the boozing

Säufer *m*, **Säuferin** *f*
(Alkoholiker) boozer

Sauhund *m beleidigend
(nichtswürdige Person)* bloody
bastard; **du Sauhund!** you bloody
bastard!

säuisch 1 *adj* (a) *(obszön)* filthy
  (b) *(schmutzig und unordent-
lich)* filthy
  (c) *(intensivierend)* **das ist ja 'ne
säuische Beule!** that's a bloody
great bump you've got there!
  2 *adv* (a) *(obszön)* **der hat sich
echt säuisch benommen** he
behaved like a filthy swine
  (b) *(intensivierend)* bloody; **das**

tut säuisch weh that's bloody painful; **es war säuisch kalt** it was bloody freezing

Sause *f (Party)* booze-up; **'ne Sause machen** to have a booze-up

scharf *adj* (a) *(sexuell erregt)* randy; **jemanden scharf machen** to make somebody randy
  (b) *(begehrenswert)* hot
  (c) *(toll)* wicked
  (d) **auf jemandem scharf sein** *(sehr gern haben)* to fancy somebody; **auf etwas scharf sein** *(sehr gern haben)* to be into something; **Felix ist scharf auf ein Fotohandy** Felix would kill to get his hands on a cameraphone

Scheiß *m* (a) *(Unsinn)* bollocks; **in dem Buch steht auch nur Scheiß drin** the book's a load of bollocks; **ich kann diesen Scheiß schon nicht mehr hören** I've heard enough of this bollocks; **was redest du da für einen Scheiß?** stop talking bollocks!; **red doch keinen Scheiß!** bollocks!; **Scheiß erzählen** to talk bollocks; **erzähl doch nicht so einen Scheiß!** that's a load of bollocks!
  (b) *(Minderwertiges)* crap; **für den Scheiß hast du 100 Euro bezahlt?** surely you didn't pay 100 euros for that crap?; **das Handy ist doch Scheiß** this mobile phone's a load of crap
  (c) *(ärgerlicher Zustand)* pain in the arse; **das ist ein Scheiß, jetzt muss ich alles noch mal machen** what a pain in the arse, now I've got to do it all over again
  (d) *(Unannehmlichkeiten)* shit; **den Scheiß hast du dir selber eingebrockt** you've brought all that shit on yourself; **jetzt haben wir den Scheiß** we're in the shit now
  (e) *(kritikwürdige Handlung)* **was soll der Scheiß?** what the fuck do you think you're doing?; **eh, macht mal keinen Scheiß!** oi, what the fuck do you think you're doing?; **was haben wir für einen Scheiß gemacht in den Ferien!** we got up to all sorts of shit in the holidays!
  (f) *(Redewendungen)* **so ein Scheiß, das ist doch völliger Quatsch!** *(so ein Unsinn)* Jesus bloody Christ, this is a right load of old nonsense!; **so ein Scheiß, jetzt müssen wir alles noch mal machen** *(so etwas Unangenehmes)* bollocks, now we've got to do it all over again; **ein schöner Scheiß ist das!** *(das ist ärgerlich)* it's a real pisser; **das geht dich einen Scheiß an!** *(das geht dich überhaupt nichts an)* that's got eff all to do with you; **einen Scheiß werd' ich tun** *(ich werde das nicht tun)* no effing way am I doing that; **das interessiert mich einen Scheiß** *(das interresiert mich überhaupt nicht)* I couldn't give a toss about that; **der kümmert sich einen Scheiß um meine Gefühle** *(der kümmert sich überhaupt nicht)* he couldn't give a toss about my feelings; **ich mache das für dich. – Kein Scheiß? – Kein Scheiß!** *(ganz sicher)* I'll do it for you. – Like shit you will. – No, I bloody will, honest!

Scheiß- *präfix (abwertend)*
bloody; **das Scheißauto springt
nicht an** the bloody car won't
start; **wir hatten ein Scheißglück**
we were bloody lucky; **ich hab'
keine Scheißahnung** I haven't
got a bloody clue; **er ist ein
Scheißtyp** he's a bloody bastard;
sie ist eine Scheißschlampe she's
a bloody slag; **ich hasse das
Scheißfrühaufstehen morgens**
I bloody hate getting up early
in the morning; **das ist heute
wieder ein totales Scheißwetter!**
the weather's bloody shit
again today!; **ich hatte eine
Scheißangst** I was scared shitless;
**du hast mir eine Scheißangst
eingejagt** you scared the shit out
of me; **(dein) Scheißpech!** tough
shit!

scheiß- *präfix (abwertend)*
bloody; **es ist scheißkalt** it's
bloody freezing; **das tut
scheißweh** that's bloody painful;
es ist scheißschwierig it's bloody
difficult; **ein scheißgroßer
Lastwagen** a bloody great lorry

Scheißdreck *m* (a) *(Kot)* crud
(b) *(Redewendungen)*
**das interessiert mich einen
Scheißdreck** *(das interessiert
mich absolut nicht)* I couldn't
give a crap; **der kümmert sich
doch einen Scheißdreck um ihre
Gefühle** *(kümmert sich nicht)* he
couldn't give a crap about her
feelings; **das geht dich einen
Scheißdreck an!** *(das geht dich
absolut nichts an)* that's got
sod all to do with you!; **einen
Scheißdreck hast du heut'**
gemacht *(nichts)* you've done
sod all today; **einen Scheißdreck
werde ich tun!** *(ich werde es
nicht tun)* no sodding way am I
doing that!; **jeder Scheißdreck**
(jede Kleinigkeit) the slightest
sodding thing; **die rennt doch
wegen jedem Scheißdreck gleich
zum Chef** the slightest sodding
thing and off she runs to the
boss; **mach doch nicht wegen
jedem Scheißdreck so einen
Aufstand!** there's no need to
make such a fuss about sod all!

Scheiße 1 *f* (a) *(Kot)* shit; **ich
glaube, ich bin in Scheiße
getreten** I think I've trodden
in some shit; **pass auf, da ist
Scheiße auf dem Bürgersteig**
look out, there's a shit on the
pavement
(b) *(Minderwertiges)* shit; **die
CD ist Scheiße** that CD's (a load
of) shit; **für so 'ne Scheiße zahle
ich doch keine 100 Euro** I'm not
paying 100 euros for that shit; **du
meinst doch nicht, dass ich so 'ne
Scheiße esse** surely you're not
expecting me to eat that shit?;
das Wetter war echt Scheiße the
weather was really shit
(c) *(Unsinn)* shit; **in dem Buch
steht doch nur Scheiße** the
book's a load of shit; **er hat die
ganze Zeit nur Scheiße geredet**
he just talked shit the whole
time; **Scheiße erzählen** to talk
shit; **erzähl doch nicht so 'ne
Scheiße** stop talking shit; **das
ist doch die totale Scheiße!**
that's a load of shit!; **ich kann
diese Scheiße schon nicht mehr**

Scheiße

hören I've heard enough of this shit; **was du redest ist nichts als gequirlte Scheiße!** that's a steaming pile of shit!

(d) *(Panne, ärgerlicher Zustand)* **bei den Reisevorbereitungen ist Scheiße passiert** there was a cock-up over the travel arrangements; **ich weiß, das ist Scheiße, ich hätte dir Bescheid geben sollen** I know, I fucked up, I should have told you

(e) *(Unannehmlichkeiten)* shit; **jetzt haben wir die Scheiße!** we're in big shit now!; **so eine Scheiße, jetzt muss ich alles noch mal machen** shit, now I've got to do it all over again; **die Scheiße** *oder* **eine schöne Scheiße hast du uns eingebrockt** you've gone and landed us in the shit now; **das ist doch alles Scheiße** it's a total pain in the arse; **das ist echt Scheiße mit dem Unfall!** *(das macht uns Unannehmlichkeiten)* the accident's a real pain in the arse; **der steckt bis zum Hals in der Scheiße** *(steckt in Schwierigkeiten)* he's having a really shitty time of it; **mit der Firma stecken wir bis zum Hals in der Scheiße** the company's up shit creek without a paddle; **in der Scheiße sitzen** *(in Unannehmlichkeiten sein)* to be in the shit; **mit dem neuen Mitarbeiter haben wir voll in die Scheiße gepackt** *(Pech gehabt)* we've landed ourselves right in the shit taking on that new guy at work; **das ist große Scheiße!** it's a total bummer!

(f) *(kritikwürdige Handlung)* **he,** **was soll die Scheiße?** oi, what the bloody hell do you think you're doing?; **als ich jung war, hab' ich auch so manche Scheiße gemacht** I used to get up to shit like that too when I was young; **Scheiße bauen** *(etwas schlecht ausführen)* to make a cock-up; **die Handwerker haben Scheiße gebaut** the workmen made a right cock-up of the job; **Felix hat Scheiße gebaut, der hat das Auto seines Vaters zu Schrott gefahren** Felix has bloody well gone and done it this time, he's written his dad's car off; **was hast du denn jetzt schon wieder für Scheiße gebaut?** what the bloody hell have you gone and done now?; **du baust nur Scheiße, weißt du das?** you're bloody unbelievable, you are!; **da haben wir mal wieder Scheiße gebaut** we've gone and cocked it up again; **als ich 25 war, habe ich Scheiße gebaut und musste ein halbes Jahr in den Knast** I got in the shit when I was 25 and ended up spending six months in the nick

(g) *(Redewendungen)* **es ist total Scheiße, immer so früh aufstehen zu müssen** *(es ist sehr ärgerlich)* it totally bloody sucks always having to get up so early; **so eine Scheiße!** *(Ausdruck des Ärgers)* shit!; **nichts als Scheiße in der Birne** *oder* **Rübe** *oder* **Platte haben** *(dumm sein)* to have shit for brains; *(nur Unsinn im Kopf haben)* to be a bloody moron; **schöne Scheiße!** shit!

2 *interj (Ausdruck des Ärgers)*
shit!; **Scheiße, wie oft soll ich**
dir eigentlich noch sagen, dass
du mich in Ruhe lassen sollst!
for Christ's bloody sake, how
many times do I have to tell
you to leave me alone!; **(ach,**
du) Scheiße!, ach, du liebe
Scheiße! *(das ist unangenehm,*
unglaublich, peinlich, ungelegen)
shit!

scheiße 1 *adj (sehr schlecht)*
shite

2 *adv (sehr schlecht)* **du siehst**
scheiße aus you look like shite

scheißegal *adj* **das ist**
mir scheißegal *(das ist mir*
vollkommen egal) I couldn't
give a shit; **die Schule ist ihm**
scheißegal he couldn't give a
shit about his schoolwork; **seine**
Meinung ist mir scheißegal
I couldn't give a shit what
he thinks; **das ist ihm alles**
scheißegal he couldn't give a shit
(about anything)

scheißen *vi* **(a)** *(Darm entleeren)*
to have a shit; **sie muss mal**
scheißen she needs a shit; **ich**
muss mal übelst scheißen I'm
busting for a shit

(b) *(Redewendungen)*
da scheiß' ich drauf!, darauf
scheiß' ich! *(ich schätze es*
gering) screw that!; **auf**
solche Freunde scheiße ich
(ich schätze sie gering) with
friends like that, who needs
bloody enemies?; **scheiß drauf!**
(Unwillensbekundung) screw
that!; **scheiß drauf, machen**
wir's doch einfach screw it, let's

just do it; **schon wieder keine**
Gehaltserhöhung, scheiß der
Hund drauf, mir reicht das, was
ich verdiene *(das ist mir egal)*
I haven't got a pay rise again,
but screw it, I've got enough
with what I earn at the moment
anyway; **eigentlich sollte ich**
die Arbeit noch fertig machen,
aber scheiß der Hund drauf, ich
geh jetzt lieber schwimmen I
really ought to finish my work
but screw it, I'm off for a swim
instead; **scheiß der Hund drauf,**
was sie sagen, lass uns trotzdem
gehen! screw what they say,
let's go anyway!; **dir haben sie**
wohl ins Gehirn geschissen (und
vergessen umzurühren)? *(du bist*
nicht bei Verstand) have you got
shit for brains? → **Hose**

Scheißer *m beleidigend*
(nichtswürdige Person) dickhead;
du Scheißer! you dickhead!

Scheißerei *f (Durchfall)* the
shits *pl*; **die Scheißerei haben/**
kriegen to have/get the shits

Scheißhaus *nt (Toilette)* bog;
auf dem Scheißhaus sein to
be on the bog; **ich muss aufs**
Scheißhaus I need (to go to) the
bog

Scheißkerl *m beleidigend*
(nichtswürdige Person) bastard;
du Scheißkerl! you bastard!

Schicht *f* **(a)** *(Arbeit)* work [*nicht*
Slang]; **ich muss jetzt auf Schicht**
I've got to go in to work now
(b) *(Schluss)* **Schicht, Jungs** time
to knock off, lads; **noch fünf**
Minuten Arbeit, dann ist Schicht

five more minutes, then I'm out of here

schiffen vi (a) (urinieren) to have a slash; **hast du geschifft?** have you had a slash?; **ich muss schiffen** I need a slash; **schiffen gehen** to go for a slash

(b) (stark regnen) to pee down; **draußen schifft's!** it's peeing down outside!

Schiss m (a) (Portion Kot) turd

(b) (Ausscheiden von Kot) shit; **ich freue mich erst mal auf einen schönen Schiss** I'm looking forward to having a good shit

(c) (Angst) **vor lauter Schiss wollte er gar nicht mehr nach Hause** he was so shit-scared he didn't dare go home; **hast du schon wieder Schiss?** you're not bloody scared again are you?; **ich hatte schon Schiss, du kommst nicht mehr** I was bloody scared you weren't going to come; **Schiss kriegen** to get the wind up

Schisshase m (ängstlicher Mensch) **der Franz, das ist ein richtiger Schisshase** Franz is a flipping chicken

Schlampe f (a) (Prostituierte) slag

(b) (unmoralische Frau) slag; **du (alte) Schlampe!** you (old) slag!

(c) beleidigend (nichtswürdige Frau) slag; **du (alte) Schlampe!** you (old) slag!

(d) (unordentliche, schmutzige Frau) filthy cow

Schläuche npl (lange Brüste) droopy tits

Schleifstein → Affe

schleimen vi (schmeichlerisch reden) to creep; **bei jemandem schleimen** to creep up to somebody

Schleimer m, **Schleimerin** f (Schmeichler) creep

Schlitten m (Auto) pimpmobile

Schluchtenjodler m (Gebirgsdeutscher) yokel from the mountains

Schluchtenscheißer m, **Schluchti** m rassistisch (Österreicher) bloody Austrian

Schluckspecht m (Mensch, der viel trinkt) pisshead

schmalzig 1 adj (sentimental) schmaltzy

2 adv (sentimental) **er hat plötzlich angefangen, total schmalzig zu reden** he suddenly came over all lovey-dovey

Schmatz m, **Schmatzer** m (Kuss) snog; **jemandem einen Schmatz geben** to snog somebody

schmeißen vt (a) (werfen) to chuck; **Werbung schmeiße ich immer direkt in den Papierkorb** I always chuck junk mail straight in the wastepaper basket

(b) (abbrechen) to chuck in; **du kannst doch nicht einfach dein Studium schmeißen!** you can't just chuck your studies in!

(c) (Pillen, Drogen) to do; **der schmeißt alles, was ihm zwischen die Finger kommt** he'll do absolutely anything he can get his hands on

(d) sich auf etwas schmeißen *(gierig ergreifen)* really to go for something; **die haben sich auf meine Eierkuchen nur so geschmissen** they really went for my pancakes

(e) *(souverän bewältigen)* to handle; **die schmeißt ihren Haushalt neben Job und Kindern** she manages to handle running the household as well as holding down a job and looking after the kids; **wir werden die Sache schon schmeißen** we'll get it sorted

(f) eine Lage schmeißen *(Getränke spendieren)* to get a round in

Schmiere *f* **Schmiere stehen** *(bei Einbruch usw. aufpassen)* to be lookout; **du stehst Schmiere** you be lookout

schmieren *vt* **(a)** *(bestechen)* to buy off; **der Schiri war geschmiert worden** the ref had been bought off

(b) jemandem eine schmieren *(jemanden schlagen)* to clock somebody one

schnallen *vt* *(verstehen)* to get; **jetzt hab' ich's geschnallt** now I get it

schnarchen *vi* *(schlafen)* to kip

Schnauze *f* **(a)** *(Mund)* **die** *oder* **eine große Schnauze haben** *(aufschneiden)* to be a bigmouth; **er hat nur guten Tag gesagt, und schon hat er ein paar auf die Schnauze gekriegt** all he did was say hello but he still got his head kicked in for it; **du kriegst gleich was in** *oder* **auf die**

Schnauze! d'you want a smack in the gob or something?; **auf die Schnauze fallen** *(hinfallen)* to go arse over tit; *(Misserfolg haben)* to screw up; **mit dem Projekt bin ich voll auf die Schnauze gefallen** I really screwed the project up; **jemandem eins in** *oder* **auf die Schnauze geben** *(jemanden schlagen)* to do somebody's head in; **jemandem die Schnauze einschlagen** *(Prügel verabreichen)* to kick somebody's head in; **halt die Schnauze!** *(sei ruhig)* shut your face!; **(von etwas) die Schnauze (gestrichen) voll haben** to be bloody fed up (with something); **den Kuchen habe ich frei (nach) Schnauze gebacken** *(ohne Anleitung, Maßangaben)* I made up the recipe for the cake as I went along; **sie strickt die meisten Pullis frei (nach) Schnauze** when she knits her jumpers she normally just makes up the pattern as she goes along

(b) *(Gesicht)* face [*nicht Slang*]; **Mann, hat der 'ne hässliche Schnauze!** Christ, he's got an ugly mug!

Schnecke *f* **(a)** *meist sexistisch* *(weibliches Geschlechtsorgan)* minge

(b) *(begehrenswerte Frau)* gorgeous bit of fluff

(c) *beleidigend (nichtswürdige Frau)* tart

(d) *(Redewendungen)* **jemanden zur Schnecke machen** *(scharf rügen)* to give somebody a bollocking

Schnee

Schnee *m* (a) *(Kokain)* snow
(b) *(Redewendungen)* **das ist doch Schnee von gestern** *(das ist überholt)* that's all ancient history

Schnickse *f beleidigend (aufgedonnerte Frau)* Christmas tree; **jetzt guck dir bloß die Schnickse an** Christ, look at the state of her, she looks like a bloody Christmas tree

Schniedel *m*, **Schniedelwutz** *m scherzhaft (Penis)* little man

Schnitte *f (Frau)* babe

Schnodder *m (Nasenschleim)* snot

Schnuckelchen *nt* (a) *(attraktive Frau)* gorgeous bird; **seine neue Freundin ist ein Schnuckelchen** his new girlfriend's gorgeous
(b) *(als Anrede)* gorgeous; **na Schnuckelchen, wie wär's mit uns beiden?** how about it, gorgeous?

schnuckelig 1 *adj (nett)* gorgeous
2 *adv (nett)* **sie hat ihre Wohnung echt schnuckelig eingerichtet** she's done her flat up so it looks just gorgeous; **sie sieht schnuckelig aus** she looks gorgeous

schnüffeln *vi (sich an Klebstoffduft berauschen)* to sniff glue

schnurzegal *adj* **das ist mir schnurzegal** *(das ist mir vollkommen egal)* I couldn't give a monkey's; **die Schule ist ihm schnurzegal** he couldn't give a monkey's about his schoolwork; **seine Meinung ist mir schnurzegal** I couldn't give a monkey's what he thinks; **das ist ihm alles schnurzegal** he couldn't give a monkey's (about anything)

schön → Mist

Schonzeit *f* **die hat Schonzeit** *sexistisch (sie menstruiert)* she's on the rag

Schorre *f (Heroin)* scag

Schuss *m* (a) *(gespritztes Heroin)* shot; **hast du dir schon wieder einen Schuss gesetzt?** have you been shooting up again?; **der goldene Schuss** *(tödliche Überdosis)* OD; **gestern hat sich wieder einer in der öffentlichen Toilette den goldenen Schuss gesetzt** someone OD'd in the public toilets again yesterday
(b) *(Redewendungen)* **einen Schuss haben** *(nicht bei Verstand oder geistesgestört sein)* to be mental; **ich in Frieder verliebt sein, du hast wohl 'nen Schuss!** me, in love with Frieder? Are you completely mental or something?; **seit seinem Nervenzusammenbruch hat er einen Schuss (weg)** he's been a bit mental since he had his nervous breakdown

Schüssel → Sprung

schwafeln *vi (viel und wirr reden)* to waffle on

schwallen *vi (viel und wirr reden)* to witter on

Schwanz *m (Penis)* dick

schwänzen 1 *vt (Unterricht)* to skive off; **die Schule schwänzen** to skive off school
2 *vi (von Schule)* to skive off

Schwänzer *m*, **Schwänzerin** *f (jemand, der nicht zur Schule geht)* skiver

Schwanzlutscher *m* (a) *homophob (Homosexueller)* arse bandit
(b) *beleidigend (nichtswürdiger Mann)* fuckface; **von dir kleinem Schwanzlutscher lass' ich mir doch nicht sagen, wie ich meine Freundin behandeln kann oder nicht!** listen, fuckface, you don't get to tell me how I treat my girlfriend!

schwedisch → Gardine

Schwein *nt* (a) *(unhygienischer Mensch)* pig; **du Schwein!** you filthy pig!
(b) *(unmoralischer Mensch)* pig; **du Schwein!** you pig!; **er behandelt seine Frau wie ein Schwein** he's a real pig to his wife; **er ist ein Machoschwein** he's a male chauvinist pig
(c) *(Mensch)* **armes Schwein!** *(glücklose Person)* poor sod!; **das interessiert doch kein Schwein!** *(interessiert niemanden)* nobody gives a shit about that!; **kein Schwein lacht über deine Witze!** *(niemand)* nobody ever laughs at your bloody jokes!; **kein Schwein ruft mich an!** *(niemand)* I've had bugger all phone calls!; **das kann doch kein Schwein glauben** there's bugger all chance of anyone believing that

(d) *(Redewendungen)* **Schwein haben** *(unverdientes Glück haben)* to be jammy; **Mensch, hat der ein Schwein!** God, he's so jammy!; **jemandem aufs Schwein gehen** *(ärgern, nerven)* to get on somebody's wick; **Mann, das Gequatsche geht mir aufs Schwein** God, their chattering is really getting on my wick; **geh mir ja nicht aufs Schwein!** you're really starting to get on my wick!; **ich habe geblutet wie ein Schwein** *(heftig geblutet)* I bled like a stuck pig; **der wollte doch einen Hunderter von mir, ich glaub', mein Schwein pfeift!** *scherzhaft (das ist unerhört)* he wanted me to give him a hundred euros, is he for real?; **was, ich soll den Ede zu meiner Party einladen, ich glaub', mein Schwein pfeift!** ask Ede to my party? Get real! → **fressen**

ⓘ It is common for people to make up their own variations on the expression **ich glaub', mein Schwein pfeift** (literally, I think my pig is whistling), in order to express surprise or incredulity. Some examples would include: **ich glaub', mein Hamster bohnert** (I think my hamster is polishing the floor), **ich glaub', mich knutscht ein Elch** (I think an elk is snogging me) and **ich glaub', ich steh' im Wald** (I think I'm standing in a forest).

Schweinefraß *m (schlechtes Essen)* pigswill

Schweinehund *m beleidigend*

(nichtswürdige Person) bastard; **du Schweinehund, gib mir sofort mein Geld zurück!** give me my money back this instant, you bastard!

Schweinepriester *m* *beleidigend (nichtswürdiger Mann)* son of a gun; **du Schweinepriester!** you son of a gun!

Schweinerei *f* **(a)** *(Skandal)* flipping scandal; **das ist eine Schweinerei, was die mit den Steuergeldern machen** it's a flipping scandal what they get up to with taxpayers' money
(b) *(unmoralische Handlung)* **die machen doch nur Schweinereien in dem Film!** that film's full of nothing but filth!
(c) *(unanständige Geschichte)* filthy story; *(unanständiger Witz)* filthy joke; **erzählst du schon wieder Schweinereien?** are you telling your filthy little stories again?
(d) *(unhygienischer Zustand)* filthy mess; **was ist das denn für eine Schweinerei in deinem Zimmer?** what's this filthy mess in your room?; **ich finde, das ist eine Schweinerei, dass die Hunde da überall hinscheißen!** I think it's flipping disgusting that the dogs shit all over the place!

schweinisch *adj* **(a)** *(unsauber)* filthy
(b) *(unanständig)* filthy; **er liest immer so schweinische Heftchen** he's always reading dirty mags

Schweinkram *m (unanständige Handlung oder Gegenstände)* filth

Schweißerdrähte → **Arm**

Schwengel *m (Penis)* dipstick

Schwimmreifen *m*, **Schwimmringe** *npl (dicker Bauch oder Fett auf den Hüften)* spare tyres

Schwuchtel *f homophob (Homosexueller)* fairy

schwul *adj (homosexuell)* queer; **ich denke, er ist schwul** I think he's queer; **ich bin schwul** I'm gay; **schwule Sau** *homophob (Homosexueller)* fucking poof

ⓘ **Schwul** can be used somewhat offensively by homophobic people to denote a homosexual, in which case the most appropriate translation is *queer*. However, when it is used by homosexuals to describe themselves, or by heterosexuals in a completely non-offensive way, then the best translation is *gay*. The examples above show this difference in usage.

Schwuler *m (Homosexueller)* poof; **wir müssen den Schwulen mal einen Denkzettel verpassen** we need to teach the poofs a lesson; **Schwule und Lesben** gays and lesbians; **die Ehe zwischen Schwulen** gay marriage

ⓘ **Schwuler** can be used offensively by homophobic people to denote a homosexual, in which case the most appropriate translation is *poof*. However, when it is used by homosexuals to describe themselves, or by heterosexuals in a completely non-offensive way, then the best translation is *gay*. The examples above show this difference in usage.

Schwuli *m homophob (Homosexueller)* poofter

Schwulibert *m homophob (Homosexueller)* mincer

Schwuppe *f (Homosexueller)* gayboy

sechen *vi (urinieren)* to make a pit stop

Seele → **kotzen**

Semmel *f sexistisch (weibliches Geschlechtsorgan)* chuff

Senkel *m jemandem auf den Senkel gehen (ärgern, nerven)* to get on somebody's wick

Sense *f (Schluss)* **das war das letzte Mal, dass du mich betrogen hast, jetzt ist Sense!** that's the last time you're going to be unfaithful to me, it's time we knocked it on the head!; **und dann war Sense!** and that was it, finito!

Sesselfurzer *m beleidigend (Büromensch)* drone

Sexprotz *m (besonders triebaktiver Mann)* stud

Sitzpinkler *m (langweiliger Mann)* girlie wuss

Sohn *m*, **Söhnchen** *nt (Anrede an jüngeren Mann)* sonny Jim

Sonne *f* **geh mir aus der Sonne**

(mach Platz) get out of my road

Soße *f (Sperma)* come

spack *adj (dünn, schwächlich)* **spack sein** to be a weed

Spack *m*, **Spacken** *m (dünner, schwächlicher Mann)* weed

Spaghettifresser *m rassistisch (Italiener)* spag

Spasti *m*, **Spastiker** *m*, **Spastikerin** *f beleidigend*
(a) *(dummer Mensch)* spastic; **he, Spastiker!** oi, spazzy!
(b) *(seltsamer Mensch)* mutant; **he, Spastiker, soll das tanzen sein, was du da veranstaltest?** oi, you mutant, d'you call that dancing?

ⓘ Originally coined as a medical term for people with cerebral palsy, the term **Spastiker** *(spastic, spazzy)* is now highly offensive if used to denote the medical condition and is mainly used as a general insult for clumsy or stupid people.

Speed *nt (Droge)* speed; **Speed ziehen** *oder* **schmeißen** *(Speed konsumieren)* to do speed

spinnen *vi (nicht bei Verstand sein)* to be crazy; **der spinnt ja** he must be crazy; **sag mal, spinnst du?** are you having me on?; **ich glaub', ich spinne** *(Ausdruck des Erstaunens)* no way!; *(Ausdruck der Empörung)* are you having a laugh?; **ich glaub', ich spinne, das ist doch Claudia Schiffer!** that's Claudia Schiffer, no way!; **du kannst doch nicht so einfach**

mein Auto nehmen, ich glaub',
ich spinne! are you having a
laugh? You can't just take my car
like that!

Spinner m, **Spinnerin** f
(*verrückter Mensch*) loony

spitz adj (*sexuell erregt*) steamed
up; **auf jemandem spitz sein** to
have the hots for somebody

Spitze 1 f **Spitze sein** (*toll sein*)
to be ace
2 interj ace!

spitze adv (*toll*) **das habt ihr
wirklich spitze gemacht!** you've
done a really ace job there!; **Seb
kann spitze Mathe** Seb is ace
at maths; **Lars hat sich spitze
verhalten** Lars was dead good

splitterfasernackt,
splitternackt adj (*nackt*)
starkers

Spritti m (*alkoholabhängige
Person*) pisshead

Sprung m **einen Sprung in
der Schüssel haben** (*nicht bei
Verstand sein*) to be off one's
head; **ich soll dir Geld leihen?
Du hast doch einen Sprung in
der Schüssel!** lend you some
money? Are you off your head or
something?

spuckebillig adj (*sehr billig*) dirt
cheap

Ständer m (*Erektion*) **einen
Ständer haben/bekommen** to
have/get the horn

Stange f **eine Stange Wasser
in die Ecke stellen** scherzhaft
(*urinieren*) to point Percy at the
porcelain

stänkern vi (a) (*necken,
provozieren*) to act up; **hör
endlich auf zu stänkern!** stop
acting up!; **die Amerikaner
sollten endlich aufhören, mit
den Russen zu stänkern** the
Americans should stop needling
the Russians
(b) (*sich beklagen*) to whinge

Staub m **sich aus dem Staub
machen** (*fliehen*) to do a runner;
**zuerst macht er ihr einen dicken
Bauch, und dann macht er sich
aus dem Staub** first he knocks
her up and then he does a
runner

Stecher m (a) (*sexuell
erfolgreicher oder aktiver Mann*)
der ist der totale Stecher he
screws around big time
(b) beleidigend (*männlicher
Sexualpartner*) fuck buddy

steif adj (*betrunken*) paralytic

Steifer m (*Erektion*) stiffy; **einen
Steifen haben/bekommen** to
have/get a stiffy

stibitzen vt (*stehlen*) to pinch

stink- präfix **sie ist stinkreich**
(*sehr reich*) she's filthy stinking
rich; **das war doch eine
stinknormale Beerdigung**
(*völlig normal*) it was a bog-
standard funeral; **der Film war
stinklangweilig** (*sehr langweilig*)
the film was a total yawn

Stinkefinger m **der hat mir den
Stinkefinger gezeigt** (*er hat eine
beleidigende Geste gemacht*) he
gave me the finger → **Vogel**

stinkig adj (a) (*schlecht gelaunt*)

stroppy; **das ist doch kein Grund, gleich so stinkig zu sein** there's no need to get all stroppy about it

(b) *(stinkend)* minging

Stoff *m* (a) *(Drogen)* gear; **schlechter Stoff** bad shit

(b) *(Heroin)* smack; **Stoff beschaffen** to score some smack

(c) *(Alkohol)* booze

stoned *adj* **stoned sein** *(unter Drogen stehen)* to be stoned

Stoß *m* **du hast wohl 'nen Stoß zu wenig gekriegt** *(du bist dumm)* you must be one stick short of a bundle or something

straff *adj (betrunken)* steaming

streben *vi (gewissenhaft und intensiv lernen)* to be a swot

Streber *m*, **Streberin** *f* (a) *(jemand, der gewissenhaft und intensiv lernt)* swot

(b) *(jemand, der im Berufsleben rücksichtslos nach oben kommen will)* careerist git; **jetzt schleimt sich dieser Streber wieder beim Chef ein!** look at that careerist git sucking up to the boss again!

striffeln *vi (masturbieren)* to beat one's meat

sturmfrei → Bude

Stuss *m (Unsinn)* bollocks; **red keinen Stuss** stop talking bollocks

Stütze *f (Sozialhilfe)* dole; **ich lebe von der Stütze** *oder* **ich kriege Stütze** I'm on the dole

Suffkopf *m (notorischer Trinker)* pisshead

sülzen 1 *vi (viel reden)* to waffle

2 *vt (dumm reden)* to spout; **sülz hier nicht so einen Mist!** stop spouting garbage!

Sumpfhuhn *nt (Mensch, der viel trinkt)* alkie

super 1 *adj (großartig)* great

2 *adv (großartig)* **das habt ihr super gemacht!** you've done a great job there!; **sie kann super tanzen** she's a great dancer

3 *interj* great!

T

Techtelmechtel *nt scherzhaft (sexuelle Beziehung)* **ein Techtelmechtel mit jemandem haben** to have a thing going with somebody

Tee *m* **einen im Tee haben** *(leicht betrunken sein)* to be a bit woozy

Teil *nt* **(a)** *(Gegenstand)* job; **was hast du denn für das Teil bezahlt?** how much did you pay for that job?; **das war ein Riesenteil!** it was a whopper!; **was is 'n das für 'n Teil?** what's that when it's at home?; **neues Handy? Geiles Teil!** is that a new mobile you've got there? Cool piece of kit!
(b) *(Penis)* thing; **der hatte ja so ein Teil!** Christ, he had a big one!
(c) *(Pille)* tab → **potthässlich**

Teppichkante *f* **die würde ich nicht von der Teppichkante stoßen** *(ich finde sie attraktiv)* I wouldn't mind doing her a favour

Teufel *m* **was zum Teufel...?** *(was um Himmels willen?)* what the hell...?; **wer zum Teufel...?** *(wer um Himmels willen?)* who the hell...?; **hol dich der Teufel!** *(lass mich in Ruhe)* give me a flaming break!; **hol's der Teufel!** *(ist doch egal)* to hell with it!; **geh** *oder* **scher dich zum Teufel!** *(verschwinde und lass mich in Ruhe)* go to hell!; **weiß der Teufel** *(keine Ahnung)* how the hell should I know?; **wie wir das schaffen sollen weiß der Teufel** I haven't a flaming clue how we're going to do it; **Teufel auch!** *(bewundernd)* flaming hell!; **jemanden zum Teufel jagen** *(fortschicken)* to send somebody packing; **zum Teufel mit ihm/damit!** *(der/das kann mir gestohlen bleiben)* to hell with him/it!; **du musstest ja auf Teufel komm raus nach Mallorca fahren** *(unbedingt)* you were the one who was hell-bent on going to Majorca; **er wollte die auf Teufel komm raus abschleppen** *(unbedingt)* he was hell-bent on getting off with her; **nach dem Bombenanschlag war dort der Teufel los** *(es ging chaotisch zu)* all hell broke loose there after the bombing; **wenn der rausfindet, dass ich sein Auto geschrottet habe, dann ist der Teufel los** *(es gibt Ärger)* all hell's gonna break loose when he finds out I've written off his car; **du wirst dich jetzt bei ihr**

entschuldigen. – Den Teufel werd' ich tun! *(ich werde es auf keinen Fall tun)* you're going to go and apologize to her now. – Like hell I am!; **der Chef sagt, du musst Überstunden machen. – Den Teufel werd' ich tun!** the boss says you've got to put in some overtime. – To hell with that!; **er ist gefahren wie der Teufel** *(sehr schnell)* he drove like a maniac; **wir haben uns beeilt wie der Teufel** *(wir haben uns sehr beeilt)* we really shifted it → **fressen**

texten *vi (viel reden)* to spout

ticken 1 *vt (verkaufen)* to deal **2** *vi* **(a)** *(mit Drogen handeln)* to deal

(b) nicht ganz richtig ticken *(nicht bei Verstand sein)* to be round the bend; **der will 200 Euro dafür, der tickt ja nicht ganz richtig** he wants 200 euros for it, he must be round the bend

Ticket *nt (auf Papier geträufelte Einzeldosis LSD)* wrap

tierisch 1 *adj (intensivierend)* **das ist ja 'ne tierische Beule!** that's a hell of a bump you've got there!

2 *adv (intensivierend)* **der hat sich gestern tierisch aufgeregt** he got in a hell of a strop yesterday; **das tut tierisch weh** that hurts like hell; **es war tierisch kalt** it was dead cold; **der war tierisch grob zu ihr** he was dead rude to her; **ich habe tierisch geschwitzt** I was sweating buckets

Tinte *f* **in der Tinte stecken** *(in Bedrängnis sein)* to be up the creek

Tintenkopf ‼ *m rassistisch (Schwarzer)* spade

Titte *f (weibliche Brust)* tit

Ton *m* **große Töne spucken** *(aufschneiden)* to shoot one's mouth off

Topf *m (Toilette)* bog; **ich muss mal auf den Topf** *(ich muss auf die Toilette gehen)* I've got to go to the bog

Torfstecher *m homophob (Homosexueller)* Marmite miner

tot → **Hose**

totlachen *reflexiv* **sich totlachen** *(herzlich lachen)* to kill oneself laughing; **ich hab' mich fast totgelacht** I nearly died laughing; **Franz und heiraten, ich lach' mich tot!** Franz getting married, that's a good one!

Traummann *m*, **Traumtyp** *m (attraktiver Mann)* studmuffin

Trine *f homophob (weiblich wirkender Homosexueller)* femme

Trip *m (Drogenrausch)* trip; **sie ist auf dem Trip** she's tripping *oder* on a trip

Tripper *m (Geschlechtskrankheit)* **den Tripper haben** to have the clap

Tritt → **Arsch**

Trottel *m beleidigend (dumme Person)* pillock; **du Trottel!** you pillock!; **ich bin mir wie der letzte Trottel vorgekommen** I felt a right pillock

tun

tun → es

Tunte *f homophob (weiblich wirkender Homosexueller)* queen

> ⓘ Although **Tunte** is offensive if used with homophobic intent, the gay and transvestite communities have embraced it as a term of pride or humorous endearment.

Tuss *f beleidigend (Frau)* cow; **die Ulla ist 'ne blöde Tuss** Ulla's a stupid cow; **sag der Tuss, sie kann mich mal** tell the stupid cow to get stuffed

Tussi *f beleidigend (Frau)* woman [*nicht Slang*]; **haste die Tussi da gesehen?** Christ, look at *her*!; **es waren mehr Tussis als Typen auf der Party** there were more girls than guys at the party; **der Kevin ist mit 'ner neuen Tussi gekommen** Kevin turned up with some new woman; **eigentlich ist die Tussi ganz in Ordnung, nur ein bisschen dumm** she's all right, actually, even if she is a bit stupid; **die Ulla ist 'ne blöde Tussi** Ulla's a stupid cow; **sag der Tussi, sie kann mich mal** tell the stupid cow to get stuffed

Typ *m* (a) *(Mann)* bloke (b) *(unbekannter, verdächtiger Mann)* character

U

umlegen *vt* (a) *(koitieren mit)* to screw
  (b) *(töten)* to whack

umsonst *adv* das hast du nicht umsonst gemacht! *(Drohung)* you're gonna pay for that!

Untersatz *m* fahrbarer Untersatz *(Auto)* wheels; ist mir doch egal, wie das Ding aussieht, Hauptsache, ich hab' einen fahrbaren Untersatz I don't care what it looks like, the main thing is that I've got (some) wheels now

V

verarschen *vt* (a) *(sich lustig machen über)* **jemanden verarschen** to take the piss out of somebody; **willst du mich verarschen?** are you taking the piss?; **fünfzig Euros für eine Pizza? Die wollen uns wohl verarschen** fifty euros for a pizza? Are they taking the piss?; **versuch nicht, mich zu verarschen!** don't screw with me!; **verarsch mich nicht!** *(das glaube ich nicht)* my arse!; **verarschen kann ich mich selbst!** *(erzähl mir keinen Unsinn)* give me a bloody break!

(b) *(betrügen)* to shaft

(c) *(hinhalten)* **jemanden verarschen** to piss somebody around

verdammt 1 *adj (sehr ärgerlich)* damn; **bei diesem verdammten Wetter kann man ja gar nichts unternehmen** you can't do anything in this damn weather; **immer deine verdammten Ausreden** I've had enough of your damn excuses

2 *adv (intensivierend)* damn; **das tut verdammt weh** that's damn painful; **er hat sich verdammt angestrengt** he tried damn hard; **das kostet verdammt viel Geld** it costs a flaming fortune

3 *interj (Ausdruck des Ärgers)* damn!; **verdammt noch mal!** damn it!; **hör mir verdammt noch mal zu!** listen to what I'm saying, damn it!; **verdammt und zugenäht!** flaming hell!; **du tust, was ich sage, verdammt und zugenäht!** you'd flaming well better do as I say! → **Mist**

verfatzen *reflexiv East German* **sich verfatzen** *(sich entfernen)* to naff off; **verfatz dich!** naff off!

verfickt *adj* (a) *(schlecht)* fucked up; **das ist total verfickt!** that's so fucked up!

(b) *(sexuell überaktiv)* ‼ **die ist total verfickt** she fucks around big time

verflucht 1 *adj (verdammt)* sodding; **bei diesem verfluchten Wetter kann man ja gar nichts unternehmen** you can't do anything in this sodding weather; **immer deine verfluchten Ausreden** I've had enough of your sodding excuses

2 *adv (intensivierend)* sodding; **das tut verflucht weh** that's sodding painful

3 *interj (Ausdruck des Ärgers)* sod it!; **verflucht noch mal!** sodding hell!

Vogel

verhökern vt (verkaufen) to flog

verkloppen vt (verkaufen) to flog

verknacken vt (verurteilen) to put away; **Thomas haben sie zu drei Jahren verknackt** Thomas has been put away for three years

verknallt adj (verliebt) **in jemanden verknallt sein** to have got it bad for somebody

vernaschen 1 vt (koitieren mit) **jemanden vernaschen** to have it away with somebody
  2 reflexiv **sich vernaschen** to have it away

verpetzen vt (denunzieren) **jemanden (bei jemandem) verpetzen** to split on somebody (to somebody)

verpfeifen 1 vt (denunzieren) **jemanden (bei jemandem) verpfeifen** to grass on somebody (to somebody); **das Schwein hat unseren Plan verpfiffen!** the little shit has gone and given our plan away!
  2 reflexiv **sich verpfeifen** (sich entfernen) to scarper; **los, verpfeif dich!** go on, scarper!

verpissen reflexiv **sich verpissen** (sich entfernen) to fuck off; **verpiss dich!** fuck off!

verramschen vt (verkaufen) to flog

verrecken vi (sterben) to buy it

versacken vi **ich bin gestern Abend mit Ute versackt** (wir haben viel und lange getrunken) me and Ute were on the piss till late last night

versauen vt (a) (schlecht ausführen) **etwas versauen** to bugger something up
  (b) (kaputtmachen) to bugger; **ich hab' mir den Rücken versaut** I've buggered my back

versaut adj (a) (mit allen Obszönitäten vertraut) **versaut sein** to have a filthy mind
  (b) (obszön) filthy

verticken vt (verkaufen) to flog

verwamsen 1 vt (verprügeln) to biff
  2 reflexiv **sich verwamsen** (sich prügeln) to scrap

verziehen reflexiv **sich verziehen** (sich entfernen) to take off; **ich glaub', ich verzieh mich mal** I think I'm gonna hit the road; **verzieh dich!** clear off!

viehisch 1 adj (intensivierend) **das ist ja 'ne viehische Beule!** that's a frigging great bump you've got there!
  2 adv (intensivierend) **der hat sich gestern viehisch aufgeregt** he got in a right frigging strop yesterday; **das tut viehisch weh** that's frigging painful

viel pron **viel haben** (große Brüste haben) to have big ones

vier → **Buchstaben**

Visage f (Gesicht) face [nicht Slang]; **guck mal, hat der nicht 'ne eklige Visage?** has he got an ugly mug or what?

Vogel m **einen Vogel haben** (nicht bei Verstand sein) to be off one's block; **der hat ja einen Vogel, wenn der meint, ich mache das noch mal** he must be off his block if he thinks I'm going to do it again; **jemandem den Vogel zeigen** *(eine beleidigende Geste machen)* to tap one's index finger against one's forehead in contempt at somebody

ⓘ In Germany, the traditional gesture for expressing your contempt for or dislike of somebody is to tap your index finger against your forehead, known as **den Vogel zeigen** (literally, *to show the bird*). It is only more recently, as a result of English influence, that it has also become common for people to stick their middle finger up at each other (**jemandem den Finger/den Stinkefinger zeigen**). This particular gesture is also known as an **Effenberg** in honour of the German footballer, Steffen Effenberg, who was caught on camera giving the German fans the finger in the 1994 World Cup.

vögeln 1 *vt (koitieren mit)* to shag
2 *vi (koitieren)* to shag; **ich hätte mal wieder Lust zu vögeln** I fancy a shag; **mit jemandem vögeln** to shag somebody

voll 1 *adj* **voll sein** *(unter Alkohol stehen)* to be blotto; **ich hab' mich voll laufen lassen** I got blotto
2 *adv (intensivierend)* **der ist voll gut drauf** *(er ist sehr gut gelaunt)* he's a happy bunny today; **voll krass** *(großartig)* fierce; **eh, Mann, das Auto ist ja voll krass** that's one fierce car, man; **voll krass, wir fahren im Sommer auf die Malediven!** fierce, we're going to the Maldives this summer!

voll kotzen *vt* (a) *(erbrechen über)* to puke all over; **der hat mir die ganze Jacke voll gekotzt!** he puked all over my jacket! (b) *(verbal belästigen)* **jemanden voll kotzen** to blah on at somebody

voll labern *vt (viel reden)* **jemanden voll labern** to spout on at somebody

voll texten *vt (viel reden)* **jemanden voll texten** to spout on at somebody

Vorbau *m scherzhaft (Brüste)* jugs *pl*; **die hat 'nen ganz schönen Vorbau!** she's got a nice pair of jugs on her!

W

Waffel f einen an der Waffel haben *(nicht bei Verstand sein)* to be a nutjob; **ich soll dir Geld leihen? Du hast doch einen an der Waffel!** lend you some money? Get real!

Wahnsinn 1 m (a) *(beeindruckendes Ereignis)* **der Wahnsinn sein** to be totally mind-blowing; **wie der Gitarre spielt, das ist der blanke Wahnsinn** his guitar-playing's totally mind-blowing

(b) *(Unvernunft)* **der Wahnsinn sein** to be madness; **das ist doch der helle Wahnsinn!** it's total madness!

2 interj *(Ausdruck der extremen Qualität)* far out!

Wald m **ich komm nach Hause, und die Kids machen eine Riesenparty. Ich hab' gedacht, ich steh' im Wald** scherzhaft *(das ist unerhört)* I get home and find the kids having a massive party. Unbelievable!

Walze f beleidigend *(dicke Person)* tub of lard

Wampe f *(Bauch)* gut

Wamse f *(Prügel)* **Wamse kriegen** to get duffed up

wamsen 1 vt *(verprügeln)* to biff

2 reflexiv **sich wamsen** *(sich prügeln)* to have a scrap

Wanne f *(Bauch)* gut

warm adj homophob *(homosexuell)* bent; **warmer Bruder** *(Homosexueller)* bender

Warmduscher m *(langweiliger Mann)* girlie wuss

Waschlappen m *(Schwächling)* wimp

weg adv **weg sein** *(unter Drogen stehen, betrunken sein)* to be out of it → **hin**

wegfressen vt *(aufessen)* to scoff; **wer hat die ganzen Erdnüsse weggefressen?** who scoffed all the peanuts?

weggetreten adj **weggetreten sein** *(unter Drogen stehen, nicht bei klarem Verstand sein)* to be out of it

Weichei nt *(langweilige, verweichlichte Person)* wimp

Weisheit → **fressen**

Wellen npl **Wellen machen** *(sich aufspielen)* to get one's knickers in a twist; *(auffällig in Erscheinung treten)* to kick up a fuss; **wir müssen jetzt aber ganz schnell los, sonst kommen wir zu spät! – Mann, mach keine**

Wellen, wir haben doch noch jede Menge Zeit we really need to get a move on or we'll be late – Hey, don't get your knickers in a twist, we're in plenty of time; **mach mal hier keine Wellen, ja?** I don't want any fuss, OK?

wenig *pron* **wenig haben** *(kleine Brüste haben)* to have little ones

werfen *vi sexistisch (Kind gebären)* to drop a sprog

Wessi *m rassistisch (Bewohner der alten Bundesländer)* bloody West German; **die Wessis sind eben mal eingebildet** those bloody West Germans are all so full of themselves; **das ist unser Wessi im Büro** this is our western German colleague

> **ⓘ** **Wessi** can be used offensively by East Germans to denote a person from West Germany, in which case the most appropriate translation is *bloody West German*. However, when it is used by West Germans to describe themselves, or by East Germans in a non-offensive way, then the best translation is *western German*. East Germans often say **Besserwessi** to refer to the typical arrogant West German who considers himself to be superior to **Ossis**.

wichsen 1 *vi (masturbieren)* to wank

2 *reflexiv* **sie hat mich ertappt, als ich mir gerade einen wichste** *(als ich masturbierte)* she caught me having a wank

Wichser *m beleidigend (nichtswürdiger Mann)* wanker; **du Wichser! – Selber einer!** wanker! – Takes one to know one!; **he, du Wichser, wie geht's denn so?** how's it going, you old wanker?

Wichsgriffel *m (Finger)* finger [*nicht Slang*]; **nimm deine unegalen Wichsgriffel von meiner Alten!** keep your grubby fucking paws off my missus!

Woche → rot

Würfelhusten *m* **Würfelhusten haben** *meist scherzhaft (erbrechen)* to blow chunks; **er hatte Würfelhusten** he was blowing chunks

Wurst *f (Kothaufen)* poo; **eine Wurst machen** *(Darm entleeren)* to do a poo

Wüste *f* **jemanden in die Wüste schicken** *(sich von jemandem trennen)* to chuck somebody

arter m homophob (Homosexueller) pansy

eiger m jemandem auf den Zeiger gehen (nerven) to get up somebody's nose

icke f (launische, streitsüchtige Frau) miserable cow

ickig adj (schwierig) grouchy

iege f (hochnäsige Frau) old bag; **sie ist eine doofe** oder **dumme Ziege** she's a stupid old bag

iehen vt einen ziehen (exzessiv Alkohol trinken) to get slaughtered; (Droge durch Röhrchen in die Nase ziehen) to snort a line; **einen ziehen lassen** (Wind abgehen lassen) to let one go → **Leine**

iehung f (Alkoholexzess) eine Ziehung machen to get twatted

ifferblatt nt (Gesicht) face [nicht Slang]; **der hat in der Kneipe so lange Streit gesucht, bis er eine aufs Zifferblatt gekriegt hat** he kept looking for trouble down the pub until in the end somebody clocked him one

inken m (Nase) conk

inker m, **Zinkerin** f (a)
(Falschspieler) con artist
(b) (Verräter) snitch

zischen vt (trinken) ein paar zischen to have a few bevvies; **ein Bier zischen gehen** to go for a beer

zocken 1 vt (stehlen) to nick
2 vi (a) (spielen) to gamble [nicht Slang]
(b) (stehlen) to nick stuff

zu adj zu sein (betrunken sein, unter Drogen stehen) to be smashed

zudröhnen reflexiv sich zudröhnen (sich betrinken) to get out of one's face; (Drogen exzessiv einnehmen) to get stoned

zugekifft adj zugekifft sein (unter Haschisch stehen) to be doped up to the eyeballs

zulabern vt (viel reden) jemanden zulabern to spout on at somebody

zulöten reflexiv sich zulöten (sich betrinken) to get wazzed; (Drogen exzessiv einnehmen) to get loaded

zusammenscheißen vt (streng rügen) jemanden zusammenscheißen to give somebody a bollocking

zutexten *vt (viel reden)*
jemanden zutexten to spout on
at somebody